LOS ANGELES'S BUNKER HILL

PULP FICTION'S MEAN STREETS AND FILM NOIR'S GROUND ZERO!

JIM DAWSON

THE History PRESS

Published by The History Press
Charleston, SC 29403
www.historypress.net

Cover image from the film *Cry Danger*. Courtesy of the Academy of Motion Picture Arts & Sciences. Back cover image copyright George Mann.

First published 2012
Second printing 2013
Third printing 2015

Manufactured in the United States

ISBN 978.1.60949.546.6

Library of Congress Cataloging-in-Publication Data

Dawson, Jim, 1944-
Los Angeles's Bunker Hill : Pulp fiction's mean streets and film noir's ground zero! / Jim Dawson.
p. cm.
Includes bibliographical references.
ISBN 978-1-60949-546-6
1. Bunker Hill (Los Angeles, Calif.)--History. 2. Los Angeles (Calif.)--History. 3. Bunker Hill (Los Angeles, Calif.)--In motion pictures. 4. Los Angeles (Calif.)--In motion pictures. 5. Motion picture locations--California--Los Angeles--History. 6. Film noir--History and criticism. 7. Bunker Hill (Los Angeles, Calif.)--In literature. 8. Los Angeles (Calif.)--In literature. 9. Pulp literature, American--History and criticism. I. Title.
F869.L86B8645 2012
979.4'94--dc23
2012024384

Contents

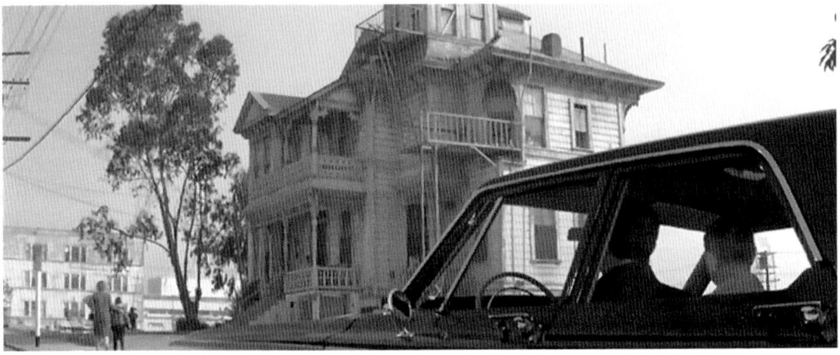

Los Angeles detectives Glenn Ford and Ricardo Montalban stake out the old Brousseau place on Bunker Hill Avenue in *The Money Trap* (1966). *Courtesy of Warner Bros.*

Acknowledgements

Thanks to Rick Mechtly for generously sharing his deep knowledge and Sanborn maps of Bunker Hill; to Nathan Marsak, Marc Wanamaker and Earl Reinhalter for their invaluable assistance; to Richard Schave and Kim Cooper for keeping noir Los Angeles alive; to Thom Andersen and John Bengtson for their archeological inspiration; and to the late photographers Arnold Hylen, George Mann and William Reagh who so beautifully documented Bunker Hill during its last decades. I'd also like to thank Mary Katherine Aldin, Susan Arosteguy (Criterion Collection), Lynne Bateson, Leonard Bernstein (Caravan Book Store), Bob Birchard (American Film Institute), Claire Brandt (Eddie Brandt's Saturday Matinee), Kathleen Correia (California State Library), Byron Dillon, Dino Everett (USC School of Cinematic Arts), Art Fein, Bill Kay, Marianne Leach (California State Library), Gary Leonard, Mary Mallory (Motion Picture Academy of Arts & Sciences), Jeff Mantor (Larry Edmunds Books), Eddie Muller (Film Noir Foundation), Tony Nittoli, Gordon Pattison, Paul Politi, Robert Porfirio, Ray Regalado, Christina Rice (Los Angeles Public Library), Alan K. Rode, Phil Stufflebean, Andy Schwartz, Alain Silver, James Ursini, Alexx VanDyne, John Welborne (Angels Flight Railway Foundation), Ian Whitcomb and last but most certainly not least, Dianne Woods.

INTRODUCTION

In his 2003 film documentary *Los Angeles Plays Itself*, Thom Andersen observed, "In a city where only a few buildings are more than a hundred years old…a place can become a historic landmark because it was once a movie location." That's only a slight overstatement. An iconic film that's loved by millions or worshiped by a determined few can turn the most prosaic street or structure into a cultural reference point. Pilgrims from all over the world will come to visit as if something really happened there.

To a location nut like me, the quality of the film is often beside the point. One early morning not long ago, I was watching a 1941 B movie called *Double Cross*, produced by a Santa Monica Boulevard slum operation that disappeared decades ago. If I told you the actors' names, you wouldn't recognize them. Like most cheap indies of that era, *Double Cross* was shot mostly on rotting studio sets left over from the early talkies. Just sitting through it was a slog. But then, just as I was ready to give up and go to bed, the screen brightened to a distant white sunlight as a motorcycle cop rode up to a parked car on what looked like a Hollywood residential street. The car's owner, a woman, came out of an apartment building whose ground-floor facade had a simple Egyptian or Mayan design. Suddenly, as the camera panned down the street, I recognized where they were. At the end of the block was a distinctive three-story art deco tower that still stands today at 5620 Hollywood Boulevard. I put the DVD on "still," pushed my feet into my shoes, ran out to my car and hurried the short distance—little more than a mile—from my Beachwood Canyon digs to the Sir Launfal Apartments still standing at 1848 North Gramercy Place, just below Franklin Avenue.

The next-door Tudor homes in the film were gone, replaced by 1950s apartments, but the front of the Sir Launfal was unchanged.

As I stood in the same spot as those long-dead ghosts frozen at that very moment on my TV screen, I felt like I'd made some physical connection with the past, as if the gravity of the Sir Launfal had momentarily folded time in on itself. Or at least that's how it seems on a dark and misty early-morning street you've only just visited seventy years ago, before you were even born.

Living in Hollywood, I'm accustomed to stepping into movie history. The long hillside stairway leading up from 2744 Westshire Drive to the 2800 block of Hollyridge Drive, where Kevin McCarthy and Dana Wynter fled from the townspeople in the original *Invasion of the Body Snatchers* (1956), is a three-minute stroll from my front door, and I frequently hike up or down its 149 steps. If I choose to go in another direction along Beachwood Canyon's western ridge, within twenty minutes I'm walking past 6301 Quebec Street, the hillside Spanish Colonial exterior of the house where Fred MacMurray said, "Goodbye, baby," and shot Barbara Stanwyck in *Double Indemnity* (1941). (As a bonus, novelist James M. Cain, who wrote *Double Indemnity*, once lived in a French-Norman house just up the hill from me in the 2900 block of Belden Drive, flush with the road, so that any passing pedestrian can glance into the corner sunroom where he probably wrote *Mildred Pierce*.)

But one famous location I can't visit is Bunker Hill. Oh, I can go downtown and stroll the charmless pedways and concrete parking caverns of a fortress called Bunker Hill, but it's Bunker Hill in name only, not *the* Bunker Hill. Except for the Second Street tunnel—now one of L.A.'s busiest locations for car commercials—and the older Third Street tunnel; the sealed-off Pacific Electric subway tunnel running diagonally beneath them; a funny little incline railway that was moved half a block from its original location; the stocky 1938 zigzag deco Southern California Edison Building at Fifth and Grand (dubbed One Bunker Hill); a couple of large 1920s office buildings near Fifth and Hill; and a section of the old Fremont Hotel's stone wall on Olive Street just below Fourth, that wonderful, sprawling movie set called Bunker Hill has been *struck*. Knocked down and hauled away to distant landfills. Even its little railway, Angels Flight, was mothballed in warehouses for nearly thirty years before they brought it back and put it in the wrong place. Simply put, Los Angeles's mandarins set out to obliterate Bunker Hill as resolutely as the Enola Gay's bombardier leveled Hiroshima. You can't even stand on a street corner today and point your finger and say, "That house was right *here*"—unless you're pointing straight *up*—because they lopped off the original hilltop just like the army turned Elvis's pompadour into a buzz cut back in '58. Then they laid down a new grid of streets stacked on top of each other and planted Los Angeles's first skyline—a vertical maze of steel, marble and opaque, palladium-silver glass—deep enough within the hill's guts that in some places their piles punctured the old subway tunnel. If you want to see the original Bunker Hill, you're out of luck, unless you're satisfied with two-dimensional representations: paintings, photos, postcards, a handful of novels and short stories and several dozen old movies and TV shows.

That's the only Bunker Hill worth visiting, if you ask me.

CHAPTER 1

REEL LIFE ON THE STREETS

"Every scene was filmed on the actual location depicted!"
—advertisement line for the realistic 1947 film noir Kiss of Death.

How important is filming on location, rather than at the studio?

The answer lies in the opening scene of a 1960 Paramount film called *The Rat Race*. Tony Curtis has been playing his saxophone for tips on Midtown Manhattan's kinetic Times Square. He gathers the coins from his open case on the sidewalk, packs up his horn, and walks around the corner—to Paramount's "New York" street in Hollywood.

In an instant, you've entered a dead zone. Your suspension of disbelief disappears in a poof. If you're Wile E. Coyote spinning your legs running nowhere above empty air, you look down, gape in shock at the audience and plummet out of frame. You're stuck on a lousy backlot you've seen a hundred times, and you don't give a damn what happens to Tony Curtis anymore.

The problem is that Times Square is real, and Paramount's street is phony. Times Square is a random collection of architectural quirks by different builders from different periods of time, haphazardly repaired, visibly cracked and worn down and given an accretion of grime; it's a chaotic, noisy place where countless people have worked, dreamed, passed by and passed on. Paramount's street, on the other hand, is a prop, a facade. Nobody ever lived there. It has blank windows and doorways, like an Edward Hopper painting of a Midwestern downtown at midnight. A director can dress it up, hide it in shadows, add cars and send in a phalanx of extras (known in the business as "atmosphere"), but he can't make it look real, especially when the editor later mashes it up with a street that *is* real. Tiny details, especially the ones that register just below consciousness, matter when you're trying to build a world.

Another element that's lost when you go from New York to "New York" is tension. At Broadway and Forty-second Street, the cast and crew must contend with changing light conditions, traffic, unreliable power sources and disruptive shop owners who feel they haven't been properly compensated. Teamster drivers and crowd control cops are costing the production extra, and so will the union crew if they go into golden time. It's essential that everyone, especially the actors, get the scene right and move on, because another day of shooting on Times Square requires more city permits and another full day's pay for everyone, and who knows, maybe tomorrow will be rainy or the sky won't look anything like it does today.

But back at Paramount, the cast and crew can spend as much time as they need to properly light the shots without worrying about the time of day. There's no traffic, no curious pedestrians, no city noise, no permits and no excitement. If Tony Curtis keeps flubbing his lines, they can always come back tomorrow. The anxiety of getting it right the first or second time is gone. That's why, when the two scenes—one on location, the other on the pristine and placid backlot—are juxtaposed on film, the difference between them is palpable. One has a lived-in feel, and the other is lifeless.

Los Angeles Times film critic Kevin Thomas noted just such a difference when he reviewed a 1966 Glenn Ford detective drama called *The Money Trap*, which interspersed scenes shot on both Bunker Hill and on MGM's backlot. The film's already "tenuous" credibility, Thomas wrote, "is completely undermined by the poor matching of actual Los Angeles locations with some of those old New York street scene sets with the familiar brownstone walkups. How can we accept Ford as a victim of environment—the poor boy who doesn't quite make good—if we can't believe in that environment itself?"

"The tremendous advantages of shooting on location, as opposed to studio, is you're dealing with reality," director Peter Bogdanovich says in his DVD commentary for the 1952 film *Clash By Night*, which was shot in Monterey, California. "It gives an authenticity and verisimilitude, immediately." As a bonus, "The actors like it because they feel it's real." Bogdanovich recalls that Otto Preminger once told him that shooting on location forces a director to be more inventive "because you can't move the walls." In other words, unlike a studio designed for the sake of the camera, a real location restricts where that camera, along with the lights and the actors, can go. It challenges the director to try something new.

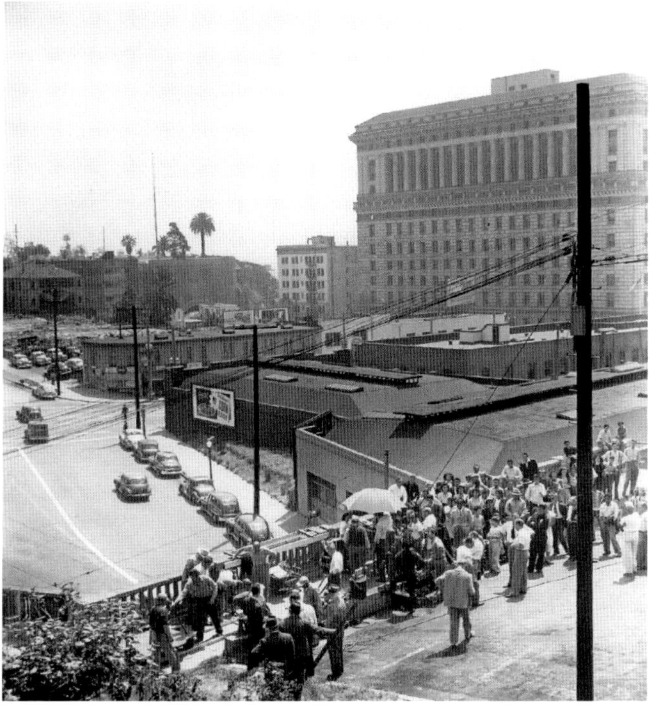

The crew of *Criss Cross* (1949), a seminal Los Angeles film noir, sets up a shot on the balustrade above the north end of the Hill Street tunnel. To the right is the Hall of Justice on the northeast corner of Temple Street and Broadway. *Courtesy of Bison Archives.*

Veteran cinematographer James Wong Howe agreed. "Artistically, I would always rather be on real sets, on location, in the natural setting versus sets built in a studio," he told film critic Alain Silver in 1970. "It's rather ridiculous when you have light from a single source, whether it's the sun or a solitary candle, and the set is lit so that objects cast three or four shadows. A real house has a ceiling and four walls, and one has to change the way of lighting. In a studio, without a ceiling, it's easier and faster for a cameraman to light. But to me these are false lights."

If "authenticity and verisimilitude" seem irrelevant within a theatrical medium, consider that general film audiences are much more literal in their tastes than live theater audiences. They wouldn't tolerate a movie version of *Waiting for Godot* with just a cardboard tree on an otherwise empty stage. (In fact, they probably wouldn't tolerate sitting through *Waiting for Godot.*) They need the illusion of quotidian reality, especially on the big screen, where actors must overcome the unnaturalness of being oversized creatures formed out of light and shadow.

Consider also that letting in the flow of reality can offset or soften the improbability of oddball characters, farfetched plots and the artificial mood lighting so important to many films. *The Christian Science Monitor*'s Edwin F. Melvin, reviewing the 1951 film noir *Cry Danger*, observed that its circuitous story "may not be quite so believable as the realistic photography in some of the less pretentious sections of Los Angeles." The January 14, 1951 edition of the *Hollywood Reporter* praised the film's director for choosing "to shoot all exterior footage against backgrounds of downtown Los Angeles [and] creating an air of authenticity difficult to capture on celluloid." In early 1953, the *Los Angeles Times*'s Philip K. Scheuer wrote: "Where [*The Turning Point*] gains the most conviction is from its on-the-spot locations"—namely Bunker Hill. Probably the best example of locations significantly enhancing the viewer's illusion of reality is the original *Invasion of the Body Snatchers*, a science fiction film noir. Director Don Siegel's use of real suburban homes and neighborhoods in Hollywood, Burbank and Sierra Madre (a small town east of Pasadena) provided enough authenticity to an otherwise ridiculous story about alien pods replicating humans that the movie has been giving audiences the willies for sixty years. If the script had been shot on a studio backlot, *Body Snatchers* would be just another campy fifties creature feature.

Thomas Edison built the first movie studio, a dark little barn, in New Jersey in 1893 because he saw the medium as simply another way of presenting theater as it had existed since Sophocles, but despite being an ingenious contraption with wheels and fulcrums, it was still a barn. More creative artists couldn't wait to test the limits of cinematic storytelling outside the soundstage box where the camera's eye could free audiences from their seats and let them accompany the actors on San Francisco streetcars or in balloon gondolas soaring over France. Why settle for a static view of a painted backdrop when the whole world is available?

Moviemakers migrated to semitropical Southern California to shoot beneath perpetual sunshine. Los Angeles in those days was a suburban city of newly paved white streets lined with young pepper trees, palms, scattered frame houses and architectural detritus from all over the world. Wide-open spaces looking like almost anywhere were no more than a few hours away. Some directors took this freedom to its solipsist extreme by journeying to historical locations and making "accurate reproductions" of events that happened there, often with real participants, as when the legendary frontier marshal Bill Tilghman and Dalton Gang desperado Arkansas Tom (paroled from prison for the project) portrayed themselves in *Passing of the Oklahoma Outlaws* in 1915. (Soviet filmmakers, given the power to commandeer entire cities for locations, would later, in the 1920s, fetishize historical replication in films like *Ten Days That Shook the World* and *Battleship Potempkin*.) Robert

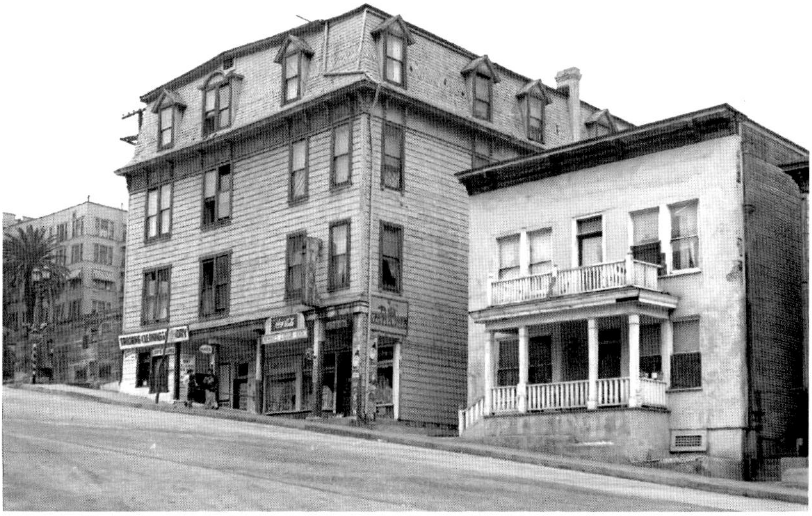

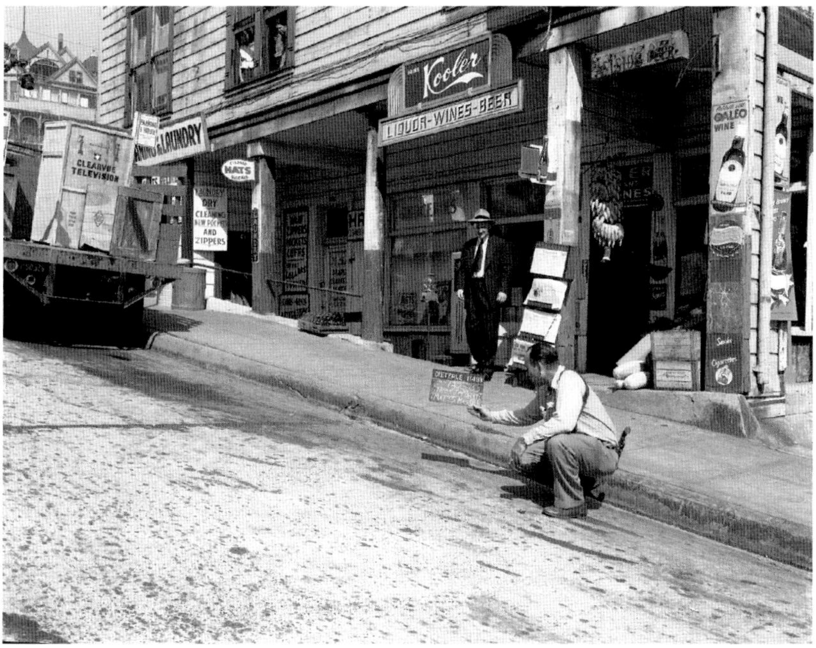

The Argyle Apartments at the northeast corner of Second and Olive Streets (left, in the top photo) had once been a well-appointed hotel, but by 1950, when this photo was taken, it was a rundown boardinghouse. The storefront dry cleaners at 431 West Second was used as Cesar Romero's bookie joint in *Once a Thief* (1950), and the next door grocery store at 427 West Second is where Sally Forrest tried to steal a baby in *Not Wanted* (1949) and Tom Tully (above) was shot to death in *The Turning Point* (1952). Next to the Argyle is the boxy Rio Grand Apartments at 425 West Second. *Courtesy of the California History Room, California State Library, Sacramento, above; and Bison Archives.*

Flaherty, on a different tack, took a camera into the Arctic Circle, filmed a family of Eskimos for a year and edited his hundreds of hours of footage into a documentary-like, dramatic narrative called *Nanook of the North* (1922).

Unfortunately, the arrival of a primitive and cumbersome sound technology in the late 1920s curtailed this freedom and forced directors back into the studio for a few years. That's why, for example, 1930s gangster films like *Scarface*, *Little Caesar* and *East Side* were shot on cramped, imaginary streets scaled to fit within the camera's eye—and they all look as phony as a grifter's three-dollar bill. During those years, the only on-location footage was normally placed at the very beginning of the movie as an "establishing shot," a first impression of realism meant to lull the audience into accepting the studio illusion that followed.

But then along came World War II and the rationing of vital resources that forced Hollywood to rethink the way it made pictures. According to the December 16, 1942 issue of *Variety*, the War Production Board had placed a $5,000 limit—effective on the first day of 1943—on each film's set construction budget, down from a previous average of $50,000 for A-films and $17,000 for Bs. (The dichotomy of A and B films came from the early days of the Depression, when a drop-off in theater attendance prompted the studios to lure back their audiences with "double features"—one major movie with star power plus one minor genre movie, roughly an hour in length, to provide "extra value" to the program—and the policy endured well into the 1960s.) This sudden belt-tightening favored the many European refugee directors schooled in the earlier German Expressionist style that substituted expensive sets with the use of "low key" mood lighting—so called because instead of using direct "key" lights, it depended on illumination coming into a darkened scene from an angle, highlighting the contours of faces and objects and creating stark shadows around them. Rationing also gave an advantage to B-movie directors already accustomed to using cheap cinematic shortcuts like mist, fog, rainy streets and the creative recycling of old sets to make them look new again. Since the sources of these secondary movies were often pulp novels bought at bargain rates, like the $2,000 that RKO paid for Raymond Chandler's *Farewell My Lovely*, the studio bosses had less regard for them and therefore allowed the screenwriters and directors a freer hand.

Right after the war, these crime movies caught the attention of French film critics who saw them not as trashy programmers but stylized examinations of the dark American soul and a welcome relief from all the over-lit singing, dancing and romantic fluff of the Betty Grable and Van Johnson movies. Nino Frank, in an article in the August 26, 1946 issue of *L'Ecran Francaise*

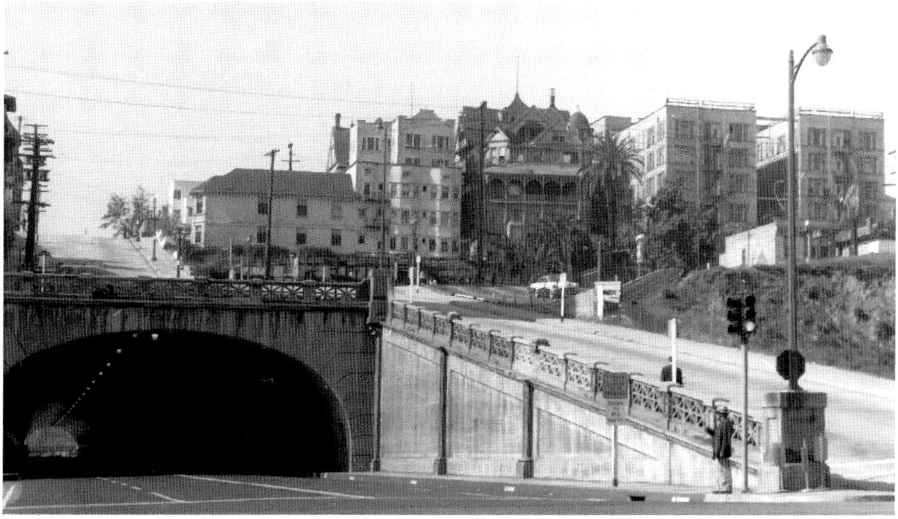

Looking west from Hill Street through the Second Street tunnel and up Bunker Hill's Second Street in 1960, the Koster house at 507 West Second (featured in *Shockproof*, 1948) is in the left center of the photo. To its right are the backs of the Richileau Hotel and the Melrose Hotel (both its 1881 building and 1891 double-wing addition) on Grand Avenue. *The California History Room, California State Library, Sacramento.*

called "Un Nouveau Genre 'Policier': L'aventure Criminell," bestowed upon them the label *film noir*—black film, though that term wouldn't penetrate the American lexicon for another ten years.

Wartime restrictions also created a parallel development outside the soundstage. In the newsreels that played before the regular features, cameramen accompanying the troops in Europe and the South Pacific used small, hand-held cameras whose roving, realistic images subtly exaggerated the staginess of the Hollywood dramas that followed them on the bill. As early as the spring of 1945, *American Cinematographer* writer Ezra Goodman commented how sixteen-millimeter war images "taken under the most trying conditions, have put Hollywood's professional 'realism' to shame." Directors began to ask themselves, "Since we can't build decent sets, why don't we go into the streets with these new cameras and shoot the way Chaplin, Keaton and the others used to do in the silent days?" Stage sets would always be necessary for period pieces and detailed interior work, but if you're filming a contemporary story set in the city, why not use the city?

Italian directors had already come to the same conclusion, though for different reasons. Nazi occupation, a collapsed economy and the Allied bombing of Mussolini's Cinecitta studio complex in Rome had seriously hamstrung movie production. In 1943, Luchino Visconti adapted James M. Cain's *The Postman Only Rings Twice* into *Ossessione* (*Obsession*) and shot it like a deranged tourist all around the Adriatic coastal towns of Ancona and Ferrara. The story of a beauty named Giovanna (Cora in the novel) enlisting a drifter to murder her husband had all the traits of what would become film noir—a dangerous woman, a passive man crippled by guilt and the inevitability of their doom—but the drama played out on dusty streets where the desperation of what passed for normal wartime life went on in the background. Critics later called Visconti's film a progenitor of a neo-realist school of cinema because he deliberately used the documentary style to strip away theatrical artifice; his characters seemed genuine because their acting was natural and their environments were real. Three years later, when Roberto Rossellini's *Open City*—shot on the streets and stairways and roofs of Rome—won Best Picture at the 1946 Cannes Film Festival, neo-realism became Italy's signature film style.

The first postwar American producer to take advantage of the neo-realist vision was Louis de Rochemont, who had begun his career in the 1930s creating a newsreel series called *The March of Time*. In 1945, he produced *The House on 92nd Street* by mixing documentary footage with staged recreations, overlaid with a patrician voice that told the "true" story about a federal counterintelligence agent infiltrating a German spy ring in Manhattan. Hollywood character actors like Lloyd Nolan shared the screen with FBI personnel (including J. Edgar Hoover himself), oftentimes in naturalistic settings like the brownstone where the real spymaster had lived. Audiences were willing to overlook the lighting inconsistencies and the boomy sound that microphones picked up in real rooms and hallways, as long as they could get that "you are there" sensation. The film's success despite its tiny budget sent screenwriters combing through government and police files to create a new genre of documentary-style procedural dramas—*T-Men*, *He Walked By Night*, *The Street With No Name* and *Walk East on Beacon*—that were stylishly similar to film noir (and often shot by the same people), though generally they presented a much more conservative worldview. Crime novelist James Ellroy calls them "public service noir" because they took the side of authority, whereas normal film noir was as morally ambiguous as Hollywood's prim little nanny, Joseph Ignatius Breen of the Production Code Administration, would allow.

The breakthrough was an early 1948 blockbuster called *The Naked City* that used what it proudly advertised as 107 different locations around New York City in recounting a fact-based homicide investigation in the midst

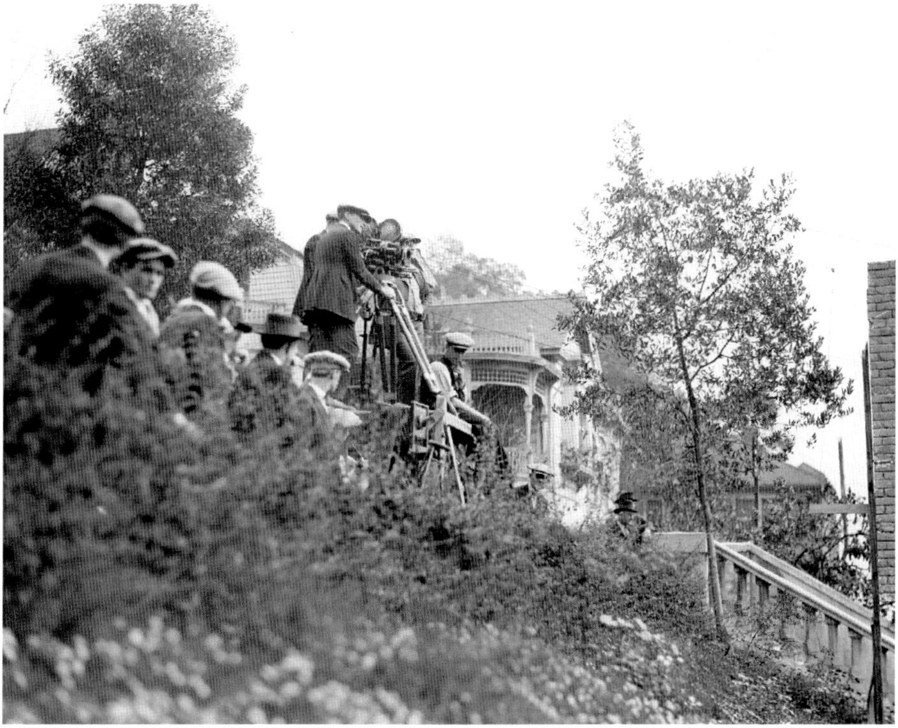

In Buster Keaton's *Three Ages* (1923), director Eddie Cline prepares a shot from the top of the Hill Street terrace steps above the south end of the Hill Street tunnel. The house behind them was at 134 North Hill Street. *Bison Archives.*

of normal urban life, culminating in a dramatic foot chase across the Williamsburg Bridge above the East River. To take full advantage of the streets, cinematographer William Daniels, a veteran of silent films, used a wide-angle lens and crisp "deep focus" to give them more texture. (Deep-focus photography, a staple of film noir, was perfect for location shooting because it revealed more detail, not less, and therefore enhanced the impression of real life.) He also shot some of the film's montages from a "candid camera" hidden in a special trailer, so that people within his frame weren't aware of it. Universal Pictures's media blitz touting *The Naked City*'s on-location realism created a cause célebre that not only sold millions of tickets but also prompted critics to wonder if the film would do to backlot streets what sound had done twenty years earlier to actors with squeaky voices.

Of course, the effectiveness of on-location filming didn't discredit the value of studio sets if they were well designed and properly shot. Two early classics of the film noir genre—*The Maltese Falcon* (1941) and *The Big Sleep* (a 1945 film with scenes added in 1946)—were filmed on Warner Bros soundstages that respectively recreated San Francisco and Los Angeles. As a rule, however, looking back from a twenty-first-century perspective, American crime movies shot on location in the 1940s and '50s tend to hold up better today than their stage-bound contemporaries. As film noir historian Foster Hirsch put it in his seminal *The Dark Side of the Screen*, studio sets were "deliberately lacking the fullness and density of a real city." They were abstractions of rooms, corridors and streets that may have served the

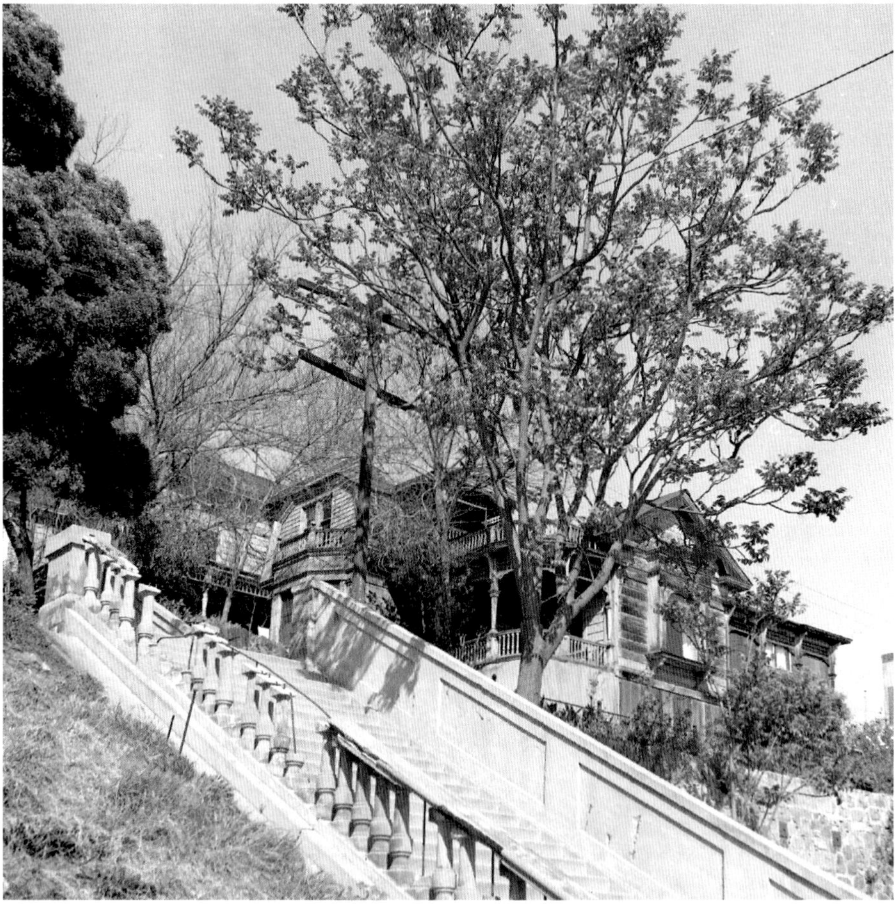

The terrace steps above the southern (First Street) end of the Hill Street tunnel were used in many silent films. Audrey Totter walked down these steps in *The Set-Up* (1949), and Ross Elliot witnessed a murder there at the beginning of *Woman on the Run* (1950). The house on the right, 134 North Hill Street, was Cornell Wilde's mother's house in *Shockproof* (1948). *The California History Room, California State Library, Sacramento.*

mood of the picture but were otherwise unconvincing, unless dazzling acting and crackling dialogue created enough misdirection to make them real.

On the other hand, scenes filmed on the streets create the impression that real life is going on outside the frame of the lens. They are literally and figuratively concrete. Their textures make you believe you're not only in the picture, but that you could take the streetcar home after the "Cut!" As director Otto Preminger told film scholar Robert Porfirio in 1975, cinematography is "an absolutely realistic medium. And I think that the more real you can make the film, the more people will believe it, because the camera, it is photography, it is not painting." To put a finer point on it, director-screenwriter Paul Schrader, in a landmark 1972 essay called "Notes on Film Noir," said that "the public's desire for a more honest and harsh view of America would not be satisfied by the same studio streets they had been watching for a dozen years."

On the commentary track of the DVD release of the now-classic *Crime Wave*, a low-budget quickie shot on the streets of L.A. in 1952 and released two years later, film noir maven Eddie Muller muses, "It's incredible the difference it makes—if you really think about this screenplay, if this thing was shot…in a studio, it would be a D-minus picture." *Crime Wave* director Andre deToth didn't disagree. "I like to show real life, which means I like to work on real locations," he told Alain Silver in 2001. "The real is the simplest and the best. Why build sets or imagine the locations to fit some sketches you did…When you can find a real place to hear dialogue, isn't that enough?"

James Ellroy probably summed it up best in that same *Crime Wave* commentary: "Location, location, location—there is no substitute."

CHAPTER 2
BUNKER HILL, LOS ANGELES

"It was an odd part of the city, but I liked it. It was a strictly no-questions-asked area, people minding their own business and letting you mind yours."
—Edward G. Robinson, Night Has a Thousand Eyes *(1948)*

The opening cast credits of United Artists's *Once a Thief* (1950) give fifth billing to "The City of Los Angeles"—and why not? Film noir titles are often a tip-off to their reliance on urban atmosphere: *The Naked City*, *Night and the City*, *Cry of the City*, *While the City Sleeps*, *The Phenix City Story* and *The City Is Dark* (the original title of *Crime Wave*). Others—*The House on 92nd Street, The Asphalt Jungle*, *Down Three Dark Streets*, *Panic in the Streets*, *Get Outta Town* and *Where the Sidewalk Ends*—leave little doubt where the viewer is going. Some of these films rely so heavily on their locations that the name of the city should be *above* the title.

In the case of *Once a Thief*, the more correct film credit should have been "The Neighborhood of Bunker Hill," because that's where nearly every outdoor scene was filmed, from the 200 block of Clay Street just north of Angels Flight to the storefronts beneath the Argyle Apartments in the 400 block of Second Street.

Filmmakers had been running around Bunker Hill at least since 1914, when Charlie Chaplin staged a fistfight for *Making a Living* in the middle of the intersection of Fourth Street and Grand Avenue. Hal Roach co-owned a movie studio in the Lewis Bradbury mansion at the corner of North Hill and Court Streets, where Chaplin, Harold Lloyd, Snub Pollard, Bebe

Daniels and other silent comics shot hundreds of early one- and two-reelers, including Chaplin's *Work* (1915) and Lloyd's *Haunted Spooks* (filmed mostly inside the mansion in 1920). Bunker Hill was visually dramatic with its two picturesque incline railways, several tunnels, numerous stairways, beautiful (if fading) Victorian homes and trapezoidal apartment buildings that rambled down the hillsides, adding new stories as they went. In a 1920 comic short called *All Jazzed Up*, director Al Christie used Angels Flight, one of the incline railways, as an amusement ride. Harold Lloyd visited the corner of Third Street and Grand Avenue in seven different films, including *Never Weaken* (1921), in which he flooded the intersection in front of the Angels Flight Pharmacy with enough soapy water to send everyone, including the cops, slipping and sliding and falling on their fannies. Many comics took advantage of several vertical drop-offs, especially on the terrace above the double-barrel Hill Street tunnel between First and Temple Streets, to create an illusion of dangerous height. But Bunker Hill never got beyond being a bit player until the end of World War II, when film noir's new strain of down-on-their-luck antiheroes required a down-on-its-luck section of the

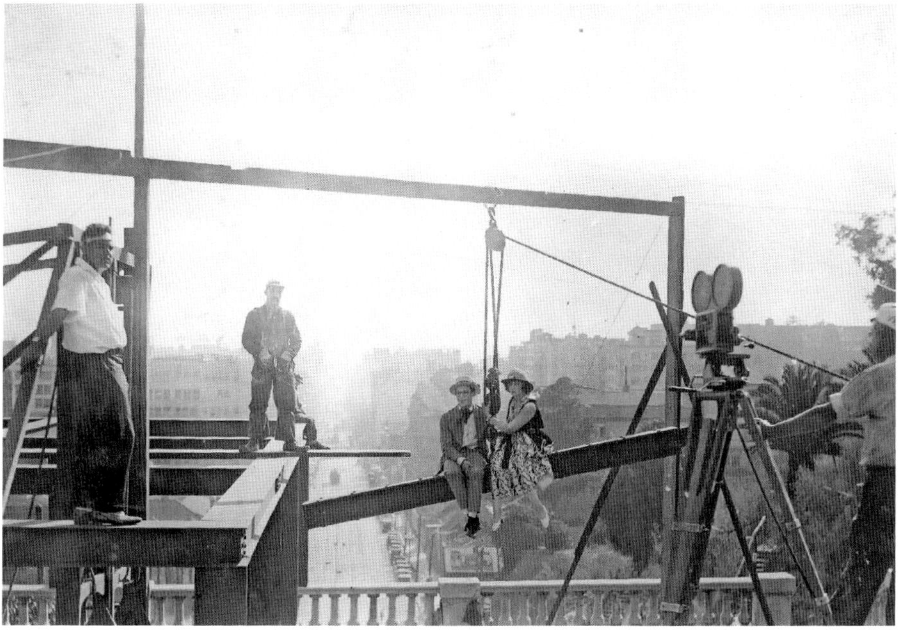

Director Hal Roach (left) and comics Snub Pollard, Harold Lloyd and Bebe Daniels prepare for a shot "high above the city" on top of the Hill Street tunnel in *Look Out Below* (1919). *Bison Archives.*

city that convincingly portrayed sunlit desolation or nightscape menace. Bunker Hill was aging and had lost much of its charm. Some people even called it a slum, though most of its neighborhoods were hardly that.

Bunker Hill was probably an island six million years ago when the Los Angeles basin was at the bottom of a warm sea. It certainly seemed like an island of tranquility in the nineteenth century, even as the little El Pueblo de la Reina de Los Angeles, founded half a mile away in 1781, gradually enveloped it like water rising around a boulder. It was an aloof, treeless promontory of sagebrush and chaparral, not much good for grazing livestock or growing crops, and its steep grades stymied horse-drawn wagons. Outside of some clay deposits on the eastern bluff, nobody thought the hill had much worth at all.

But then one day in 1867, a French-Canadian named Prudent Beaudry bought a big chunk of it—twenty acres—for $517 at a sheriff's auction on the courthouse steps, with the idea of developing a residential neighborhood

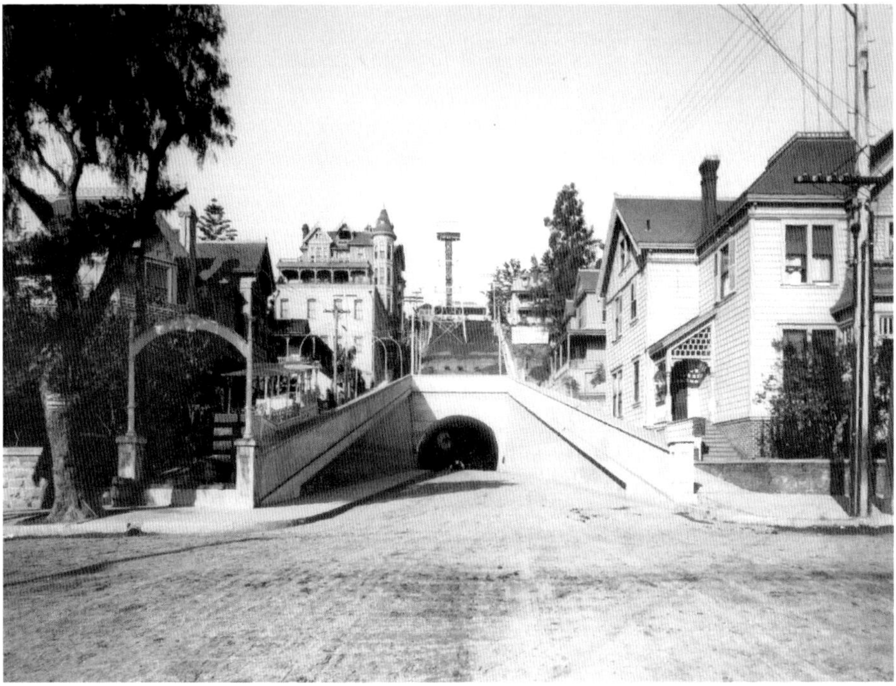

In 1901, the Angels Flight incline railway opened beside the new Third Street tunnel to ferry passengers from Hill Street at the bottom to the Olive Street station at the top. In its original configuration, seen here around 1903, Angels Flight's open gondolas passed each other in the middle of Clay Street. Owner J. Ward Eddy elevated the railway above Clay in 1905 and replaced the gondolas with enclosed cars. *Jim Dawson.*

for the city's nascent business class. His property—known to surveyors and land assessors as the Mott Tract—was bordered by Fourth Street to the south, Charity Street (later renamed Grand Avenue) to the west, Second Street to the north and Hill Street, which lay at the bottom of the hill, to the east. Beaudry subdivided his land into lots with views of distant Pasadena to the northeast and the Pacific Ocean to the south. He built two water reservoirs, eleven miles of iron pipe and a pumping system that brought water up from the Los Angeles River. He graded streets, paved them and planted elm trees. Other speculators developed adjacent properties and softened the hill's northern edges to make it more accessible. In time, they expanded the neighborhood west to Figueroa, north to Temple and south to Fifth Street. After Beaudry became the city mayor, he celebrated America's 1875 centennial commemoration of the Revolutionary War's Battle of Bunker Hill in Massachusetts by officially conferring the name upon his hilltop community.

As Los Angeles boomed in the 1870s and into the '80s, many of the local bankers, lawyers and wealthy merchants who were anxious to display their exalted place in the firmament began building dream castles on Bunker Hill. A fairly new type of housing construction called "balloon-frame," using light, factory-milled lumber that could be hammered together with iron nails, allowed architects to abandon the massive timbers that required thick bearing walls and build mansions at a reasonable cost. Many of their clients, or more likely the clients' wives, were drawn to the hot new Queen Anne Revival and Eastlake styles introduced at the British Pavilion of the 1876 Centennial Exhibition in Philadelphia. Queen Anne (named after an early eighteenth-century monarch) was the more ostentatious of the two: pure bric-a-brac, with steep Gothic roofs, jutting gables, wraparound verandas, cupolas, gawky chimneys, elaborate spindlework and any other "gingerbread" that might add a few extra dollops of grandiosity or whimsy. If architecture is "frozen music," as the German writer Goethe once said, then Queen Anne was a warm and kooky symphony of oboes, piccolos and tubas. Since the (mostly pine) wooden parts were pre-cut and advertised in factory catalogs, architects could mix and match and create unique houses, each unlike any other, limited only by the enthusiasm and daring—and money—of their patrons. A skyline like Bunker Hill flaunted these showboats for miles around. Among the most impressive of them were the Crocker mansion at Third and Olive, which would later loom above the Angels Flight incline railway; Daniel F. Donegan's "Castle" at 325 South Bunker Hill Avenue, with added touches of simpler Eastlake lines; the Robert Larkin mansion at 142 South Grand, later converted into the Richlieu Hotel in

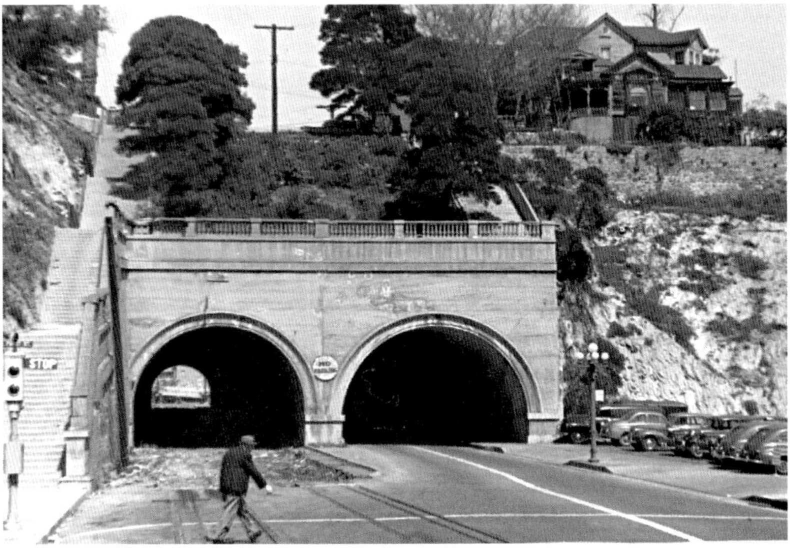

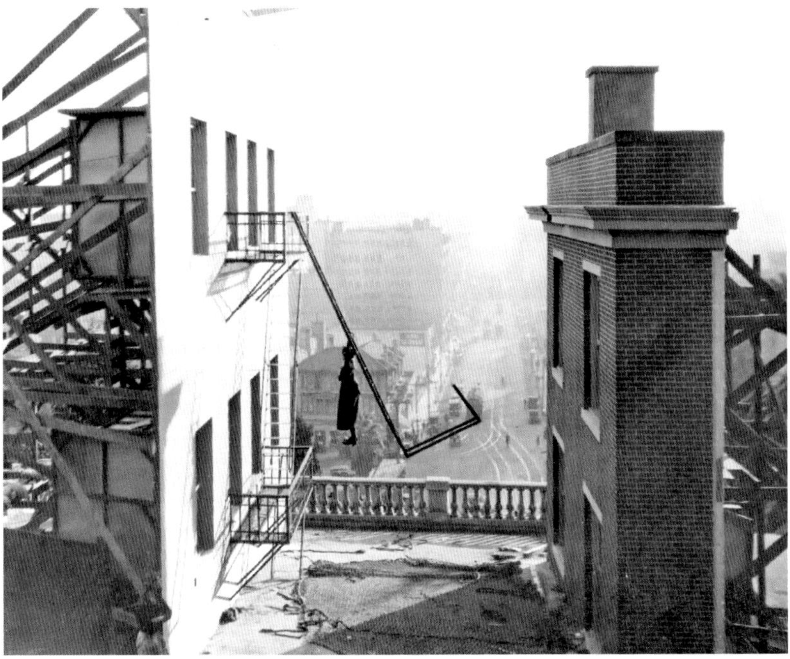

This page: The Hill Street tunnel, seen here in 1953 after the streetcar tracks had been torn up, ran from near First Street (where the photographer, Arnold Hylen, is standing) to Temple Street on the other side. The area just behind the balustrade was popular with silent comedians, who built sets to give an illusion of height above the city. Actress Eileen Sedgwick hangs from a fire escape ladder at what looks like the top of a building in *The Terror Trail* (1921). *The California History Room, California State Library, Sacramento, above; and Bison Archives.*

1891; and Dr. Edmund Hildreth's house at 357 South Hope Street. Three other Bunker Hill homes—Leonard J. Rose's mansion at Fourth Street and Grand Avenue, Pierre Larronde's mansion at 237 North Hope and the Lewis Bradbury mansion at 139 North Hill on the corner of Court Street—were built in a San Francisco elaboration of Queen Anne excess called American Renaissance, whose wood patterns mimicked California vegetation.

But within just a few years, as Los Angeles's bustling commercial district intruded upon the streets below, Bunker Hill lost much of its cachet. As John D. Weaver noted in *El Pueblo Grande*, the "men who had grown old and rich buying and selling, lending and speculating, healing and suing, abandoned Bunker Hill to fling up French chateaux and English manor houses on the recycled beanfields of Beverly Hills," not to mention the West Adams district, Chester Place and Hancock Park, leaving their high-maintenance mansions to be broken up into apartments for lesser folks. Then, in the late 1890s and into the new century, came the construction boom of more than one hundred hotels and rooming houses to accommodate the city's new swarm of workers and tourists. By 1900, Bunker Hill was a thriving middle- and working-class community.

You had to climb a hill from any direction, but one of Bunker Hill's more impassable grades was just below where Third Street dead-ended at Olive Street. Below Olive was a grassy drop-off leading down to a parallel alley called Clay Street, where a short, residential block of Third picked up again on its way down to Hill Street. It was there that a mining engineer named J. Ward Eddy built Angels Flight, an incline railway (what Europeans call a funicular) run from a station house at the top. It was comprised of two counterbalanced cars attached to a cable system, one going up as the other came down, so that each car helped pull or slow the other on its 325-foot journey. Angels Flight opened on the afternoon of New Year's Eve 1901, right next to the new Third Street tunnel, and became a thriving enterprise over the next six decades. In 1904, Samuel Vandergrift built a second incline railway, Court Flight, three blocks north of Angels Flight, linking the top of northern Bunker Hill with the Los Angeles County Courthouse on Broadway.

During the next forty years, as vast new tracts of housing opened up in the western and northern parts of Los Angeles, the strivers gradually moved out of Bunker Hill and the rents got cheaper. The residents who enjoyed their lives there or couldn't afford to leave stayed put and grew old. Other retirees living on limited incomes moved in, along with artists and writers, Italian and Mexican immigrants, Dust Bowl refugees, low-wage downtown workers and poor folks in general. By the end of World War II, when Hollywood came calling, many of the old houses and hotels had deteriorated into

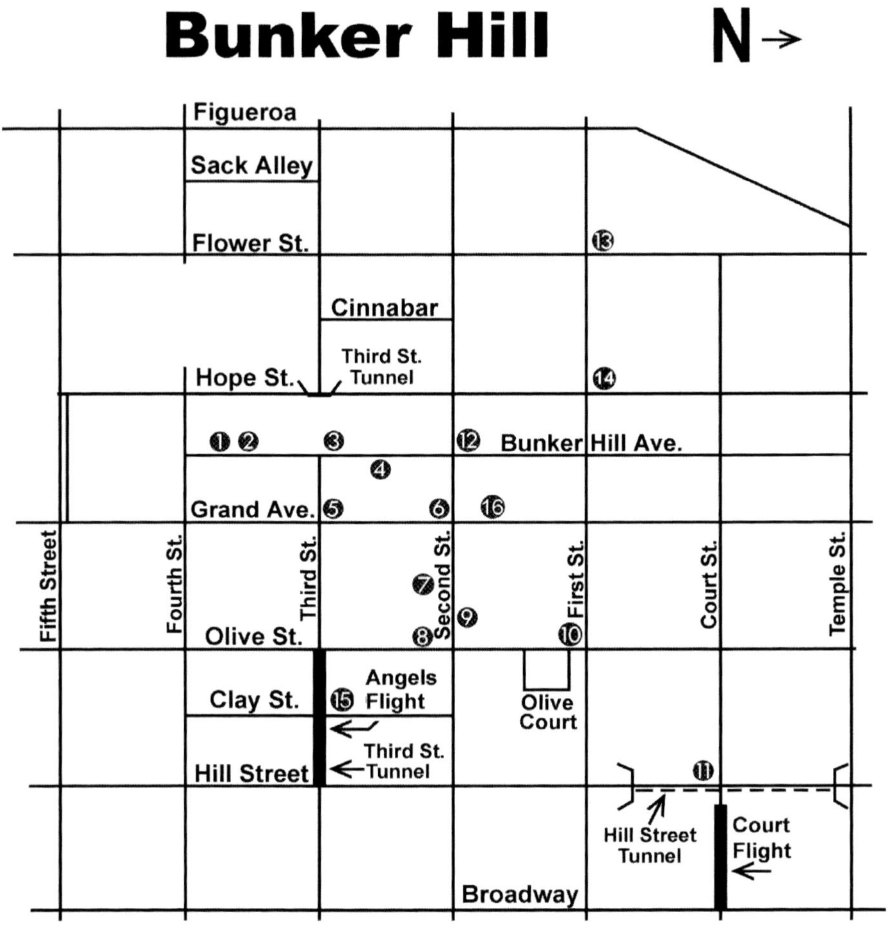

1. The Castle
2. The Heindel house
3. The Alta Vista
4. The Brousseau mansion
5. The New Grand Hotel
6. The Dome
7. The Chaspeak Apts
8. The Mission Apts
9. The Koster house
10. The Gladden Apts
11. The Bradbury mansion
12. The Berke/Warncliffe
13. The Lancaster Apts
14. The Auburn Apts
15. The Sunshine Apts
16. The Melrose Hotel

Map by Earl Reinhalter.

spectral figures in need of a good paint job. Bunker Hill looked like a place that might seep into the souls of the desperate or struggling people who lived there. Central casting couldn't have picked a better "rough neighborhood" for its new genre of dark and stark crime dramas, in which the last scene never faded out on a kiss—unless it was the kiss of death.

CHAPTER 3
HARD-BOILED MEMORIES

"But down these mean streets a man must go who is not himself mean, who is neither tarnished nor afraid."
—Raymond Chandler, "The Simple Art of Murder" (1950)

Before film noir, there was pulp fiction. In fact, film noir was mostly pulp fiction lifted off the page and cast in jagged shadows upon the screen.

In his essay "Notes on Film Noir," Paul Schrader pointed out that if the genre got its visual style from the German expatriates who fled to Hollywood in the 1930s, it got its characters and snappy dialogue from the American pulp magazines of the 1920s, so named because they were printed on cheap wood-pulp paper that started turning brown the moment the pages were opened. These magazines were strictly for the working-class, a couple of rungs down from the "slicks" like the *Saturday Evening Post* and *Cosmopolitan*, but boys and men of all ages and backgrounds devoured them. They had names like *Argosy*, *Astounding Stories*, *Weird Tales* and *Double Action Western*. Especially popular were the crime chronicles like *Detective Fiction Weekly*, *Thrilling Detective*, *Dime Detective* and the gold-standard *Black Mask*, which published John Carroll Daly (credited as the first successful hard-boiled writer), Erle Stanley Gardner, Dashiell Hammett and Raymond Chandler. Writing for the pulps was piecework, usually at one penny a word, though some paid more and many paid less.

Tawdry broadsheets and magazines, originally called "penny dreadfuls," had been around since the 1840s, catering to a newly literate public with a taste for sensation. These publications relied on a new breed of scrivener—the hack, short for hackney: a hired drudge, or a prostitute—capable of cranking out formula plots within genres as rigid as a schoolmarm's corset. The prose was usually mock-heroic and ornate, sometimes called "purple" because of its faux royal pretensions, to overcompensate for its lack of freshness and literary worth.

By the 1920s, Americans wanted something with a little more punch. The coupling of a booming economy with the federal government's unpopular prohibition of alcohol had created an era in which any goodtime Charlie who took a drink was a criminal. Otherwise respectable people were obliged to rub elbows in speakeasies with foul-mouthed flappers, colorful gangsters and politicians on the take. They developed a taste for fiction that was as hot and syncopated as the new jazz and as current as that morning's shocking headlines. According to veteran pulp writer Frank Gruber, his compatriots were the ones who streamlined the American literary tradition. "They stripped [their writing] of verbiage, blue-penciled the descriptive passages, kept their stories moving. The characters became strong, silent men. The stories became more violent, the prose became sparser." *Black Mask* editor Joseph Shaw told his writers, "Prune and cut, don't use a single word that you

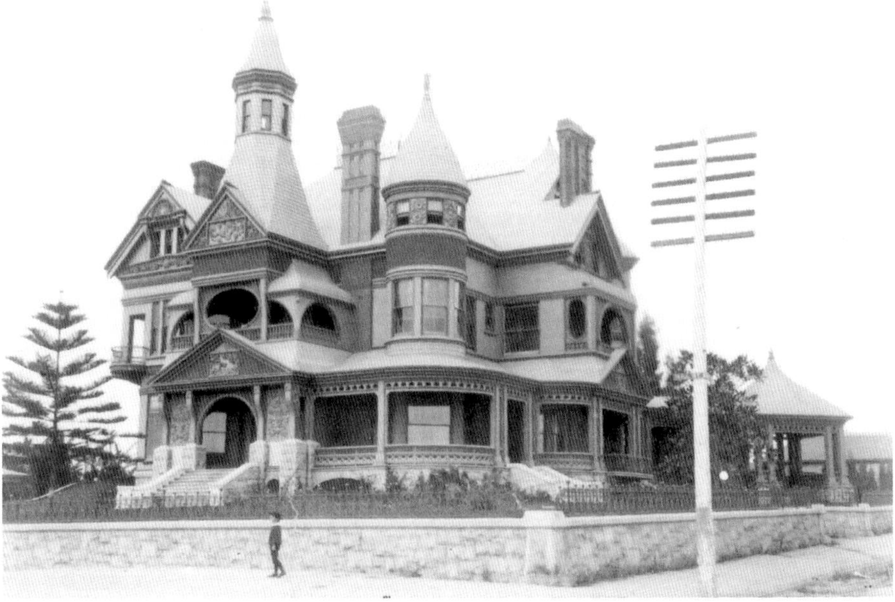

Mining magnate Lewis Bradbury is best known today for building what was then called the Bradbury Block at the southeast corner of Third and Broadway in downtown Los Angeles, but he also built the impressive Bradbury mansion at the southwest corner of North Hill and Court streets. The house later became Hal Roach's film studio. It was razed in 1929. *Security Pacific Collection/LAPL.*

can do without." One of Shaw's exemplars was Dashiell Hammett, a former operative of the Pinkerton's National Detective Service, whose terse sentences read like telegrams to his home office. The style came to be known as hard-boiled, a term used as a character trait within the pulp stories themselves. Originally a method of cooking eggs to a solid consistency, hard-boiled's use as a human descriptive (callous, unfeeling, with a heart the size of a blister) was probably an update of the eighteenth-century *hard-bitten*, meaning "given to hard biting; tough in a fight," to quote the Oxford English Dictionary.

It's hard to touch upon hard-boiled fiction, not to mention film noir, without quoting Raymond Chandler's "mean streets" line from near the end of his essay "The Simple Art of Murder." It's like an article of the crime writer's constitution, excerpted so often that it's gone beyond cliché. Chandler was making the case that Hammett was the first true artist of the American crime genre because he moved the murder scene out of the vicar's garden and "into the alley" where it belonged. When Hammett began writing for *Black Mask* in 1923, his detective—the Continental Op from the Continental Detective Agency—wasn't the traditional sleuth in silk pajamas solving parlor-game puzzles with his knowledge of arcane tobaccos and Ming vases. Nor did he gather all the suspects in one room to spring a climactic "gotcha," known as the *denouement*, complete with fancy French pronunciation. The Op was just an underpaid working stiff who, in the course of his job, dealt with cutthroats, punks, grifters, fallen angels, dirty municipal functionaries and plenty of bum steers. Such a man, said Chandler, had to be tough but not mean, street-wise but not bitterly cynical, as honest as a dollar and "fit for adventure." He didn't have to be a private detective. He could be a cop, a newspaper reporter, a knob-jostling hotel dick or simply a put-upon average Joe seeking his own redemption. But he couldn't be a chump, unless a beautiful siren had temporarily (with the stress on *temporarily*) clouded his judgment. And he had to talk like he meant business.

Most of these stories took place in a nameless metropolis, because the writers found it easier to make up geographical details as they went along. But Hammett's Continental Op worked out of San Francisco and sometimes described landmarks by name. As for Los Angeles, not until Chandler shouldered his way through the door with similes blazing did any pulp writer appreciate that it was more than a remote farm-town resort of retired Iowans and motion picture people or that malfeasance was as much a part of the terrain as Mexican palms, Japanese gardens and motley European architecture.

One of the first distinctly "Los Angeles" novelists of the twentieth century was Don Ryan (1889-?), a columnist for the *Los Angeles Record* and the *Evening*

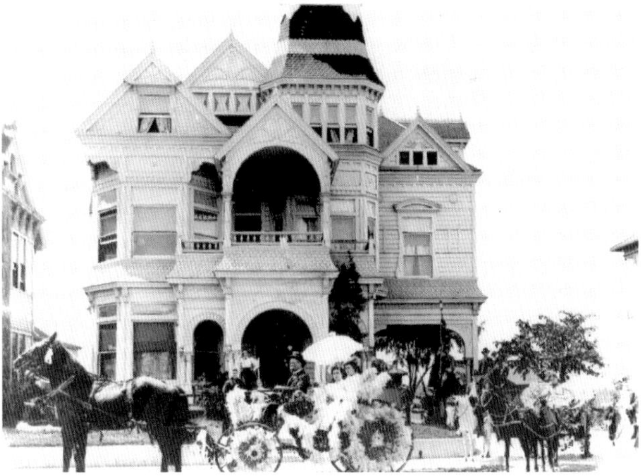

The Castle at 325 South Bunker Hill Avenue was for many years the residence of Daniel F. Donegan, who paved most of Bunker Hill's streets, but after he moved out around 1902, the new owners divided the 1882 mansion into apartments. Fifty years later, it was used in the film *Kiss Me Deadly* (1955). *Courtesy of Security Pacific Collection/Los Angeles Public Library.*

Herald whose beat was personal interest stories. A southern Ohio-born alumnus of West Virginia University and a veteran of the World War, Ryan had moved west to the city around 1920. He would write four novels between 1927 and 1930, before settling into Hollywood's Beachwood Canyon (two blocks from where I live today) to write B-movie scripts like *Tear Gas Squad* for Warner Bros. The first of Ryan's books was *Angel's Flight*, an olio of memoir, free verse and pulp fiction as told by his alter-ego, William Pence, a speakeasy habitué who consorts with bootleggers, witnesses an ambush murder and lands a job as a newspaper writer. *Angel's Flight* was the first of more than half a dozen novels with that title and one of the first novels of any title to contrast Los Angeles's booster-driven promises of Sunkist paradise and movie star magic with the threadbare realities. *Angel's Flight* was also the first to note Bunker Hill's growing popularity among bohemians and older citizens, especially war veterans, fleeing the winter seasons of past lives. During a visit to Pershing Square, a block-sized park on Fifth Street at the foot of Bunker Hill, he notices that the benches are "filled with grotesque cripples, abandoned hulks of men, gray invalids, impish hobo anarchists who taunt the furious apostles of fundamentalism." It's likely that many if not most of these displaced men lived in Bunker Hill rooming houses.

When J. Ward Eddy built Angels Flight along the impassable 400 block of Third Street in 1901, he took advantage of Bunker Hill's panoramic view by building an observation tower called Angels View, one hundred feet high, with a *camera obscura*—a small room, literally a camera—at the top. Los Angeles's Board of Public Works closed the tower in the 1920s because the ground beneath it was unstable, but not before Don Ryan paid a visit. The

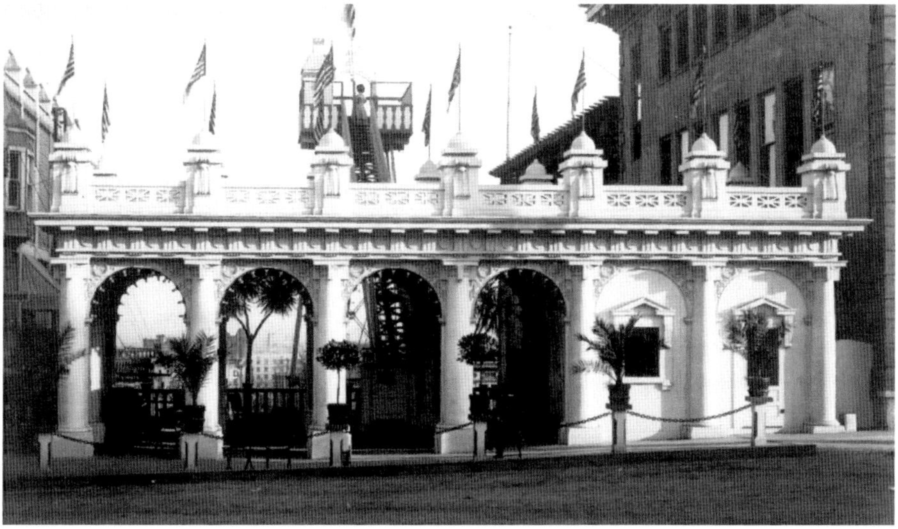

Angels Flight owner J. Ward Eddy attached a one-hundred-foot-high observation tower, Angels View, to his railway's Olive Street station (seen here around 1910) and placed a room-sized camera at the top. The price of admission was a nickel. Local newspaper columnist Don Ryan visited the tower in his 1927 novel *Angel's Flight*. Most of the station's pavilion had to be removed within several years because of unstable ground (only the two bays on the right survived—and are still being used today), and the tower was torn down in the 1930s. *Jim Dawson.*

camera provided him with a metaphor of disembodied angels looking down upon a faded image of a city.

His character Pence stumbles upon the little railway during a celebratory amble after being hired by a local paper:

> *ANGEL'S FLIGHT.*
> *The letters printed large across an archway shunted my train of thought with a jerk on to a siding…*
>
> *The groaning cable car landed me above the tops of brittle palms and loquat trees. On the cracked concrete [of the station pavilion deck] gray invalids were sunning themselves, wheelchairs parked in a row along the railing, over which they could look down at the city below.*
>
> *Another sign inviting another ascent. With legs. An ascent impossible to the occupants of the wheelchairs. A long flight of wooden steps. Perhaps, beyond, another sign will tempt a rebellious angel to try his wings… Angel's flight.*
>
> *The summit. A sentry-box penciled over with paltry memories of Iowa, Michigan, Massachusetts, Ohio.*

> *A contrivance labeled Camera Obscura. One of those had been a toy of Leonardo da Vinci. I am alone, I close the door. It is dark inside the box.*
>
> *My eyes grow accustomed by degrees to the darkness. Something is moving on the white surface in front of me. Colors appearing—faintly. It is a reflection in miniature of the city above which I am hovering. The Camera Obscura has given me wings.*

Pence imagines himself as a professional fly on the wall, deputized by his newspaper to report on every nook of the city. His trips up to Bunker Hill keep this mental fiction alive.

> *One day I felt my steps turning in the direction of Angel's Flight. I had been below for weeks and I felt the need for orientation. I wished to hover over the city again and from the heights to laugh.*
>
> *Again I paid a nickel to ride in the groaning cable car. Again I passed through the ranks of gray invalids in wheelchairs and mounted the long flight of wooden steps.*
>
> *Alone at the summit, I entered the box and closed the door. Darkness giving way to moving shadows—colors appearing—a city of pigmies taking on life in the streets below.*
>
> *Los Angeles, city with aspirations for the Los Angelicizing of the world…Jazz Baby of the Golden West, I greet you.*

Perhaps the first crime novel that visited Bunker Hill was Paul Cain's *Fast One* (1933), five *Black Mask* serialized stories combined into a high-velocity kill-fest that Raymond Chandler later, in a 1953 letter to critic James Sandoe, called "some kind of high point in the ultra-hardboiled manner." Cain (1902–1966) himself was as slippery as his characters. Born in Iowa as George Sims, he changed his name to Peter Ruric and wrote a few B-movie scripts, including Universal Pictures's *The Black Cat*, starring Boris Karloff and Bela Lugosi. Paul Cain was his *Black Mask* nom de mayhem. His *Fast One* protagonist is Gerry Kells, a hardheaded gambler who can't go more than two pages without getting shot at or knocked cold. Though most of the action takes place around Hollywood, Kells visits the Bunker Hill area a couple of times without naming it. Many vacant areas on the hill had been turned into parking lots to accommodate the expanding downtown district below, beginning in 1917 with Andrew Pansini's "auto park" at the northwest corner of Fourth and Olive—perhaps the first private parking lot in Los Angeles. "Kells drove up Fourth to the top of the hill. His eyes were

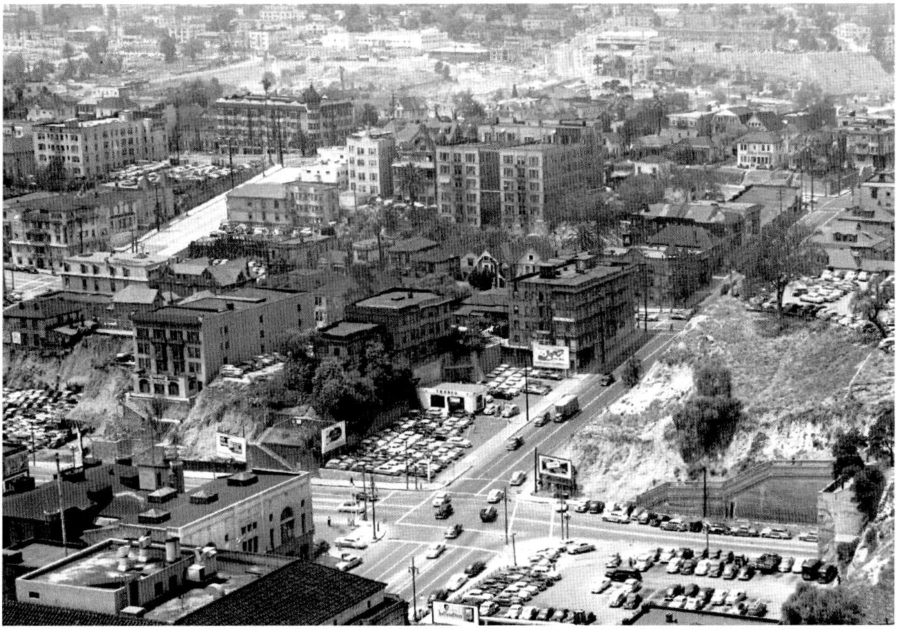

This southwestern view from the top of Los Angeles City Hall shows that Bunker Hill was still fairly intact in 1953. Hill Street is running across the bottom (note the south end of the tunnel at far right) and First Street runs diagonally up the page. Gerry Kells parked on the southwest corner in writer Paul Cain's *Fast One* (1933) when he went to the arch-windowed Central Division Police Station across the street, at 318 West First. In 1916 Raymond Chandler lived at the Gladden Apartments at First and Olive, just right of the photo's center. Second Street runs diagonally up the left side of the photo; the Dome Hotel Apartments at the southwest corner of Grand Avenue is plainly visible near the top. The California History Room, California State Library, Sacramento.

half closed and there was an almost tender expression on his face. He swore softly, continuously, obscenely. His anger had worn itself out by the time he had parked the car on Grand and walked down the steep hill to the rear entrance of the Biltmore."

Later on, his girlfriend gets kidnapped on the Bunker Hill side of Hill and First, across the street from the Central Division Police Station at 318 West First.

> *Their cab was across the street. Kells looked up First Street to where the second cab had been parked on the other side of Hill Street. It had gone. He stood there a moment looking up First, then he said, "Come on," and crossed the street, asked the driver, "What happened to the other cab?"*
>
> *The driver shook his head. "I don't know. It was there a minute ago an' then I looked up an' it was gone."*

The closest thing Bunker Hill had to a tough-guy poet was Raymond Chandler (1888–1959), who didn't have much good to say about it. He was born in Chicago and raised in England, but his Philip Marlowe novels and his noir screenplays for *Double Indemnity* and *The Blue Dahlia* put Los Angeles at the heart of the hard-boiled universe. Three years after Chandler arrived in the city in 1913, he and his mother moved to Bunker Hill's Gladden Apartments at 100 South Olive Street, a former Jewish hotel once called the Cecil, not far from the Los Angeles Creamery Company on Towne Avenue downtown where he worked as a bookkeeper. In 1937, Chandler returned to Bunker Hill with his wife, "Cissy," to live for a short time at the Palm Terrace Apartments at 625 West Fourth Street, in a neighborhood that was still fairly genteel, despite the hill's overall decline. That's where he may have written his now-famous novella "The King in Yellow" for the March 1938 issue of *Dime Detective* magazine, in which he made his first full-on indictment of Bunker Hill.

But it was not his first fictional visit. In one of his earlier stories, "Spanish Blood" (from the November 1935 issue of *Black Mask*), when a Filipino cokehead went to kill a stoolie at a cheap Bunker Hill hotel, Chandler didn't mention the area's name. "Ceferino Toribo strolled along Spring Street, trailing smoke over his neat shoulder from a chocolate-colored cigarette. At Fourth he turned west, went three blocks more, turned into the side entrance of the Mansfield, by the barbershop." Though another character says the Mansfield is on Grand Avenue, anyone familiar with downtown L.A. knows that three blocks west of Spring is Olive Street, where the Fremont Hotel stood on the southwest corner of Fourth. Grand is a block further west, where the Zelda occupied the southwest corner. Either place works in the story because both were residential hotels on Bunker Hill. But Chandler's inconsistency shows either carelessness or obfuscation, which becomes apparent when he later recycles the following pungent description of Bunker Hill from "The King in Yellow":

> *Court Street was old town, wop town, crook town, arty town. It lay across the top of Bunker Hill and you could find anything there from down-at-heels ex-Greenwich-villagers to crooks on the lam, from ladies of anybody's evening to County Relief clients brawling with haggard landladies in grand old houses with scrolled porches, parquetry floors, and immense banisters of white oak, mahogany and Circassian walnut.*
>
> *It had been a nice place once, had Bunker Hill, and from the days of its niceness there still remained the funny little funicular railway, called the Angel's Flight, which crawled up and down a yellow clay bank from Hill*

> *Street. It was afternoon when Steve Grayce got off the car at the top, its only passenger. He walked along in the sun* [north on Olive Street for three blocks], *a tall, wide-shouldered, ranging-looking man in a well-cut blue suit.*

Grayce, a hotel detective on a personal mission, turns west and begins looking for the Ridgeland Apartments at 118 Court Street. It's across the street from the Paolo Perrugnini Funeral Home, where a "swarthy iron-gray Italian in a cut-away coat stood in front of the curtained door…smoking a cigar and waiting for somebody to die."

> *One-eighteen was a three-storied frame apartment house. It had a glass door, well masked by a dirty net curtain, a hall runner eighteen inches wide, dim doors with numbers painted on them with dim paint, a staircase halfway back. Brass stair rods glittered in the dimness of the hallway.*

Upstairs, Grayce picks Apartment 211's lock and discovers the woman who lives there lying dead under a pull-down Murphy bed. He goes downstairs to see the manager. When he knocks, a "sharp voice" calls him in.

> *In the middle of the room a woman rocked in an old Boston rocker, her body in the slack boneless attitude of exhaustion. She had a mud-colored face, stringy hair, gray cotton stockings—everything a Bunker Hill landlady should have. She looked at Steve with the interested eye of a dead goldfish.*

Before Grayce leaves the building, a man is shot to death in the hallway by a couple of thugs. Grayce chases after them down the back alley, and as their car gets away he keeps running to put distance between himself and Court Street. He sees a nearby lunchroom.

> *He went in, sat at the counter and ordered coffee. In a little while there were sirens.*
>
> *Steve drank his coffee, asked for another cup and drank that. He lit a cigarette and walked down the long hill to Fifth, across to Hill, back to the foot of the Angel's Flight, and got his convertible out of a parking lot.*

When Chandler graduated to novels in 1939 with *The Big Sleep* and the new first-person voice of Philip Marlowe, he sometimes took shortcuts by rewriting and elaborating upon scenes from his old pulp stories. Grayce's

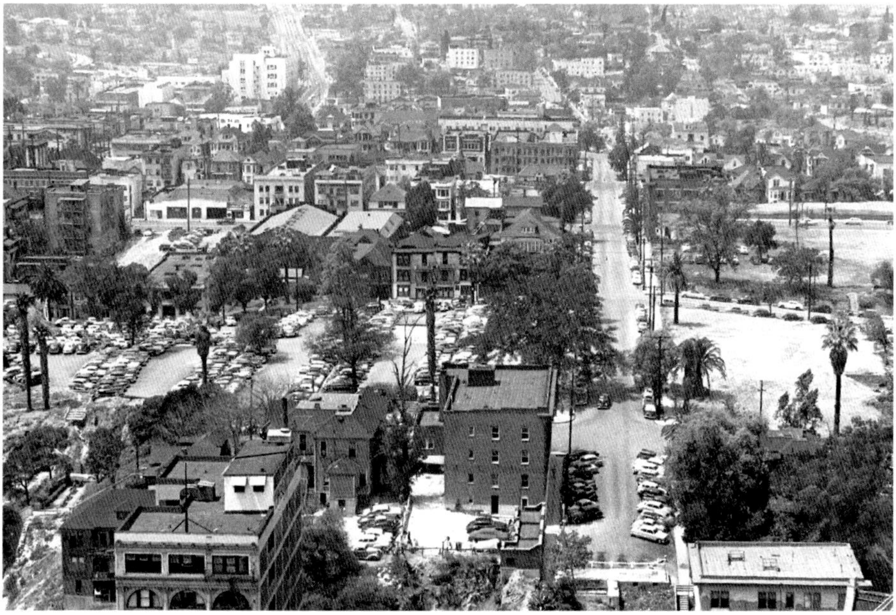

In this westward shot from the top of Los Angeles City Hall in 1953, most of Court Street is still intact, though some of the old houses have been torn down. In *The High Window*, Philip Marlowe parked where it dead-ends near the bottom of the photo, just above the now defunct Court Flight incline railway. The cross street is North Hill. The Florence Apartments would have been on the left side of the street, near the photo's center. *The California History Room, California State Library, Sacramento.*

foray to 118 Court Street in "The King in Yellow" found its way into *The High Window* (1942), but this time the more loquacious Marlowe, expressing Chandler's own disappointment over the changes he'd noticed in the twenty years between his residencies on Bunker Hill, lingered in a bitter monologue that has been repeated many times since—probably too many times—by Los Angeles historians and film noir explicators, because Chandler so deftly crystallized the neighborhood's slide into seediness.

> *Bunker Hill is old town, lost town, shabby town, crook town. Once, very long ago, it was the choice residential district of the city, and there are still standing a few of the jigsaw Gothic mansions with wide porches and walls covered with round-end shingles and full corner bay windows with spindle turrets. They are all rooming houses now, their parquetry floors are scratched and worn through the once glossy finish and the wide sweeping staircases are dark with time and with cheap varnish laid on over generations of dirt.*

> *In the tall rooms haggard landladies bicker with shifty tenants. On the wide cool front porches, reaching their cracked shoes into the sun, and staring at nothing, sit the old men with faces like lost battles.*
>
> *In and around the old houses there are flyblown restaurants and Italian fruit stands and cheap apartment houses and little candy stores where you can buy even nastier things than their candy. And there are ratty hotels where nobody except people named Smith and Jones sign the register and where the night clerk is half watchdog and half pander.*
>
> *Out of the apartment houses come women who should be young but have faces like stale beer; men with pulled-down hats and quick eyes that look the street over behind the cupped hand that shields the match flame; worn intellectuals with cigarette coughs and no money in the bank; fly cops with granite faces and unwavering eyes; cokies and coke peddlers; people who look like nothing in particular and know it, and once in a while even men that actually go to work. But they come out early, when the wide cracked sidewalks are empty and still have dew on them.*
>
> *I was earlier than four-thirty getting over there, but not much. I parked at the end of the street, where the funicular railway comes struggling up the yellow clay bank from Hill Street, and walked along Court Street to the Florence Apartments.*

That's the inconsistency mentioned earlier. In *The High Window*, the address he's looking for has changed from 118 to 128 Court Street, but neither one makes sense geographically. First of all, in transferring the scene from "The King in Yellow" to the novel, Chandler conflated the two Bunker Hill incline railways, even though they were three blocks apart. Angels Flight did indeed climb up from South Hill Street, but Chandler's description indicates that Marlowe parked his car just east of *North* Hill Street on a dead-end spit of Court Street (an area of Bunker Hill that locals called Court Hill), directly above the Court Flight railway that ran down to the 200 block of North Broadway. Court Flight lacked Angels Flight's charm and tourist appeal and mostly served the Los Angeles County Courthouse and Hall of Records. It ceased operation in 1943.

Also, in real Los Angeles, both the 118 and 128 Court Street addresses would have been located between Main and Spring Streets, *inside* the familiar Los Angeles City Hall, if Court Street had extended off Bunker Hill into downtown. Was this Chandler's way of insinuating the corruption of Los Angeles politics? Did he suspect that the machinations of power players within that bone white art deco obelisk would, within twenty years, doom Bunker Hill and obliterate that section of Court Street completely?

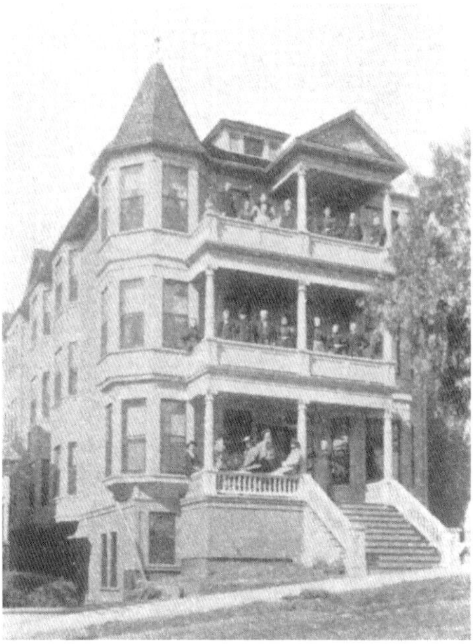

The Carroll at 343 South Olive was typical of Bunker Hill's many small Victorian tourist hotels that began renting furnished rooms and apartments to downtown workers in the early 1900s. It was dilapidated by the time it was torn down in the 1960s. *Jim Dawson.*

Having parked near the corner of Court and North Hill Streets, Marlowe should have been walking west in the 400 block of Court Street. Furthermore, though a Florence Apartments did exist in Los Angeles in 1942, it was miles away. Perhaps Chandler replaced the earlier, nondescript Ridgeland Apartments in "The King in Yellow" with the Florence in *The High Window* because he'd once lived with his mother, Florence Chandler, a block south of Court Street at the Gladden Apartments at First and Olive. Coincidentally, in 1947, when Twentieth Century Fox adapted *The High Window* into *The Brasher Doubloon*, a lackluster B film starring George Montgomery as Marlowe, one of the few real locations he visited was that very Gladden Apartments building, with the Los Angeles City Hall gleaming in the background, in a pan shot that inspired a nameless *Los Angeles Times* reviewer (June 2, 1947) to gush that "there is a breathtaking street view of a Los Angeles rooming house." Five years later, in Paramount's *The Turning Point*, the Gladden is a gangster haven that looks worn down, its stucco plainly broken in places and patched in others. But in all fairness, Chandler's description of the Florence doesn't quite fit the four-story Gladden, which had front bay windows and a small columned porch:

> *It was dark brick in front, three stories, the lower windows at sidewalk level and masked by rusted screens and dingy net curtains. The entrance door had a glass panel and enough of the name left to be read. I opened it and went down three brass bound steps into a hallway you could touch on both sides without stretching. Dim doors painted with numbers in dim paint. An alcove at the foot of the stairs with a pay telephone. At the back of the hallway a screen door and in the alley beyond it four tall battered garbage pails in a line, with a dance of flies in the sunlit air above them.*

Here's how *The Brasher Doubloon* screenwriter Leonard Praskins plundered Chandler's style to describe the place in George Montgomery's narration: "The Florence Apartments was a rooming house on Bunker Hill, which used to be the choice place to live in Los Angeles. Nowadays people live there because they haven't got any choice."

Apparently none of the Florence residents sit around reciting Edgar Guest poems over tea cozies. The manager is a nasty drunk who tells Marlowe to shove off until he learns there's a bribe involved, and the other tenants are loudly abusive to each other. When the manager threatens one man that he'd better turn down his blaring radio or else, they end up pulling guns on each other. The manager also tells Marlowe that Mr. Palmero, the mortician he saw across the street, owns the Florence and most of the neighborhood, which suggests that the innocent-looking Italian we first met as Paolo Perrugnini in "The King in Yellow" is some kind of Bunker Hill slumlord godfather. (This offers another explanation why Chandler moved his 400 block action to the fake 100 block; a large, real-life funeral home, the Alvarez and Moore Mortuary, had been operating at 500 West Court, on the southwest corner of Olive, since the late teens, and he didn't want them to sue him.)

The man Marlowe is looking for in *The High Window* is a down-on-his-luck shamus named George Anson Phillips, who's working for a coin dealer. In an earlier scene, Phillips had given Marlowe his card with a Hollywood address printed on it, but then he took it back and hastily scribbled his new Court Street address on the back.

> *I looked at him curiously. "Court Street on Bunker Hill?"*
>
> *He nodded, flushing all over his blonde skin. "Not too good," he said quickly. "I haven't been in the chips lately. Do you mind?"*

Chandler had also used the phony Court Street address to skewer Bunker Hill in his first novel, *The Big Sleep*, three years earlier. Two-bit chiseler Harry Jones is being pressured by a professional thug named Canino to give up the whereabouts of his unfaithful wife.

> *"Where's Agnes?"*
>
> *Harry Jones sighed. "Okey," he said wearily. "She's in an apartment house at 28 Court Street, up on Bunker Hill. Apartment 301. I guess I'm yellow all right. Why should I front for that twist?"*

Marlowe, who hears this exchange from the next room, finds Jones dead from cyanide poisoning after Canino leaves. He calls the telephone operator for the number at 28 Court Street and learns that the address is the Glendower Apartments. He calls the manager to get hold of Agnes and warn her.

> *"Is there a tall blonde with green eyes registered in the flop?"*
>
> *"Say, this isn't any flop—"*
>
> *"Oh, can it,* can *it!" I rapped at him in a police voice. "You want me to send the vice squad over there and shake the joint down? I know all about Bunker Hill apartment houses, mister. Especially the ones that have phone numbers listed in each apartment."*

Chandler had also used the 28 Court Street address in a January 1936 *Black Mask* story called "Guns at Cyrano's," even though a two-digit number wouldn't have existed in Los Angeles, where all east-west streets begin at 100 on either side of Main. On the trail of a group of blackmailers, a local operator named Ted Carmady finds the body of his buddy Tony Acosta with a bloody note he'd written in his last moments: "Tailed him…woptown…28 Court Street…over garage…shot me…think I got…him…your car…" Before Carmady can get to the address on his own, he's nabbed by a couple of henchmen and forcibly taken there on the orders of a local mobster.

> *They went through silent streets, past blurred houses, blurred trees, the blurred shine of street lights. There were neon signs behind the thick curtains of mist. There was no sky.*
>
> *Then they climbed and a feeble arc light strung over an intersection threw light on a signpost, and Carmady read the name "Court Street."*
>
> *He said softly: "This is woptown, Critz. The big guy can't be so dough-heavy as he used to be."*

This time the address isn't an apartment building but a gang hangout. "The car slowed in front of a big frame house with a trellised porch, walls finished in round shingles, blind, lightless windows. Across the street, a stencil sign on a brick building built sheer to the sidewalk said: 'Paulo Perrugini Funeral Parlors.'" The "wop undertaker," one of the crooks later tells Carmady, owns the house.

Chandler obviously had a grudge against Bunker Hill in general and Court Street in particular. To him it was a beat-down place with brutish, beat-

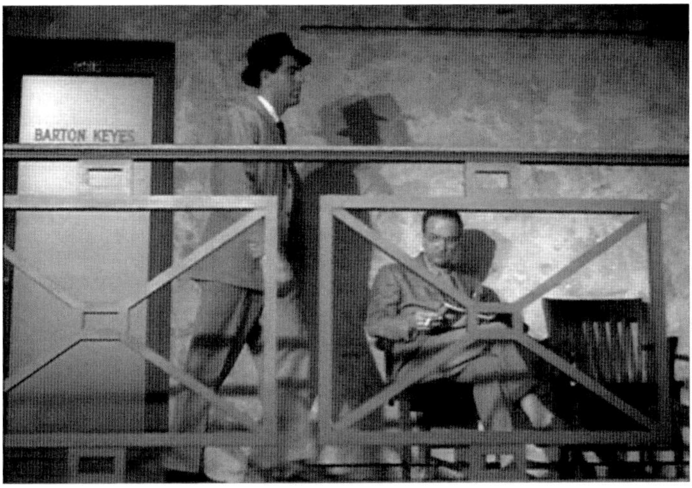

Besides writing much of its snappy dialogue, Raymond Chandler (sitting, above) made a cameo appearance in Billy Wilder's *Double Indemnity* (1944), but star Fred MacMurray rushed past him so quickly that few people noticed him. *Courtesy of Universal Pictures.*

down people, most of them woozy from alcohol and many of them packing heat. He left a few bloody corpses on Court Street. Given the popularity of Chandler's fiction, it's no wonder that Bunker Hill had a widespread reputation as a blighted crime area. Unlike the nearby beach town of Santa Monica, which Chandler called Bay City in his stories, Bunker Hill didn't even deserve a protective alias.

A section of Court Street still exists today west of the Harbor Freeway, but its Bunker Hill blocks disappeared in the mid-1950s, along with everything around them, with the extension of the Hollywood Freeway and the expansion of the L.A. Civic Center. The Department of Water and Power headquarters and the Music Center Plaza cover up part of it; the block where Marlowe walked would hang high in the air today above the gently sloping Grand Park.

Whether Chandler's shorthand use of Bunker Hill as a tough neighborhood influenced Hollywood directors to cast it in their 1940s and '50s crime movies is anyone's guess. Most likely they would have gone there anyway, because Bunker Hill was visually the perfect location for the new hard-boiled cinema that would soon enough become world famous as film noir.

CHAPTER 4

BUNKER HILL GOES HOLLYWOOD

"[Bunker] *Hill was broodingly urban and mysterious—everything that Los Angeles, suburban and banal from birth, was precisely not.*"
—Mike Davis, Dead Cities *(2002)*

After the completion of principal photography on *The Naked City* but many months before its successful March 1948 release, producer Mark Hellinger was already putting together a follow-up project—not another police procedural but a hard-boiled melodrama. It was based on Don Tracy's 1934 potboiler *Criss Cross*, the story of an armored car heist that goes bad. Though the novel took place in Baltimore, Hellinger thought it would play better and be cheaper to shoot in Los Angeles. Not the Los Angeles regularly glimpsed in A movies—Hollywood Boulevard, Sunset Strip, the "miracle mile" section of Wilshire Boulevard, anonymous residential streets with red-tiled Spanish Colonials and tidy Japanese-accented bungalows—but in some older part of the city where working-class people scraped by. When Hellinger suddenly dropped dead of a heart attack just before Christmas, Universal Pictures handed the project over to director Robert Siodmak, who was just back into town from making *Cry of the City* on the streets of New York. Before that, on an independent film called *Hollow Triumph*, Siodmak had shot several scenes in downtown Los Angeles, including Paul Henreid's escape from two murderous thugs on one of the Angels Flight railway cars, so he was clearly at home filming on location. As part of the *Criss Cross* caper package, Siodmak brought with him a young actor he'd used two years earlier in the stage-bound noir thriller *The Killers*: Burt Lancaster.

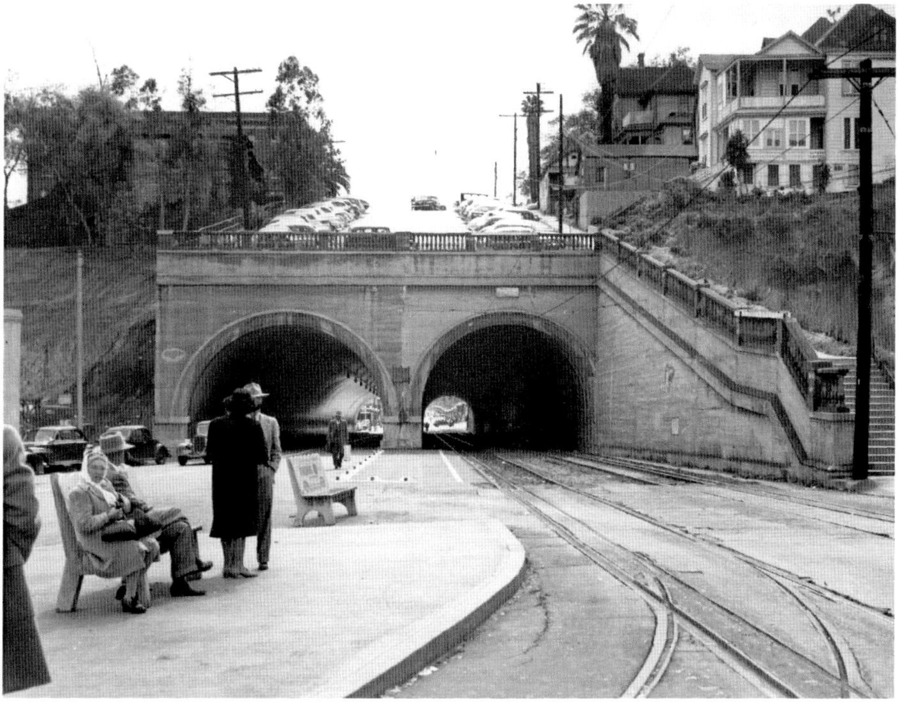

In *Criss Cross* (1949), Steve Thompson (Burt Lancaster) returns to his mother's house at 215 North Hill Street (upper right) on the terrace above the northern end of the Hill Street tunnel. The photographer is standing at the corner of Temple Street. *Security Pacific Collection/LAPL.*

Tracy's novel was pure pulp, narrated in the first-person by a German-American prizefighter using the name Johnny Thompson who's making the rent as an armored car guard. When his gold-digging Polish-American girlfriend, Anna Krebak, runs off and marries another pug—an Italian-American tough guy who fights under the name Slim Parsons—Johnny tries to win her back by setting up an inside robbery with Slim. In the end, he kills Slim, loses Anna and faces life in prison. But Siodmak and scriptwriter Daniel Fuchs jiggered the Depression-era story to give it more postwar dislocation. In the film, neither man is a boxer, the ethnic back stories are tossed, Johnny becomes Steve (Lancaster), Anna becomes Johnny's ex-wife (Yvonne DeCarlo) instead of his ex-girl and Slim Parsons is transformed into a sociopathic Aryan hipster named Slim Dundee (Dan Duryea) who eventually kills Steve and Anna. Inspired by the opening aerial shots of New York in *The Naked City* and of downtown Los Angeles in the recent *He Walked By Night*, Siodmak introduces Steve and Anna and their sticky predicament from a helicopter gliding above downtown, moving north along Spring Street past Los Angeles City Hall and then angling eastward toward Main Street until the descending camera approaches a nightclub parking lot where the lovers are locked in a secret embrace. (This area was later obliterated when Interstate 5 came through.)

To highlight the working-class milieu of his characters, Siodmak picked Bunker Hill for two of his key locations. Steve's mother's house, used for both exteriors and interiors, was located at 215 North Hill Street, on a picturesque terrace at the edge of Bunker Hill called Court Hill, directly above the block-long Hill Street tunnel between Temple and First. In fact, Siodmak establishes the lay of the land by following Steve as he gets off the Hollywood Boulevard streetcar just outside the tunnel at the corner of Temple Street and walks up the terrace stairs to the house. For the scene in which Steve and his cohorts plan the fatal heist, Siodmak chose a disreputable-looking place four blocks away called the Sunshine Apartments.

Bunker Hill's Sunshine Apartments at 421 West Third Street has been gone now for almost fifty years, but it's still one of the most familiar unknown houses in Los Angeles. Perched on a ten-foot-high retaining wall above Clay Street, it sprawled halfway up the steep hill across from Angels Flight. The Sunshine was the sort of multilevel dwelling that novelist John Fante described in *Ask the Dust* (1939) as "on the crest of Bunker Hill, built against the decline of the hill, so that the main floor was on the level with the street but the tenth floor was downstairs ten levels." The difference was that the Sunshine had only four stories and its front, not its sides, conformed to Third Street's slant, so that the

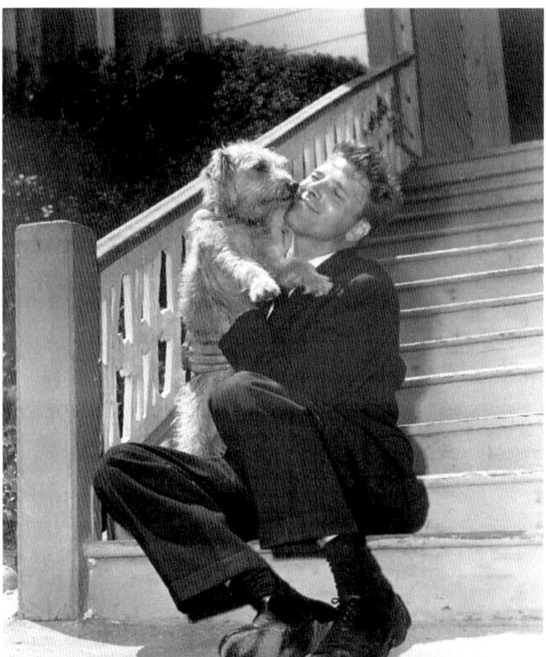

Criss Cross star Burt Lancaster plays with one of his costars, Corky, on the steps of 215 North Hill Street. *Jim Dawson.*

first floor was only half as wide as the second floor, which in turn was not as wide as the third.

Constructed on vacant property around 1905 to accommodate downtown's need for cheap housing, the Sunshine looked like a huge clapboard farmhouse, with a stack of wraparound Queen Anne-inspired porches and a couple of other filigree touches around the front entrance, which was on the third-floor. Just under the eaves of the front gable was a wooden design of a sunburst on the horizon. Midwestern migrants probably found the place comfortably familiar in its own way. Inside, a labyrinth of odd-angled hallways, step-downs and stairways connected the Sunshine's many small apartments.

Though it made its film debut as one of Angels Flight's neighbors in a 1920 comedy called *All Jazzed Up*, the Sunshine didn't get its first close-up until 1932, when director James Whale cast it as the home of two downtown working girls (Mae Clarke and Una Merkel) in *The Impatient Maiden*, his follow-up to the classic *Frankenstein* (in which Clarke played the wife of Colin Clive's Dr. Victor Frankenstein). Because sound cameras in those days were unwieldy, Whale also used a smaller silent camera, probably a Bell & Howell, to shoot the movie's opening scene on the Third Street steps as the actresses come out of the Sunshine's front door, step down off the porch and walk up to the Angels Flight station on Olive Street. (The dialogue and traffic sounds were dubbed in later.) Whale also shot another scene lower down on the Third Street steps at Clay Street and at the rear

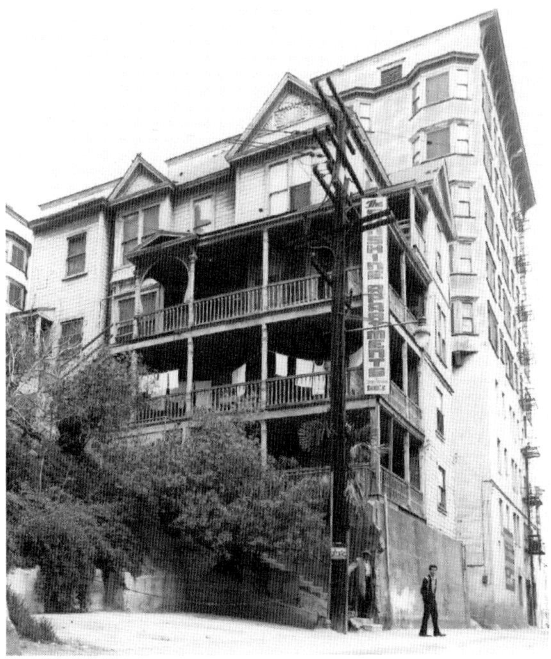

The Sunshine Apartments at 421 West Third Street and the taller Astoria Hotel behind it were getting shabby by 1960, when Arnold Hylen took this photo on Clay Street. Note the bottom of a second set of utility stairs beyond the concrete retaining wall, where at least half a dozen films were shot. *The California History Room, California State Library, Sacramento.*

of the apartments, where a second flight of concrete utility steps came down the hill from Olive between the Sunshine and the much larger Astoria Hotel. (More on these utility steps later.)

But what turned the Sunshine Apartments into a fairly steady if nameless character was film noir. And since—by the mid-1940s—Bunker Hill was a rundown neighborhood of neglected Victorians, rambling flophouses and vertiginous streets, the Sunshine was its perfect embodiment. Just as familiar character actors like Franklin Pangborn or Ted de Corsia needed no setup or backstory for contemporary film audiences to know exactly who and what they were, the Sunshine Apartments, belying its sunny moniker, announced the moment it came onscreen that here was a shabby lodging house for desperate and worn-down people.

In Paramount's *Night Has a Thousand Eyes* (1948), the Sunshine offers low-rent anonymity to a con man (Edward G. Robinson) hiding from his past. Director John Farrow pointedly establishes its location with a 180-degree pan shot—taken from a crane above Clay Street—that follows one of the Angels Flight cars up from Hill to Olive and then sweeps across the top of the hill to catch Robinson's character (a stand-in) hurrying down the Third Street steps and up onto the third-floor porch to the Sunshine's front door. A later shot, taken from higher on the steps, shows John Lund and Gail Russell coming up to the porch from Clay Street below.

Then, only a couple of months later, Robert Siodmak came to the Sunshine to shoot *Criss Cross*'s motley crew of crooks plotting their armored car robbery. The apartment interiors in the earlier films had been obvious studio creations, too spacious for a dump like the Sunshine, but in *Criss Cross* you have to look closely to see that the shots of Burt Lancaster and Yvonne DeCarlo standing next to a bay window, with the Angels Flight cars passing each other in the background, were done on a soundstage. The railway cars were filmed from the Sunshine (most likely from the third-floor porch, judging from the angle), but the building itself didn't have any bay windows facing Angels Flight, so the scene had to have been a process shot. But since the apartment looked so convincing, and since Siodmak had already shown his characters walking up the real Sunshine's outside steps and navigating its maze of dingy hallways and interior stairways—whose atmosphere one character mockingly dismisses as "Picturesque, ain't it?"—nobody noticed.

Thanks to its exposure in *Criss Cross*, the boardinghouse would go on to have another dozen years of Hollywood glory. In Paramount's *The Turning Point* (1952), crusading reporter William Holden and gal pal Alexis Smith take Angels Flight up the hill and try to reach a witness hiding there, but

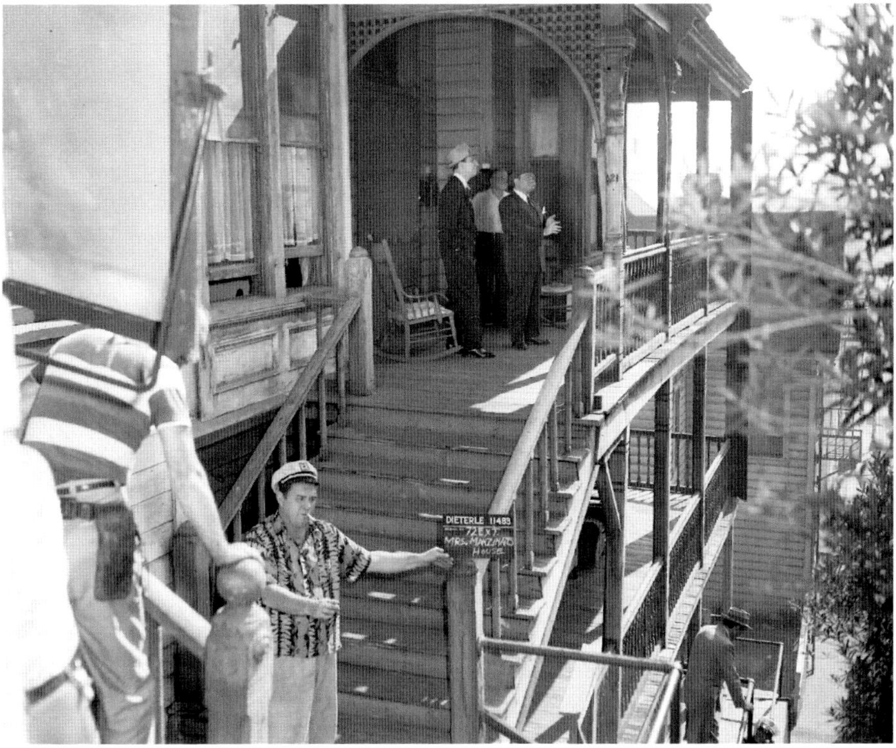

The crew of *The Turning Point* (1952) prepares a scene on the third floor porch of the Sunshine Apartments at 421 West Third Street, across from Angels Flight. *Bison Archives.*

they have to duck several torpedoes standing guard around the porch. The building also shows up briefly in *Act of Violence* (MGM, 1949), Joseph Losey's *M* (Columbia, 1951) and *Angel's Flight* (1965). In Kent Mackenzie's neo-realist *The Exiles* (1961), the female lead, an Apache Indian named Yvonne Williams, spends the night there with one of her girlfriends in a scene that takes the camera up the Third Street steps, up onto the third floor porch, through a hallway and into a tiny apartment. Documentary filmmaker Edmund Penney introduces his lyrical fifteen-minute film *Angel's Flight Railway* (1964) with a shot of the funicular cars crisscrossing from behind the Sunshine's screen door.

The aforementioned set of back steps, which separated the Sunshine Apartments and the Hillcrest Hotel above it from the larger Astoria Hotel to the north, were also a great location because of their restricted access. Connecting Olive with Clay, these steps revealed the utility entrances, back doors and trashcan landings for the three buildings (which by the 1950s were all boardinghouses despite the Hillcrest's and the Astoria's continued use of the word hotel). Among the films shot on these steps were *The Impatient Maiden* (1932), *Once a Thief* (1950), *Sudden Fear* (starring Joan Crawford, 1952), *Kiss Me Deadly* (1955), *The Indestructible Man* (1956), *My Gun Is Quick* (1957) and *Angel's Flight* (1965). These utility steps are the only location where two Mike Hammers (Ralph Meeker in *Kiss Me Deadly* and Robert Bray in *My Gun Is Quick*) walk the same ground.

The Sunshine Apartments finally had its appointment with a Caterpillar in 1964. Today, besides surviving in old movies, it can still be found in countless photo- and postcard-tableaux of Angels Flight and as the most prominent background feature—painted green—in Millard Sheets's vibrant 1931 oil painting *Angel's Flight*, one of the most famous works on permanent display at the Los Angeles County Museum of Art.

Now back to the action: To keep alive the earlier novelty of *The Naked City*'s much-touted use of locations, Universal's *Criss Cross* press book played up its reliance on L.A.'s atmosphere: "The air of realism and authenticity which pervades the film is largely due to the fact that all the outdoor scenes were filmed in their actual locale, which is the old section of Los Angeles." Never mind that the story was fiction and had no "actual locale"; Robert Siodmak's realistic use of Bunker Hill, filmed with natural light during the bright afternoons of a Southern California summer, made it look like "actual"

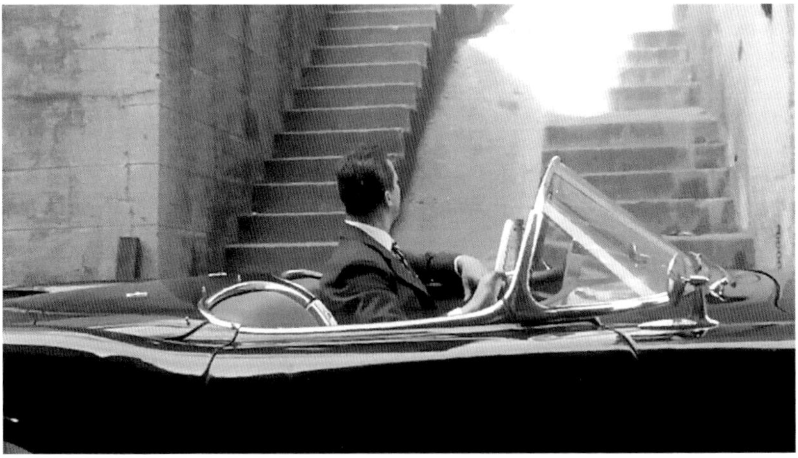

Mickey Spillane's Mike Hammer (Ralph Meeker) parks on Clay Street at the bottom of the utility stairway behind the Sunshine Apartments in *Kiss Me Deadly* (1955). Another Mike Hammer (Robert Bray) would find a murder victim on these same steps two years later in *My Gun Is Quick*. *Courtesy of the Criterion Collection.*

events had occurred there. According to the *Hollywood Reporter*, "Without being imitative [of *The Naked City*], his presentation has the same qualities of raw, exciting melodramatic action set against an authentic background." Fred Hift of *Variety* remarked, "Using many location shots in Los Angeles, [Siodmak] succeeded in giving the film an air of realism that tends to heighten the dramatic punch," and added that "LA locations at Union Station and Angels Flight give [the] picture that much sought documentary look." The *Los Angeles Times*'s Philip K. Scheuer agreed: "Director Siodmak's sure cinematic touch seldom falters, whether in casting down to the smallest bit or filming such locales as Bunker Hill, Angels Flight, Terminal Island, the Union Depot and a run-down Spring Street hotel."

One of the first modern writers who would later acknowledge Bunker Hill's recurring role as film noir's resident purgatory was Mike Davis, who in a 1990 exegesis, *City of Quartz*, noted that late-1940s directors abandoned Los Angeles's more prosperous precincts for "the epic dereliction of Downtown's Bunker Hill, which symbolized the rot in the heart of the expanding metropolis." In his later *Dead Cities*, Davis even dedicated a chapter to Bunker Hill called "Hollywood's Dark Shadow"—"a hillside slum whose decaying mansions and sinister rooming houses might have been envisioned by Edgar Allen Poe." That was an overstatement, but under the right direction, the hill's streets, buildings and back alleys could certainly look nightmarish.

Producer Dore Schary, the head of MGM's B-unit in Culver City, immediately saw the possibilities of going downtown after he watched *Criss Cross*. "I told the production units, 'We're in a different world, I want you to go down to Los Angeles and photograph some streets,'" he told Robert Porfirio in 1977. "These weren't street stories, but there were things on those streets that we had never seen on film. All our studio streets were so manicured. So I said, 'Just take the look of any street anywhere and you'll find drama on that street, because it's a little oily, it's a bit dirty, it has some character. It looks like a street.'"

Since Bunker Hill could pass for any turn-of-the-century neighborhood of rental housing in Milwaukee, Sioux City, Pittsburgh, Newark or Richmond, it was a cheap and effective stand-in, as long as the director kept the palm trees out of the shots. For example, William Dieterle shot *The Turning Point* (1952) all over Bunker Hill—on First, Second and Third Streets—and even on Angels Flight, but one of the characters in the script identified the locale as "a fine Midwestern city." Bunker Hill was also great for last-minute pickup shots for out-of-town movies. A police car prowling up First Street from Olive to Grand is the first thing we see after the credits in *The Asphalt*

Jungle (1950), which was otherwise filmed in Cincinnati. Several years later, in *Bus Stop* (1956), sunny residential Bunker Hill Avenue passed for the street where Marilyn Monroe lived in Phoenix.

But the city it most resembled, if properly framed, was San Francisco, which, along with Los Angeles and New York, was one of the three main loci of film noir, owing not only to its picturesque architecture, daunting hillside streets, cable cars climbing halfway to the stars and its fabled reputation as land's end—the end of the line—but also to its adopted native son, Dashiell Hammett, who had made the city the stomping grounds of his Continental Op and his gumshoe Sam Spade. For example, though Ann Sheridan searches for her husband through the real streets of San Francisco in *Woman on the Run* (1950), the film's lengthy opening murder scene takes place on the terrace above the south side of the Hill Street tunnel. That same area also represented the city in a scene from *The Sniper* (1952).

But Bunker Hill stood in most dramatically for San Francisco when David Miller, a former documentary maker, directed the 1952 Joan Crawford melodrama *Sudden Fear*, which earned her an Oscar nomination for gnawing on the scenery. Miller set the action on several San Francisco locations, including serpentine Lombard Street, but when it came time for the dramatic nocturnal chase finale, he moved the production to Bunker Hill's narrow Cinnabar Street, several nearby alleys and Second Street near Olive where Jack Palance in his big Packard convertible unintentionally runs down Gloria Grahame in front of the Mission Apartments. The deception was so deft that nobody noticed, despite a glimpse of a Cinnabar street sign at the corner of Third. The *New York Times*, on August 8, 1952, couldn't help rave that "San Francisco…is an excitingly photogenic area. [Miller] has taken full advantage of the city's steep streets and panoramic views. And, in his climactic scenes in a darkened apartment and a chase through its precipitous dark alleys and backyards he has managed to project an authentically doom-filled atmosphere." You can excuse a New York reviewer, of course, for not knowing San Francisco from a Los Angeles Victorian neighborhood, but not so William Hogan of the *San Francisco Chronicle*, who described the Bunker Hill scene as "a silent chase up and down the hills of Pacific Heights in dark, wet streets." Perhaps even the *Los Angeles Daily News*'s Howard McClay should have spotted his hometown ringer (just a dozen blocks from the Daily News building on Los Angeles Street) when he wrote, "[Miller's] dramatic use of silent action, mood-setting scenes and nerve-shattering bits of business, plus effective staging of the San Francisco location shots…provides the picture with a tense pace that never lets down until the final scene."

This page: The Chaspeak Apartments (right) at 512 West Second Street was the perfect exterior for the musty residence of a slightly mad spinster (Josephine Hutchinson, below, looking toward the front steps from the apartment on the left) in *Somewhere in the Night* (1946). It was one of the first film noirs shot on Bunker Hill. The Chaspeak was later the model for Arturo Bandini's rooming house in the 2006 film adaptation of John Fante's *Ask the Dust*. *The California History Room, California State Library, Sacramento, above; Jim Dawson.*

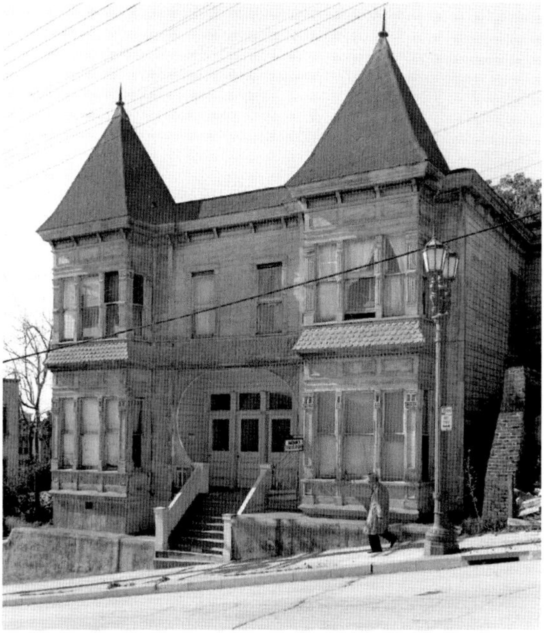

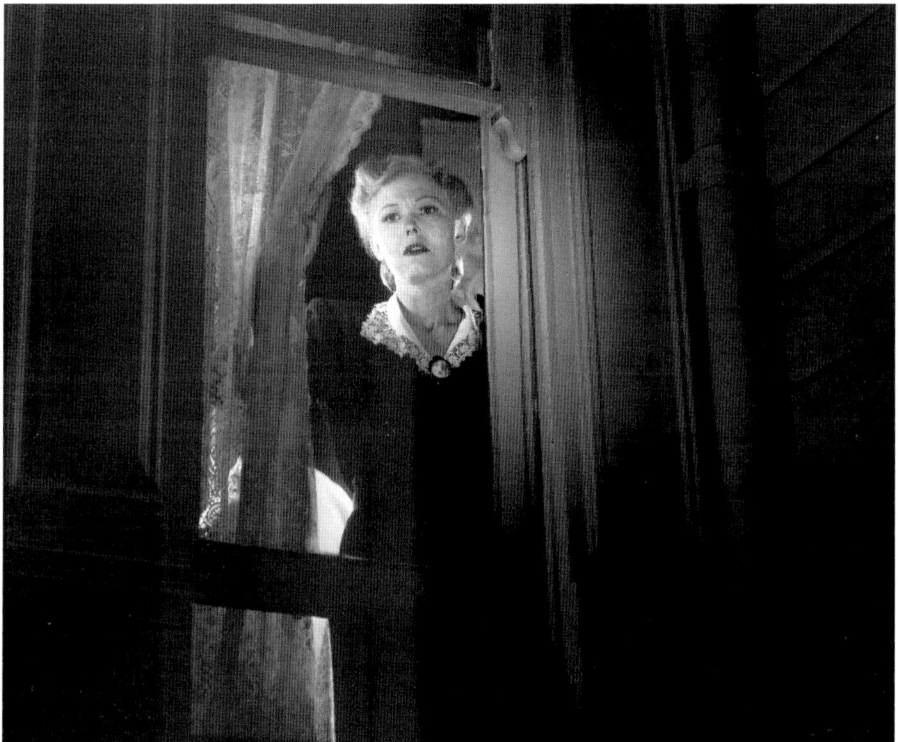

In a 1975 interview, director Joseph H. Lewis—whose on-location bank robbery and getaway in and around Montrose, California (just north of Glendale), in *Gun Crazy* (1949) is one of the most spectacularly sustained single-take scenes in film history—told Robert Porfirio that he hated to go on location outside of Los Angeles. "The only reason you go out on location, like a small town, is because you can't find what you need in the studio. And I honestly believe outside of seeing landmarks in large cities…that any location can be duplicated here [in Los Angeles]…I remember I went to San Francisco to shoot a sequence in the streets of Chinatown in San Francisco. It was dreadful. Cars stopping, people gawking, unnatural action in the background. We finally got an idea: we set up two cameras on a street corner with a 'director' there. We gave him a megaphone and a loudspeaker and what-not; and he was 'directing' one film while we were down the street actually shooting the real scene. Otherwise, because of crowds, you couldn't shoot." But using Bunker Hill was almost like being on the backlot. No wonder Lewis filmed an extended chase scene on foot through the Third Street tunnel and up Angels Flight to Olive Street in his 1953 MGM film *Cry of the Hunted*.

Real-life Bunker Hill was also a place where nobody seemed to object to Hollywood branding it as an unsavory neighborhood. After all, no less than Raymond Chandler had already put the mark of Cain—the biblical Cain, not James M. or Paul—upon it. Most of the housing and the local businesses were owned by people, some of them slumlords, who lived elsewhere. When the Fremont Hotel was built on the southwest corner of Fourth and Olive in 1902, it had proudly billed itself on colorful postcards as "The newest and most elegantly appointed family hotel in Los Angeles…on an eminence commanding a charming vista of the city and offering to its patrons the benefit of the purest air, prompt and courteous service and a cuisine unequaled in points of excellence anywhere." But by the time it showed up in Warner Bros's *Backfire* (shot in 1948 and released two years later), Fremont postcards hadn't existed for years. Despite being identified in the dialogue as "Fremont Hotel, Fourth and Olive," its lobby (on a soundstage) was threadbare and its desk clerk clearly disreputable. And when *Backfire*'s lead character (Edmond O'Brien), heading for the classy Biltmore Hotel downtown, tells the cabbie at the last minute that he's changed his mind and wants to go to the nearby Fremont instead, the driver scowls into the rearview mirror as if he'd sniffed a bad odor. Apparently the hotel management at the time didn't care how badly it was being treated at the movies.

Likewise, in *Night Has a Thousand Eyes* (1948), when Edward G. Robinson hides out at the Sunshine Apartments, he says of Bunker Hill, "It was an odd part of the city...It was strictly a no-questions-asked area." No neighborhood chamber of commerce objected.

One of the first film noir directors who went to Bunker Hill was Joseph L. Mankiewicz, who used the exterior of a witchy-looking rooming house called the Chaspeak Apartments at 512 West Second Street for the most offbeat scene in *Somewhere in the Night* (1946), the story of an amnesiac ex-marine (John Hodiak) stumbling blindly through Los Angeles trying to find out who he is. Following a lead to the Chaspeak after dark, he introduces himself to a middle-aged spinster (Broadway veteran Josephine Hutchinson) who seems to have once had a relationship with him. "For a moment I didn't know you, George," she says vaguely as she brings him from the darkness into her oppressively wallpapered parlor. "You're being so formal." But during their cryptic conversation he comes to realize that some old, jilted romance has driven her half-crazy, like Charles Dickens's Miss Havisham, and her musty turn-of-the-century hideaway is a twilight world. They've never met. What better neighborhood to introduce this lost-in-time soul than Bunker Hill?

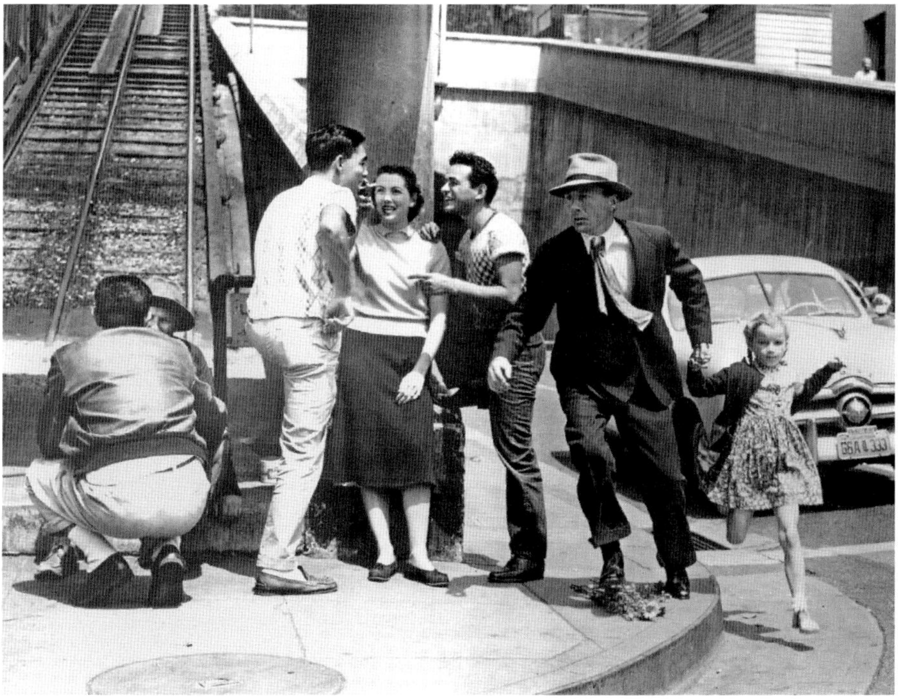

David Wayne and Janine Perreau run through the Third Street tunnel and turn the corner on Hill Street at the bottom of Angels Flight in Joseph Losey's *M* (1951). *Bison Archives.*

The shadow of the late Mark Hellinger touched Bunker Hill one last time in *Act of Violence*, a property that MGM purchased from his estate. Like *The Naked City* and *Criss Cross*, *Act of Violence* is a location-heavy project, but unlike the others, it takes place in newly opened tract-house neighborhoods—at least until the final thirty minutes, when Robert Ryan tracks Van Heflin, the man who betrayed him in a Nazi POW camp, to a hotel convention in Los Angeles. Suddenly the action descends from the bright suburbs of Southern California to a hellish, nighttime Bunker Hill, the Third Street tunnel and the dingy bars of East Fifth Street. *New York Herald Tribune* critic Otis L. Guernsey thought Fred Zinnemann, the film's Austrian director, provided "added realism [with] the casual use of outdoor settings much too unlovely to have been imagined in a studio."

One of the most interesting films that took advantage of Bunker Hill's quaint atmospherics and "no questions-asked" reputation was *M*, shot in the spring and early summer of 1950 by director Joseph Losey. Though considered a classic today, *M* at the time was a troubled project beset by the cultural and political paranoia of its day. The story behind *M* begins with Seymour Nebenzal, a cousin of Robert Siodmak and a German film producer (*The Threepenny Opera*) who had fled his country in 1933. After several years in Paris, Nebenzal immigrated to America and produced a string of low-budget independent Hollywood movies, including the 1946 film noir *Whistle Stop*, starring Ava Gardner. He also decided to produce American remakes of two of his German successes: a fantasy called *Siren of Atlantis* (which became a campy 1948 stinker starring Dominican spitfire Maria Montez) and *M*, the story of a serial child murderer that he'd made with director Fritz Lang and Hungarian actor Peter Lorre in 1931. But Joseph Breen—the Puritan gatekeeper of Hollywood's Production Code—saddled Nebenzal's American *M* with a major restriction: the only way he would tolerate a movie about a psychopath who killed little girls, as well as its underlying theme that the police and the criminal underworld were not all that different from each other, was if Nebenzal strictly followed the script of the original, which everyone agreed was one of the classics of German cinema and therefore protected by a kind of grandfather clause.

One aspect of this new *M* that would further taint it was that Nebenzal, resisting what he recognized as America's growing nationalist intolerance (not dissimilar to what he'd seen in Germany twenty years earlier), hired former Communist Party member Joseph Losey to direct it, and Losey in turn brought in several activist-leftist actors and dialogue rewrite men, including Dalton Trumbo. Like many of Hollywood's best and brightest, they would all soon enough get blacklisted. Losey, who had just finished another noir, *The Prowler*, at Universal, later admitted that he took Nebenzal's project because he needed the money and was expecting the House on Un-American Activities Committee (HUAC) in Washington, D.C., to shut down his career at any moment.

(The Hollywood blacklist's toll on film noir was considerable. Leftist writers and filmmakers, especially those who had cut their teeth on documentaries during the Depression, were more ideologically predisposed to recognize and criticize America's social, economic and psychosexual problems—the red meat of film noir. Naturally pessimistic and perhaps too cynical for their own good, they became easy targets in the early fifties when a right-wing inquisitor, Wisconsin senator Joe McCarthy, kicked the Red Scare into high gear.)

Joseph Losey compensated for the twenty-year-old script's inflexibility by changing *M*'s look and Americanizing the names of the characters. The psychopathic Hans Beckert became Martin Harrow, and rather than cast him with a gnomish character actor like Peter Lorre, Losey chose a benign-looking

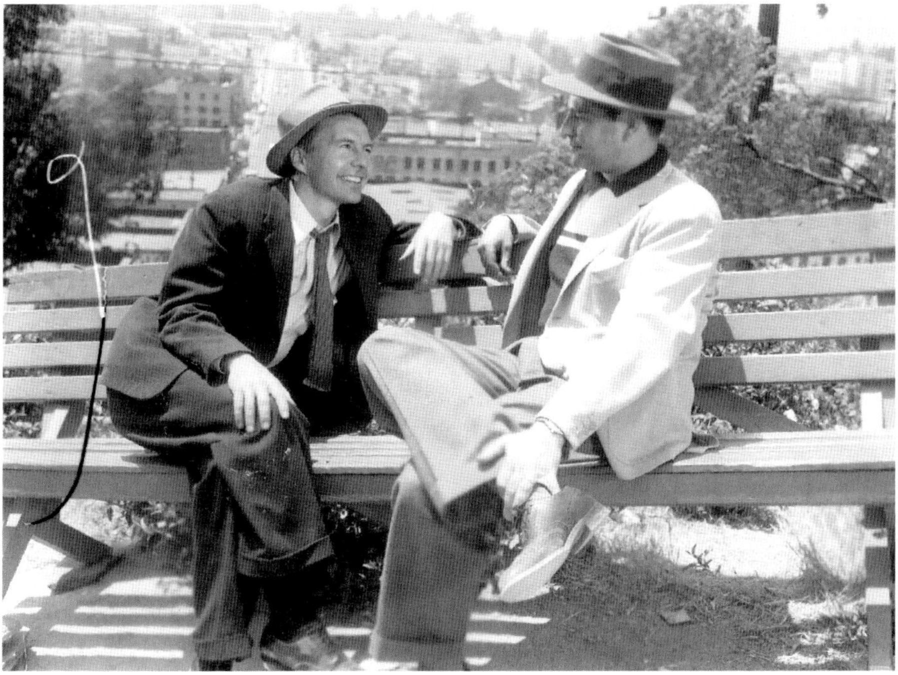

M co-producer Harold Nebenzal (in white jacket) chats with actor David Wayne on one of the several benches at the top of Third Street, on the west side of Bunker Hill Avenue. *Bison Archives.*

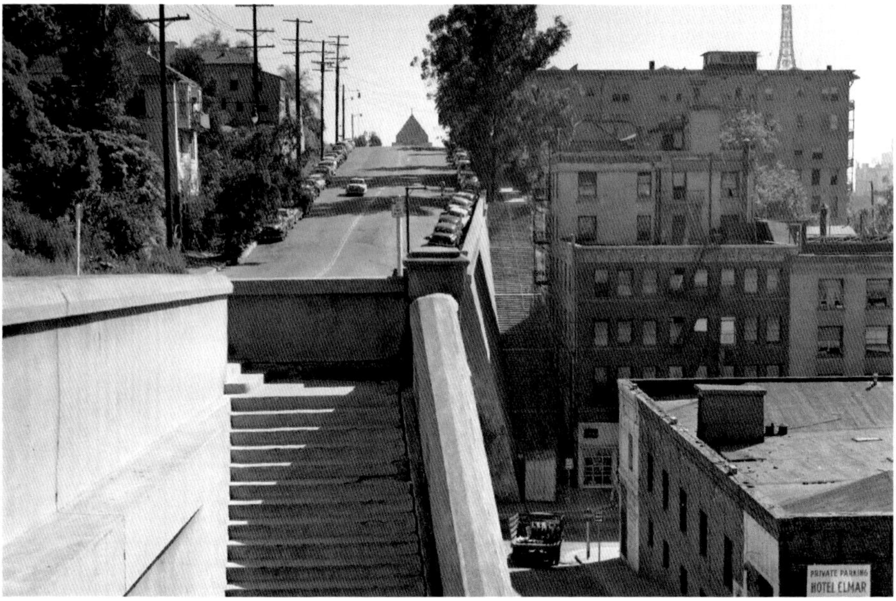

Director Joseph Losey filmed a chase on the far steps leading down from Hope Street to the western mouth of the Third Street tunnel in *M*; four years later, his former assistant director, Robert Aldrich, used the same steps when Mike Hammer (Ralph Meeker) dispatched a knife-wielding thug in *Kiss Me Deadly* (1955). *Security Pacific Collection/LAPL.*

musical comedy performer, David Wayne. Instead of Fritz Lang's eternal night, he used mostly day, which seemed logical since that was the best time to find stray children on American streets. And rather than place the story in a stylized, sound-stage city of the imagination, Losey took *M* almost exclusively into outdoor Los Angeles. Searching for a rundown American neighborhood to stand in for decadent Weimar Berlin, he settled on Bunker Hill. One of the reasons, Losey told writer James Leahy in 1966, was that he didn't know how to transpose Berlin's tightly knit multi-generational subculture of beggars and thieves to modern, socially fragmented Los Angeles. "It didn't work here," he said. "The underworld of Lang, the underworld written in the text which we had to follow basically, made no sense in terms of Los Angeles in the 1940s or early fifties, and I tried to get over this a bit by using a good deal of old Los Angeles. Bits of it are very modern, bits are very old: the old Victorian houses that were on a ridge overlooking the dividing line between the city of Los Angeles and Hollywood."

Losey practically marinates *M* in Bunker Hill's funky ambiance, though he draws a couple of downtown streets and a distant seaside amusement park—

Santa Monica's Ocean Park—into its universe through creative editing. The film opens as the camera rides up Angels Flight with David Wayne. He lives in an upstairs apartment in a quirky Victorian at 315 South Bunker Hill Avenue where an early twentieth-century occultist and astrologer named Max Heindel once lived. (The house's address in *M*, which never refers to Bunker Hill by name, is given as 1302 River Street.) The mother of Wayne's first victim lives at the Alta Vista Apartments at 255 South Bunker Hill Avenue (the same building where novelist John Fante once lived); Losey told writer Michael Ciment in the late 1970s that he chose the Alta Vista because it sat dramatically "on a ridge over a tunnel that leads into the downtown Los Angeles," and because it had an interior spiral staircase similar to one in Lang's original *M*. The child's balloon, signifying her loss, floats away above the Sunshine Apartments. In another scene next to the Alta Vista, Wayne sits on one of the park benches at the top of Third Street carving into its wooden slats with the knife he uses to

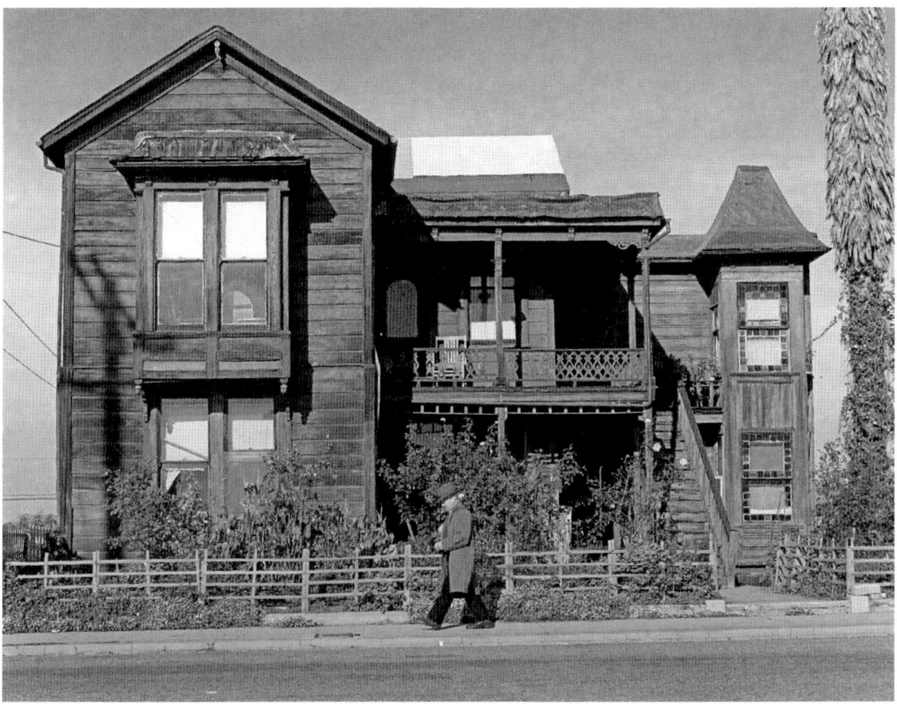

The Foss-Heindel house at 315 South Bunker Hill Avenue was the home of child killer Martin Harrow (David Wayne) in *M* (1951). Artist Leo Politi later featured the house in *Bunker Hill Los Angeles*, his 1964 book of paintings. By the time William Reagh took this photo in 1965, the house had lost much of its Victorian ornamentation. *The California History Room, California State Library, Sacramento.*

carve soap figures and, presumably, kill children. Later, he tries to lure another little girl away from a grocery store at the corner of the New Grand Hotel at Third and Grand. After successfully grabbing yet another child (Janine Perreau), he's recognized as the killer and chased down the Hope Street steps adjacent to the western terminus of the Third Street tunnel. Reaching Third Street at the bottom of the steps, Wayne flees through the tunnel with the girl and comes out on the eastern side, at the foot of Angels Flight on Hill Street. Running a block further east, he hides out in the Bradbury Building on the corner of Broadway, where a group of street criminals sets up a manhunt from the basement to the roof in what turns out to be a spectacular twenty-minute tour of the much-filmed nineteenth century landmark.

Just as the spooky old Chaspeak building in *Somewhere in the Night* is a correlative to the aging, neurotic woman hiding inside, the Bunker Hill Avenue house where Harrow lives in *M* suggests the source of his demons. Known as the Foss-Heindel house, its irregular shape—with a gable on the left, stacked porches in the middle and a little tower on the right with a distorted mansard roof—was probably considered eccentric even when William Foss built it in 1885. In re-imagining *M*, Losey wanted to go deeper into his killer because, as he told James Leahy, "Lang's villain was my hero." Losey saw Harrow as an overly sensitive and otherwise moral man who knows what he's doing is wrong but can't stop his compulsions; he's a scapegoat for America's religious irrationalism and sexual repression. Even his last name suggests torment. And a photo of his prim, grim Victorian mother, occupying a place of honor next to his bed, erases any doubt of who imbedded that torment within him. The rotting, rococo house represents her presence and its hold over him. Ten years later, when art director Robert Clatworthy designed and built a house for Alfred Hitchcock's *Psycho* that was meant to amplify the dark personality of Norman Bates's dead mother, he might have been thinking of that relic at 315 South Bunker Hill Avenue.

Released in February 1951 on a double bill with a Frances Langford musical comedy called *Purple Heart Diary*, *M* was praised mainly for its "true-to-life locations which raise the overall impact of realism," according to Red Kann of *Motion Picture Daily* (March 6, 1951). The *Hollywood Reporter* (March 5, 1951) liked "the unidentified but hugely effective backgrounds of Los Angeles." Unfortunately, protesters carrying signs like "Known Reds" picketed its Los Angeles screenings, drawing attention to the principals' left-wing politics. Several states banned *M* altogether, prompting Columbia to pull it early from distribution. Losey fled to England to avoid a HUAC subpoena. "All that emerges from the film, really," he said later, "is a couple of—I think—

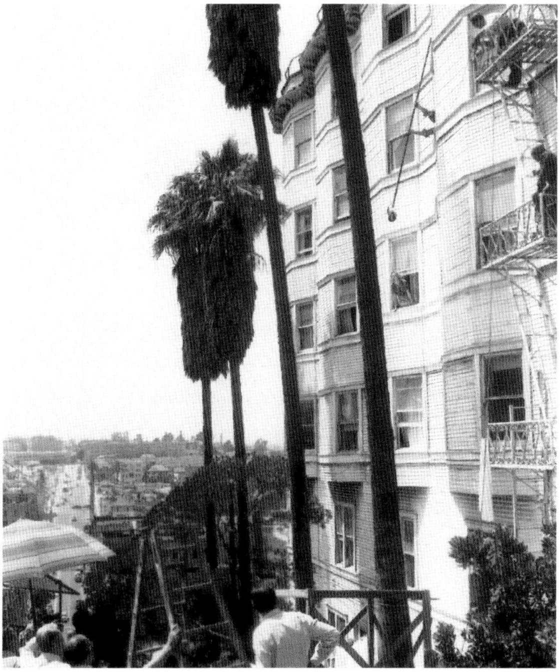

The crew of *M* (1951) readies a shot at the south side of the Alta Vista Apartments at 255 South Bunker Hill Avenue, high above the western terminus of the Third Street tunnel. *Courtesy of the Academy of Motion Picture Arts & Sciences.*

remarkable sequences, some previously unseen aspects of Los Angeles, and a fantastic performance from [David] Wayne." Most film noir aficionados put this *M* remake near the top of their must-see lists. And several academic writers, including Edward Dimendberg, have written dissertations on its use of Los Angeles to extrapolate bigger issues of society, class and urban land use.

Robert Aldrich, Joseph Losey's assistant director on *M*, had better luck four years later when he re-imagined Mickey Spillane's 1952 novel, *Kiss Me, Deadly*, by relocating the story from New York City to sunny Los Angeles, dropping the title's comma and changing a lot of the details. Basically he did to Spillane's book what Losey had done to Fritz Lang and Thea von Harbou's original *M* script. Spillane's tough guy, Mike Hammer, was busting heads up and down the *New York Times*'s bestseller list at the time, and producer Victor Saville, who owned the film rights to Spillane's works, had already cranked out a low-budget, 3-D noir of his *I, the Jury* that matched the blunt force of the prose. Though Mike Hammer's office scenes in *I, the Jury* were shot at the Bradbury Building, everything else was confined to the Samuel Goldwyn Studios' aging, dreary "New York" set. But Aldrich, with a tight budget and a twenty-two-day shooting schedule, took most of *Kiss Me Deadly* outdoors and, in collaboration with screenwriter A.I. Bezzerides, goofed on Hammer's hard-boiled persona by portraying him as a sleazy knucklehead tossing the city for some unknown item his girl Friday calls "the Great Whatzit." Mickey Spillane spent the rest of his life telling anyone who'd listen how much he hated this movie.

In Aldrich's vision, inspired by *M*, Los Angeles is a gilded, sun-blasted wasteland awaiting the apocalypse. Using *M*'s cinematographer Ernst Lazlo, he filmed on location in the finer precincts of Malibu (more specifically Point Dume), Calabasas, Beverly Hills, Westwood and Hollywood, but he paid special attention to Bunker Hill, whose atmosphere lingers far more vividly than any of *Kiss Me Deadly*'s other locales. To fix its place in the film, he used two Bunker Hill icons: the 1882 redwood Castle at 325 South Bunker Hill Avenue (the home of the opening scene's ill-fated hitchhiker, played by Cloris Leachman, and identified in the film as "325 Bunker Hill Avenue") and Angels Flight, which Hammer drives beneath in his Corvette convertible as he pulls up below the Sunshine Apartments. Aldrich was familiar with both landmarks from working with Losey on *M*: the Castle was just two doors south of the Heindel house, close enough to cast a winter's shadow upon it, and Losey had used Angels Flight as a camera "dolly" in *M*'s opening scene.

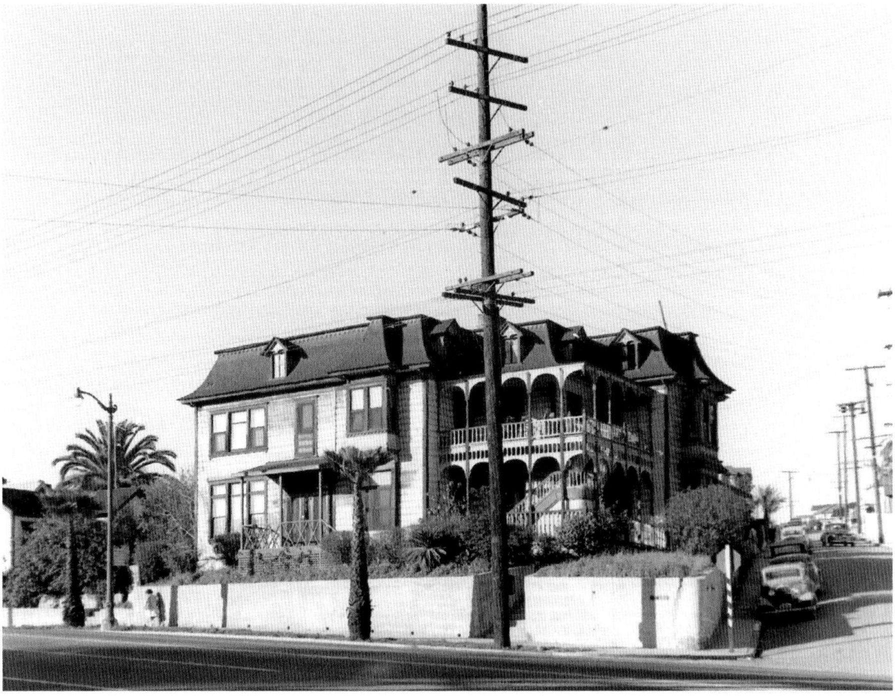

In *Kiss Me Deadly* (1955), Mike Hammer (Ralph Meeker) paid two visits to an informant on the second floor of this rambling Victorian whose address was given as "121 Flower Street, Bunker Hill." It was actually located a few blocks north of Bunker Hill at 601 West Sunset Boulevard, at the northwest corner of North Hill Place. *The California History Room, California State Library, Sacramento.*

In *Kiss Me Deadly*, Mike Hammer (Ralph Meeker) appears to walk up a set of stairs from Clay Street to the Hillcrest Hotel at Third and Olive (identified in the film as "Hillcrest Hotel, Temple Street"), but in fact Aldrich spliced together the utility steps behind the Sunshine Apartments with the Third Street steps in front of the Hillcrest, just a few steps from the Angels Flight station. Aldrich even edited other parts of town into Bunker Hill. For example, when Hammer goes looking for a science writer named Ray Diker, whose address is identified as 121 Flower Street (without a north or south designation) on Bunker Hill, he's actually walking along the 2600 block of Temple Street in the Rampart district of town, more than a mile west of Bunker Hill; but then, after a torpedo with a switchblade slips up behind him at the entrance of an alleyway (Dryden Place in real life), we quick-cut to Hammer knocking the guy down the long Hope Street steps next to the western entrance of the Third Street tunnel (the same steps Losey had used for a chase scene in *M*). Completing the scene, Hammer then walks up a dark wooden stairway to Diker's apartment in a hillside Victorian that looks every bit the quintessential Bunker Hill boardinghouse, but in fact it was located several blocks north at 601 West Sunset Boulevard on the northwest corner of North Hill Place. Likewise, to create a hideout for psycho chick Lily Carver (Gaby Rodgers), Aldrich matched up the hallway interiors of the shabby Hillcrest Hotel with a dramatic flight of interior stairs and the street exterior of the second-floor Jalisco Hotel at 616½ North Spring Street in Chinatown. From a poetic point of view, splicing together these fragmented bits of urban images to create Mike Hammer's fragmented, alienated Los Angeles makes perfect sense. But then again, it was exactly what Losey had done in *M* when he placed Bunker Hill within easy walking distance of the seaside amusement park in Santa Monica.

Shot in black and white in November–December 1954 and released the following May, *Kiss Me Deadly* came late in the film noir cycle, and though it more than paid for itself at the box office, it was roundly panned by critics and condemned by the Catholic Church's Legion of Decency because of its violence and arty nihilism. Only later did the film become a subject for festival retrospectives and essays by adoring cineastes. It's generally recognized today as one of film noir's masterpieces.

But *Kiss Me Deadly* was an anomaly in 1955. Many changes over the previous half-dozen years—the five major studios' loss of their theater chain monopolies and therefore the diminishing need for studio B movies; the explosive growth of television in the early fifties; the public taste for super-widescreen films in color (and, briefly, in 3-D); and the rise of cheap drive-

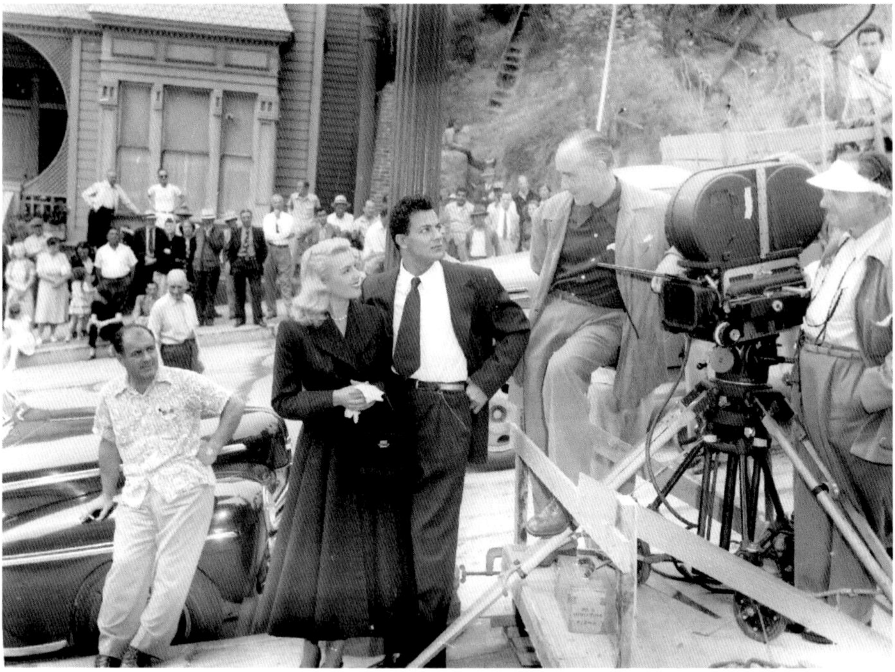

Patricia Knight, Cornel Wilde and director Douglas Sirk prepare to shoot a scene at the Koster house for *Shockproof* (1949). The building across Second Street behind them is the Chaspeak Apartments. *Bison Archives.*

in teen movies about bug-eyed monsters and high school rebels without a cause—had more or less ended the downbeat black and white theatrical crime film where light was hard and shadows harder. Instead, a more home-friendly hybrid had migrated to the smaller TV screen.

It was bound to happen. As David George later wrote in the *Jerusalem Post Magazine*, "Chases round the sewers and up and down tenement stairs; questioning of sleazy suspects by hard-eyed detectives; spoken narratives introduced by a date, place, a time; the wail of police sirens and the thud of running feet on pavements—these were fine while the impulse stayed fresh, but the moment came when all that remained was to turn the whole thing over to television and the ultimate never-never world of *Dragnet*."

Ah yes, *Dragnet*. Over the years, many well-known people had spent time on Bunker Hill while they were young and struggling. Lon Chaney Sr., "the man of a thousand faces," lived at 123 North Grand Avenue in the early twenties. Brothers Henry and Charles Greene, Southern California's most iconic architects, lived at 257 South Grand in 1906. Edith Head, Hollywood's top costume designer, lived with a family friend at 401 South Grand in 1917–18 and director Norman Taurog, probably best remembered today for his bad Mario Lanza and worse Elvis Presley movies, had an apartment just down the street at 431 South Grand a couple of years later. In 1920, when he was still Marion Morrison, John Wayne resided at the Gladden Apartments where Raymond Chandler had lived a few years earlier. For all of them, Bunker Hill was a way station, a cheap place to spend a few months or a year until their careers got going. But for Jack Webb it was home, and its memories were saturated into every molecule of his being.

Webb's mother, Maggie, was an Irish Catholic alcoholic living on county relief; he never met his father, a Jewish sailor named Sam Webb who gave Jack his dark complexion. Though born in Santa Monica's Ocean Park neighborhood in 1920, he grew up from age two in a rundown Bunker Hill rooming house, the St. Regis Apartments at 237 South Flower Street. "I lived [there] for seventeen years with my mother and my grandmother," Webb told *Cosmopolitan* writer Peter Martin in 1954. "My boyhood memories span Prohibition, bootlegging, Repeal, Franklin Roosevelt, the big California earthquake in 1933, and apartment 339, one room, third-floor rear, with bathrooms on the back porch." The back yard, Webb said, "was on 'apartment-house hill.' Half a dozen apartment houses [on Figueroa] backed up on the same rear area, filled with trash bins and garbage cans." Webb was so ashamed of the St. Regis that whenever schoolmates saw him there, he claimed he was visiting friends.

For most of his childhood, Jack slogged up Bunker Hill's streets with difficulty because of asthma. "I could not walk up even a slight incline without severe breathing pain. Flower Street was a high hill, almost painfully tough for a Model T or the iceman's horse. My mother and grandmother used to combine forces and carry me up the hill." He couldn't make it on his own power until he was ten years old. To go to the Beaux Arts movie houses on Broadway from the west side of Bunker Hill, young Jack usually took the Third Street tunnel "shortcut" under the hill. "It connected Flower Street with Hill Street…It was a gloomy tunnel, and it scared me and stirred my imagination."

He grew out of his asthma and blossomed into a popular young man with an interest in theater and radio. When he got a regular job at Silverwood Men's Store at Broadway and Sixth, he couldn't wait to move out of the St. Regis and off Bunker Hill for good. In the mid-1940s, after a stint in the Army Air Corps, he got the lead role as a San Francisco-based private eye in *Pat Novak For Hire*, first on several West Coast radio stations and then on the

Mutual Broadcasting Network, zinging listeners with witty Chandlerisms. *Time* magazine dubbed him "the ultimate radio hard boiler."

Naturally, Hollywood called. His first film, in 1948, was Eagle Lion's *Hollow Triumph* (released in the U.K. as *The Scar*), with the tagline: "The story of a man who murdered himself—and lived to regret it." Webb, uncredited, plays Bull's-Eye, one of two syndicate enforcers who at one point send the film's star, Paul Henreid, scurrying for his life up Angels Flight to the top of Bunker Hill. From there, Webb stepped into a substantial role as a police chemist in a documentary-style noir called *He Walked By Night*, based on a true story of a Los Angeles cop killer and filmed on some of the actual locations, including a housing court just off Santa Monica Boulevard, between Fuller and Poinsettia, in Hollywood. The film begins with a written disclaimer superimposed upon a map of Los Angeles: "This is a true story… The record is set down here factually—as it happened. Only the names are changed—to protect the innocent." Then comes an aerial shot of downtown Los Angeles à la *The Naked City*. The voice of Reed Hadley (a regular noir actor and narrator) intones: "This is Los Angeles, Our Lady the Queen of Angels, as the Spaniards called her." A series of clips shows Angelenos going about their business, as well as a well-framed shot of Los Angeles City Hall, which in those days housed the L.A.P.D. headquarters. After the action begins, the cops use the word "dragnet" four times in the first half hour. The film's technical adviser and a *Pat Novak For Hire* fan, Detective Sergeant Marty Wynn, suggested to Webb that he take a page from *He Walked By Night* and create a new radio cop program using real police files.

Though Jack Webb went on to make several more noirs—*Dark City* (1950), *Sunset Boulevard* (1950) and *Appointment with Danger* (1951)—he took Wynn's advice and put together a new radio show, *Dragnet*, copying *He Walked By Night*'s basic format, using himself as the narrator and main character, laconic L.A.P.D sergeant Joe Friday. As a bonus, composer Walter Schumann gave *Dragnet*'s theme march a distinctive staccato *dum-de-dum dum* musical cue that became the most famous four-note introduction since the opening of Beethoven's Fifth Symphony. (Unfortunately, Schumann lost the composer rights when a judge ruled that he'd borrowed those four notes from Miklos Rozsa's soundtrack for the 1945 film noir *The Killers*.)

Running from 1949 to 1955 on NBC, the radio show was a great success because of Webb's attention to tiny details. Realistic radio transmissions crackled in the background. Characters sometimes had to say something twice before being understood or misheard what was being said. Sometimes the dialogue rambled, going nowhere. Secondary characters had real voices

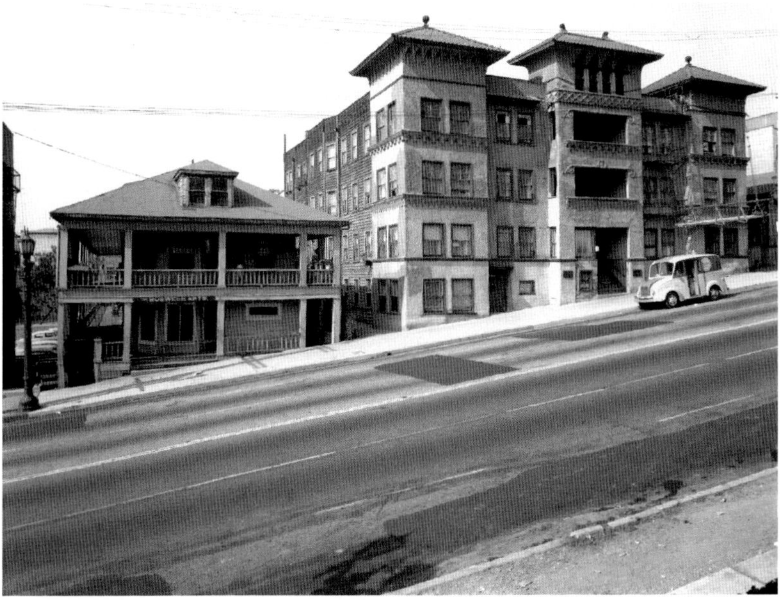

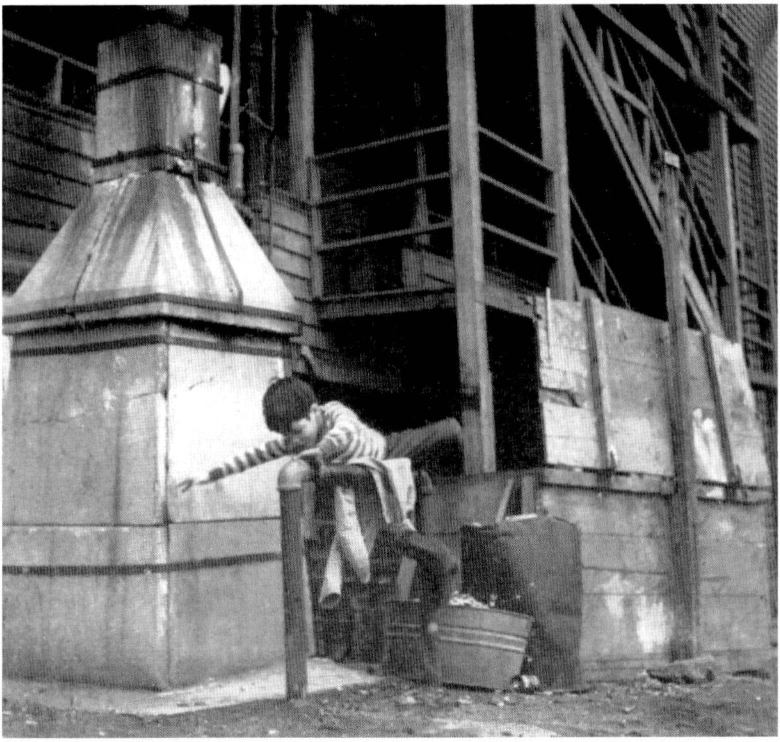

Jack Webb grew up at the St. Regis Apartments (top, right) at 237 South Flower Street, where his early playground was the trash area in back (above). *Bison Archives; Jim Dawson.*

instead of "radio voices." The cops spoke casually in jargon ("we ran his M.O. through R and I") without stopping to explain it.

When the network moved *Dragnet* over into television in 1951, the L.A.P.D. let Webb shoot inside its headquarters. But going downtown and working around real detectives was time consuming, so Webb built an exact studio duplicate down to the last detail. According to one associate, "Story locales and time periods were required to be exact. Calendars and telephone extension numbers were authentic, and even doorknobs were replicated to match those at Los Angeles City Hall." As Webb himself put it, "My thesis for the show… was realism pitched in a low key." He began each episode with a brief opening monologue: "This is the city, Los Angeles, California," over an aerial shot and a montage of everyday life around Los Angeles, including Angels Flight on Bunker Hill ("…for five cents ride the shortest railway in the world"). In effect, he moved the police procedural, the documentary side of film noir, from the dying world of theatrical B movies into the American living room, at a time when other noir-inspired programs—*Mr. District Attorney*, *Treasury Men in Action*, *Racket Squad*, *Front Page Detective*, *Ellery Queen*, *Man Against Crime*

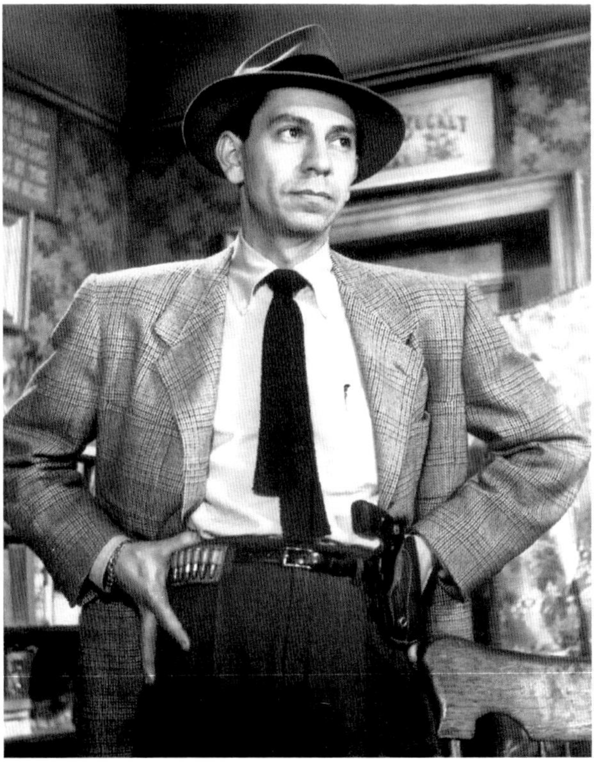

After getting his start as a radio gumshoe and a film noir actor, Jack Webb created the realistic Los Angeles police procedural Dragnet and the role of Sergeant Joe Friday, first on radio and then on TV. *Jim Dawson.*

and *Martin Kane Private Eye*—were also migrating to the new medium. The big difference was that *Dragnet* became the most popular police show in television history, at least until the multiple rerun channels began playing *Law & Order* episodes day and night forty years later. Webb controlled every aspect of the show, keeping sixteen-hour days, sacrificing friendships and marriages and chain-smoking the cigarettes that eventually killed him. Always in the back of his mind, driving him forward, was that dingy Flower Street apartment on Bunker Hill, a place where he never wanted to return. Not even Joe Friday ventured into Bunker Hill's warrens, for who knew what terrors they might unleash? There was crime enough elsewhere in Los Angeles.

The end of Hollywood's film noir period, it turns out, was not the end of Bunker Hill's golden age as a movie location. As buildings began to disappear and the population thinned out in the sixties, the neighborhood became an ideal spot for independent and low-budget filmmakers. Some of them tried to continue within the film noir tradition and others made teenage social problem movies. At least one guy made a fancy porno flick. Some referred to Bunker Hill by name and made it a character. And nearly all of them, whether they meant to or not, documented the hill being systematically taken apart.

CHAPTER 5
LAST DOUBLE BILL AND TESTAMENT

"This hill, ya know? Stories? It's loaded. Nobody's ever written 'em. Now they're tearing it down. I figured somebody oughta say something about it before it's gone."
—Jake the bartender, Angel's Flight *(1965)*

In 1947, ninety million Americans went to the movies twice a week. Four years later, attendance had dropped to fifty-four million people, and they were going only once a week. The rest had decided to stay home and watch their new television sets. Hollywood studios frantically tried to lure them back by improving the theater experience with amenities they couldn't get at home: wide-screen Cinerama and CinemaScope, three-dimensional StereoVision, four-track stereophonic sound and, of course, vivid color. Black and white theatrical film noirs, with their nearly square 1.33-to-1 screen ratio, were beginning to look as passé as Pola Negri movies from the twenties. Or like something you'd watch in the den on your tiny, snowy cathode ray tube.

Bunker Hill briefly got a boost from this brave new Hollywood in 1953 when two first-run Technicolor films were shot there. Universal Pictures's *The Glenn Miller Story*, starring Jimmy Stewart, included a couple of scenes at a pawnshop mockup at the corner of Clay Street and the Third Street steps, with the Halloween-colored Angels Flight cars passing each other on the overhead rails in the background. But the more memorable movie was Warner Bros' CinemaScope remake of *A Star Is Born*, the studio's most expensive film up to that time. Studio boss Jack Warner borrowed George

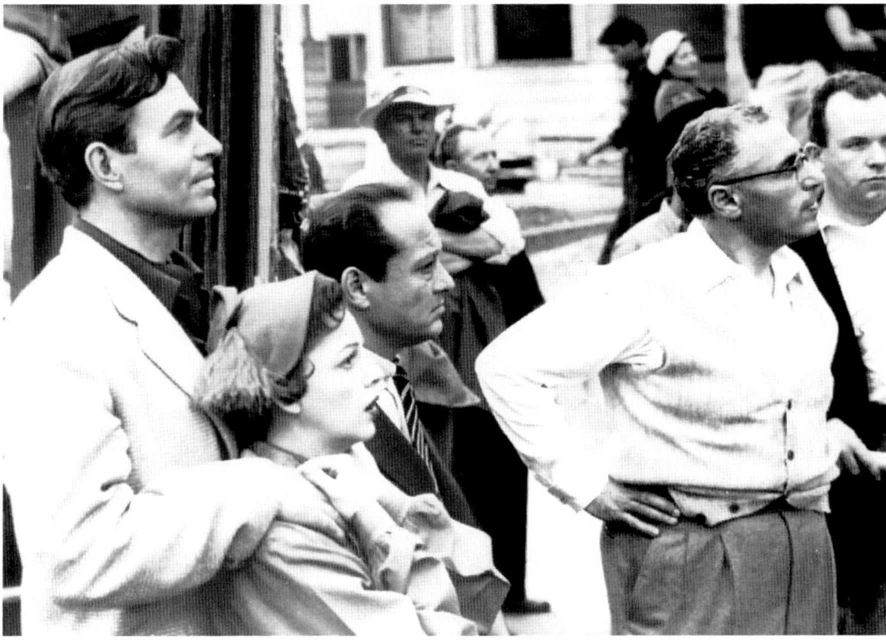

James Mason, Judy Garland and producer Sid Luft wait for *A Star Is Born* director George Cukor (wearing glasses, right) to set up the next shot at the Lancaster Hotel at 121 North Flower Street. *Jim Dawson.*

Cukor from Metro-Goldwyn-Mayer to direct Broadway playwright Moss Hart's screenplay, which itself was an update of the original 1937 script jointly written by, among others, Dorothy Parker and Ring Lardner. Unlike the earlier *A Star Is Born* with Janet Gaynor, this one was a musical drama introducing new Harold Arlen and Ira Gershwin songs. Its star (and silent co-producer) was Judy Garland, hoping to get back on top again after several years away from Hollywood.

Bunker Hill had never seen anything like it. According to film historian Ronald Haver, in late November "twenty transportation units" arrived at "the seedy Bunker Hill section of downtown Los Angeles," where Esther Blodgett, Garland's character, had moved "to a dingy rooming house in a decaying area." In the scene, James Mason comes looking for her and finds her sunbathing up on the roof. The shoot took only two days, but the expense for that caravan of vehicles and technicians was probably more than the entire budgets of some of Bunker Hill's black-and-white crime films. And Garland's legendary presence brought out crowds of otherwise blasé local residents.

The location was the four-story, thirty-eight-room Lancaster Apartments at 121 North Flower Street, on a quiet block of wood-frame apartment buildings on one side and tidy family bungalows on the other. It was hardly a seedy or decaying neighborhood, except perhaps by rarefied Beverly Hills standards. And though Haver wrote that the name of Esther Blodgett's lodgings came from Hart's script, the place had in fact been operating as the Hotel Lancaster since the 1920s.

Cukor gave Flower Street plenty of good CinemaScopic coverage as Mason drives his roadster up First Street from Figueroa, turns left, and parks across the street from the Lancaster, with the wide lens taking in the large LaBaterre Apartments on the southwest corner behind him and glimpses of the black-gold, tower-topped Richfield Building nearly six blocks away through a curtain of smog. In Technicolor, the neighborhood doesn't look shabby at all. Maybe Bunker Hill had a bright new future in the movies.

Unfortunately, Jack Warner came to believe that his musical drama had too much drama and not enough music, and to rectify this imbalance, he ordered the last-minute addition of a $250,000, fifteen-minute MGM-style showcase for his star that stretched *A Star Is Born* to nearly three hours. After the preliminary screenings in 1954, audiences said the movie was too long, theater operators complained that the reduced number of screenings per day hurt their revenues and critics called the added musical segment ("Born in a Trunk") not just a show-stopper but a dead-stopper. Prompted by Garland and her producer husband, Sid Luft, Warner decided to keep the music anyway and cut Moss Hart's carefully crafted exposition, including the Bunker Hill scene. It was a huge mistake. *A Star Is Born*, all five million dollars' worth, belly-flopped at the box office, and Judy Garland's resurrection as a film star died aborning. And so ended the neighborhood's brief tenure as an A-list location. It would take another thirty years before Ronald Haver and Doug Edwards restored *A Star Is Born* to nearly its full length for a 1983 video release, with the Bunker Hill scene mostly intact.

If the noir filmmakers of the '40s and '50s liked Bunker Hill for its memorably gritty mien, B-movie producers and independent filmmakers in the 1960s were drawn to its ready-made ghost town desolation. As long as they got their proper police permits (and not all of them did), they could shoot night and day without disturbing too many people, especially the type of pesky property owners who often interfered with productions until they were paid off. And if directors wanted an extra dose of realism, they could incorporate into their stories the slow dissolution of Bunker Hill in the background. Whatever their motives, these filmmakers chronicled the last

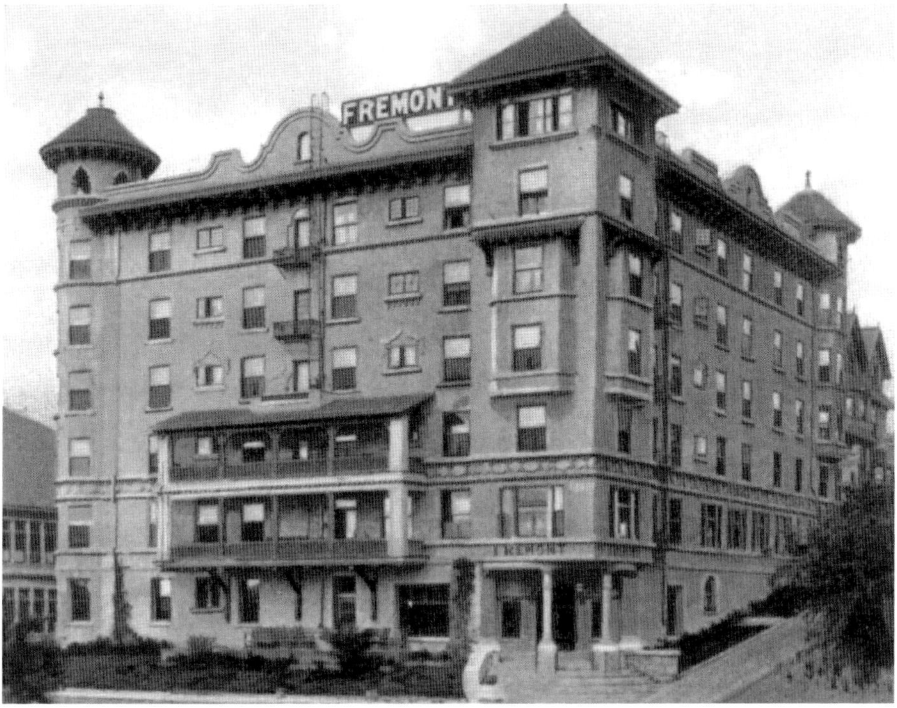

The Fremont was a first-rate hotel when it opened on the southwest corner of Fourth and Olive in 1902, but by the time Edmond O'Brien checked in nearly half a century later in *Backfire* (1950), the place was getting seedy. *Jim Dawson.*

days of Bunker Hill and created a record of a place that, by the end of the decade, ceased to exist.

Though traditional film noir was writhing in the gutter by the 1960s, a couple of holdouts still came to the hill to take a few final gasps. There was also a thriving new sub-genre of the old crime drama called the juvenile-delinquent-as-social-problem action thriller, an outgrowth of the late forties teenage potboilers like Irving Shulman's *The Amboy Dukes* and Hal Ellson's *Duke* that Hollywood carried into the fifties with *The Wild Ones* (1952), *Blackboard Jungle* (1955), *Running Wild* (1955) and *Cry Tough* (1959). And finally, as Bunker Hill faced the proliferating pendulums of wrecking balls, its mostly vacant shells and empty lots provided space for low-budget filmmakers who were as down on their luck as the neighborhood. These films included *Get Outta Town* and *The Little Shop of Horrors* (1960); *The Boy Who Caught a Crook* (1961); *The Exiles* (shot in 1958, but assembled in 1960–61); *Angel's Flight* (shot in 1962-63, released in 1965); *Incredibly Strange People Who Stopped Living and Became Mixed-*

Up Zombies!!? (1964); and an arty soft-core porn film called *The Girls of F Street* a.k.a. *The Maidens of Fetish Street* (1966). Even when the big studios came to the hill in 1960 (*This Rebel Breed*), 1963 (*Dime with a Halo*) and 1966 (*The Money Trap*), they slummed in black and white, shooting the last of their B movies with mostly television directors before movie theaters gave up on double bills altogether. Then, finally, television itself came calling, just as the final scraps were being hauled away.

One of the camp classics of ultra-low-budget filmmaking was Roger Corman's *The Little Shop of Horrors* (1960), a farce about a florist shop employee named Seymour (Jonathan Haze) who cultivates a man-eating Venus flytrap. Best known today for Jack Nicholson's cameo as a mental dental patient, the $27,000 film was mostly shot in two days on old standing sets at the Charlie Chaplin Studios at 1416 South La Brea Avenue in Hollywood. In a 2004 interview, screenwriter Charles B. Griffith told writer Aaron Graham that after they spent a full day planning the two-camera set-ups and rehearsing the actors, "Roger shot fifty pages of interiors and the next day he shot fifty [more] pages of interiors…And I directed the exteriors and street scenes." Like most of Corman's films, *Little Shop* "was a throwaway that would play downtown for forty-eight hours and that was it. There was just nothing else to do with these pictures. It would play drive-ins down South." Not until years later would midnight movie denizens turn it into a freak hit that inspired a Broadway adaptation and a $33 million Hollywood remake.

In a January 17, 2012 Internet post, Jack Warford, who played a police detective in the film, corroborated Griffith's claim: "All the exteriors except those immediately in front of the shop door were shot on location at night, mostly over two long weekends, directed by Chuck Griffith with a non-union crew. That included the scenes on Skid Row with rummies working for ten cents a shot, Angels Flight Railway, [and] Bunker Hill in L.A. before they tore it down." The scenes were shot quickly and furtively after midnight, without city permits. Since Angels Flight was already closed for the night, Griffith filmed Haze at the ticket window of the Olive Street station, as if he had just ridden up on one of the cars, and then walked a hooker (Merri Welles) into the scene to solicit him. They also shot across the street in front of the Angels Flight Café at the northwest corner of Third and Olive and at the benches at the top of Third Street on Bunker Hill Avenue.

One of the most unusual—and belatedly celebrated—Bunker Hill films is *The Exiles*, which a British-born University of Southern California cinema student named Kent Mackenzie shot in sixteen-millimeter black and white as part of a masters thesis. Filmed in 1958 but not exhibited until the 1961

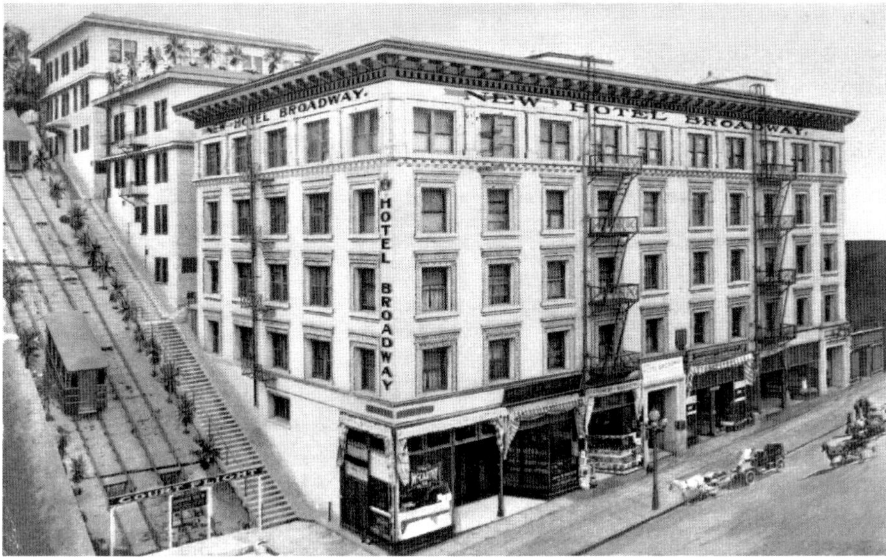

Court Flight connected the dead end of Court Street on Bunker Hill with the 200 block of North Broadway below. Located three blocks north of Angels Flight, Court Flight was shorter and steeper, and like industrial funiculars, it ran its cars on two separate sets of tracks, whereas the cars on the more glamorous Angels Flight shared only one set of tracks at the top and bottom and passed each other on little sidetracks in the middle. Court Flight ran from 1904 to 1943. *Jim Dawson.*

Venice Film Festival, it was not commercially released at the time. Mackenzie died in 1980, leaving *The Exiles* in storage, and it might have been forgotten if California Institute of the Arts professor Thom Andersen hadn't resurrected it for his 2003 film essay of movie clips called *Los Angeles Plays Itself.*

Much like Lionel Rogosin's *On the Bowery* (a 1956 New York film that followed mostly real street people as they drank themselves into oblivion), *The Exiles* is a poignant, semi-documentary ride-along starring non-actors portraying restless young people like themselves. In fact, since they contributed to the story and the dialogue, it's impossible for the viewer to discern where the "actors" leave off and their characters begin. At the film's heart are a pregnant Apache from Arizona named Yvonne Williams (called Yvonne in the film) and her "husband," a Hualapai Indian named Homer Nish (called Homer), living on the margins of society on Bunker Hill, compliments of the federal government's Urban Indian Relocation Program. (Williams's real husband was not in the movie and, in fact, was jailed on a felony charge while she was filming.) *The Exiles* takes place over roughly fourteen hours, from early dusk to late dawn, as Homer and his pals go carousing. They drop Yvonne off a few blocks away at the Roxie Theater at 518 Broadway and head off on their peregrinations, beginning with a couple of so-called "Indian bars" on Main Street near Third, then over to the Royal Liquors store on the northwest corner of Third and Hill to pick up some fortified Thunderbird wine (*The Trail of the Thunderbird* was Mackenzie's original title), through the Third Street tunnel and off to a poker game in a rambling slum apartment probably somewhere around Hope Street. Yvonne, at the end of her evening after window gazing on Broadway, trudges up the steps beneath Angels Flight (she never takes the railway, probably because the nickel fare is too expensive for her), but instead of turning left and heading back to the cramped rear apartment where she and Homer live at 334 Clay Street, she turns right and walks up to the Sunshine Apartments to spend the night with a girlfriend. There is even a tribal scene of Native Americans gathering late at night atop the recently leveled Chavez Ravine, with nighttime L.A. glittering in the distance. Mackenzie gave *The Exiles* the professional, deep-focus look of film noir, and only its plotless, seemingly cinéma vérité meanderings keep it from qualifying as such. Because it spends so much time enveloped by Bunker Hill, *The Exiles* is one of the best time capsules of the neighborhood.

When Hollywood trekked down to Bunker Hill to create a social drama about race and ethnicity in America, the result was a little more confused and much more contrived than *The Exiles*. In fact, Bunker Hill wasn't even mentioned in the script of *This Rebel Breed*, an early 1960 Warner Bros teen exploitation flick, even though most of it was shot there. Since the studio production notes put the location as being in East Los Angeles—the city's main Mexican-American neighborhood—one critic commented that *This Rebel Breed* was "photographed adequately on the streets of East Los Angeles" and another wrote, "Much of the picture was filmed at night in East Los Angeles." But credited or not, Bunker Hill was the costar in this movie about undercover cops going after a drug-dealing, racist high school gang. An unknown (pre-*Westside Story*) Rita Moreno and her Mexican family live at 227 South Bunker Hill Avenue, a modest Eastlake home. Various scenes are shot all up and down Third Street, but the most extensive footage takes place at the corner of Third and Grand in a dolly scene that begins at a liquor store on the southeast corner (formerly the Angels Flight Pharmacy), where undercover cop Mark Damon is following Moreno. She walks diagonally eastward across the street to a small house at 523 West Third Street, where she learns from her doctor that she's pregnant. Then she mopes west lost in thought, past the Philadelphia Cleaners and Laundry at 525 West Third, housed within the Lovejoy—a large, white apartment building on the northeast corner that fronts at 529 Third; she turns north on Grand, where we can see the Dome Hotel Apartments at the southwest corner of Second Street. The advantage of this long, mobile take is that it gives the neighborhood a distinct spatial and temporal reality; the audience literally walks along the street with her for a minute or so. There are also later scenes of a black neighborhood filmed at a corner house at 201 South Bunker Hill Avenue (which was also used three years later in the opening scene of MGM's *Dime With a Halo*, starring another Latina actress named Barbara Luna).

Based on a story called "All God's Children," *This Rebel Breed* was aimed at drive-ins and the type of theaters where teenagers hung out for weekend matinees, but in all fairness, it's a couple of notches above the average teen-angst film of the period. Its tagline was "The Screen Looks Squarely Into the Face of Today's Wild Teenage Emotions Caught in the Cross-Fire of Love and Hate," and indeed it did deal fairly honestly with ethnic and racial prejudice, even though the lead character, a Hispanic mulatto cop, was a white actor in brownface. The film was banned in parts of the South, especially after Warner Bros retitled it *The Black Rebels* for a 1966 reissue. Director Richard Bare and most of the film's actors went straight into television.

Get Outta Town (1960), produced by actor Doug Wilson and director Charlie Davis, was a better-than-average low-budget black and white film about an ex-safecracker named Kelly who returns to Los Angeles for his brother's funeral. (Its working title was *The Day Kelly Came Home.*) More than most Hollywood noirs of the forties and fifties, *Get Outta Town* has the gritty feel of a pulp magazine short story, with hard characters and working-class dialogue. There is an extended scene on the Spring Street side of Los Angeles City Hall and a couple of shots around Second and Olive, but what makes this movie special is that a large portion was filmed inside the Dome Hotel Apartments at Second and Grand, giving a good sense of its layout, its small apartments, its corridors and its narrow balconies and stairways. When Miller Consolidated Pictures released the film as a program padder for *The Amazing Transparent Man*, the *Hollywood Reporter* (March 15) said, "Shot on local locations, *Get Outta Town* gains from this authenticity which is the film's greatest asset." The *Los Angeles Times* likewise liked its look: "[T]he fact that it was made entirely on location around Los Angeles and was directed and photographed with care and talent does make some worthwhile difference." Beckman Film Corp rereleased it as *Gangster's Revenge* a couple of years later, but distribution has always been limited. The film was released on video/DVD as *Get Outta Town*.

Typical of the low-budget Bunker Hill programmers during this period was *The Boy Who Caught a Crook*, a 1961 indie produced by Robert E. Kent, a protégé of legendary Hollywood schlockmeister Sam Katzman (*Earth Vs. the Flying Saucers*). It was written by Nathan Juran (*Attack of the 50-Foot Woman*); and directed by Edward L. Cahn (*Creature With the Atomic Brain*). Described by *Variety* (October 12, 1961) as "another supporting item from the [Kent-Cahn] assembly line of instant melodramas," a "filler thriller" and "a routine utility 'B'," *Boy* had a television cast that included Walt Disney kid Roger Mobley and cardboard villain Johnny Seven playing the eponymous characters, respectively. The film begins with a panning shot from the corner of Second Street and Bunker Hill Avenue, but most of its location action takes place a couple blocks west: the boy's friend—a local bum named Colonel (Don Beddoe)—lives in an old house at 711 West Second Street, near the northwest corner of Hope; together they find a bank robber's briefcase just north of First Street, between Figueroa and the new Harbor Freeway, and take it to the nearby Paul Kendrick's Service Station at 117 North Figueroa. Because of the freeway, this area on the western edge of Bunker Hill has already been stripped of most of its buildings, and Colonel's house has a sign on it that says TO BE MOVED; piles of dirt and derelict houses are visible in the background, and the characters occasionally refer to the hill's creeping destruction. Colonel tells the robber that he buried his money at the top of the hill at the old Clancy place: "It's just a cellar now, the house is gone," he says. A cop (Robert Stevenson) who's searching for all of them says that the Colonel probably lives in "some cheap flop in one of these rooming houses. There's plenty of those. Hyde, get on the car radio and ask for every available unit, I want Bunker Hill sealed off tight…Must be fifty-sixty houses on the hill, we're going through every one of them." Late in the film, a local reporter (Richard Crane) looking down from the nocturnal desolation to the busy downtown below says, "Bunker Hill is like an island in the city of light." Unfortunately, as if trying to illustrate the folly of juxtaposing location and studio scenes, the filmmakers set the boy's house—whose address is alternately given as 641 and 909 Bunker Hill Avenue, neither of which would place it on Bunker Hill—on a studio soundstage whose artificiality is jarring.

One of the strangest, and cheapest, films shot on Bunker Hill was director Ray Dennis Steckler's $28,000 cheesefest, *Face of Evil* (1964), starring himself—under the name Cash Flagg—and his real-life wife, Carolyn Brandt. If this original title is unfamiliar, it's because he changed it at the last minute to capitalize on Columbia Pictures' hot new movie, *Dr. Strangelove: or, How I Learned to Stop Worrying and Love the Bomb!* When Columbia threatened to sue Steckler for using *The Incredibly Strange Creature: or, Why I Stopped Living*

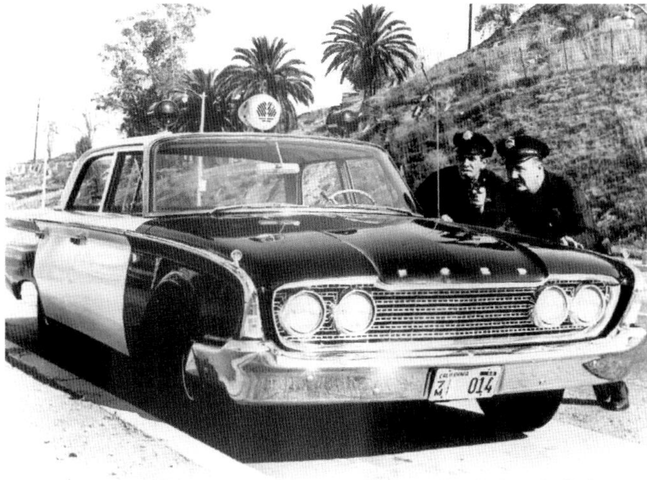

The Boy Who Caught a Crook (1961) was shot mostly around Figueroa, Flower and Hope streets, north of First Street, where many of the houses had already been torn down. This photo of two cops who were chasing bankrobber Johnny Seven was most likely taken on Hope Street. *Bison Archives.*

and Became a Mixed-Up Zombie!, he modified the title into *Incredibly Strange People Who Stopped Living and Became Mixed-Up Zombies!!?* Yes, the ending punctuation is correct. Filmed in "Terrorama," it was exactly the type of movie to which the title is everything: an amusement park gypsy named Madame Estrella, whose facial wart keeps migrating around her cheek like a pet bug, puts young men into homicidal trances with one of those old spinning spiral wheels that cost 39 cents at the five-and-dime store. At one point in all the general incoherency, Steckler, a.k.a. Cash Flagg, inexplicably finds himself roaming all around Angels Flight, up and down inside one of the cars and up and down the desolate stairways on both sides of Third Street, while a sad jazz piece plays on the soundtrack.

A couple of years later, when George Romero's *Night of the Living Dead* redefined the zombie genre, Steckler briefly renamed his opus *The Teenage Psycho Meets Bloody Mary*—in "Hallucinogenic HypnoVision." The visual process was always as important as the wacky titles in Steckler's ads; he's the guy who in 1966 shot *Rat Pfink a Boo Boo* in "RegularScope Black and White!" His cameraman on *Incredibly Strange Creatures*, incidentally, was a young Hungarian named Vilmos Zsigmond, who would go on to shoot a number of memorable films, including *Close Encounters of a Third Kind*. Comparable Hollywood success eluded Steckler, however. He eventually transformed himself into hardcore porno director "Cindy Lou Sutters," whose *oeuvre* included *Debbie Does Las Vegas* (1981), and later ran a Las Vegas video rental store right up to his death in 2009. As for *Incredibly Strange Creatures*, it found new life after a popular cable TV show, *Mystery Science Theater 3000*, gave it the so-bad-it's-good treatment in the early eighties. The Turner Classic Movies channel occasionally showcases the film during late-night trash festivals.

Perhaps the first slasher noir, not just on Bunker Hill but in Hollywood, was an independent production called *Angel's Flight*, so named, according to scriptwriter Deane Romano, because it took place around the Angels Flight railway and, more important, featured "an angel in flight" as the protagonist, a female serial killer—thus the apostrophe. (In the early days of Angels Flight, owner J. Ward Eddy wasn't grammatically consistent, but by mid-century, the subsequent owners began to drop the apostrophe.) The term film noir fits despite the timeline because *Angel's Flight* has many of the ingredients of the genre, including an idealist who has lost his way in an alcoholic fog, a deadly and psychologically damaged woman, dreary flophouse interiors and wise-guy dialogue like "How long's this maniac been prowling the moors?" and "My tom-tom's been on the blink." The film is a fascinating mess. Egyptian-born director Raymond Nassour began shooting in 1962, but the producer-star, William Thourlby, ran out of money at just about the same time the police shut down the production for not having film permits. Eventually, they sneaked back to Bunker Hill and got most of the remaining footage.

Angel's Flight played briefly on a Midwest drive-in circuit under the name *Shock Hill*, supposedly to hide its identity from its investors. Twenty years later, Romano found a negative in a Los Angeles photo lab and sued to get the rights back. Unfortunately, the final scene was either missing or never got shot, so he had to duplicate the opening credits and splice them in at the end—which means the same credits run twice. When the film was showcased at a Hollywood film noir festival in April 2006, it had to be screened in a digital format because no sixteen-millimeter or thirty-five-millimeter prints had been made.

But *Angel's Flight* remains compelling despite its limitations. A broken down reporter named Ben Wylie (Thourlby) has crashed at the Royal Apartments on the southeast corner of Third and Olive, next to Angels Flight. On a bender one night he stumbles into Liz, a local stripper (Indus Arthur), not realizing that she has just murdered a man with a straight razor and is hurrying back to her apartment at 256 South Bunker Hill Avenue, at the corner of Third. When the next morning's headlines announce that a serial killer is on the loose in the neighborhood, Ben decides to investigate the story and get his life back on track. He drinks at the Angels Flight Café at the northwest corner of Third and Olive (though the interiors were filmed on a set) and at Bob's Café at 708 West Third Street, between Hope and Flower just west of the tunnel, where he briefly runs into a rowdy barfly (Rue McClanahan). The characters refer to the neighborhood as Bunker Hill or simply "the Hill."

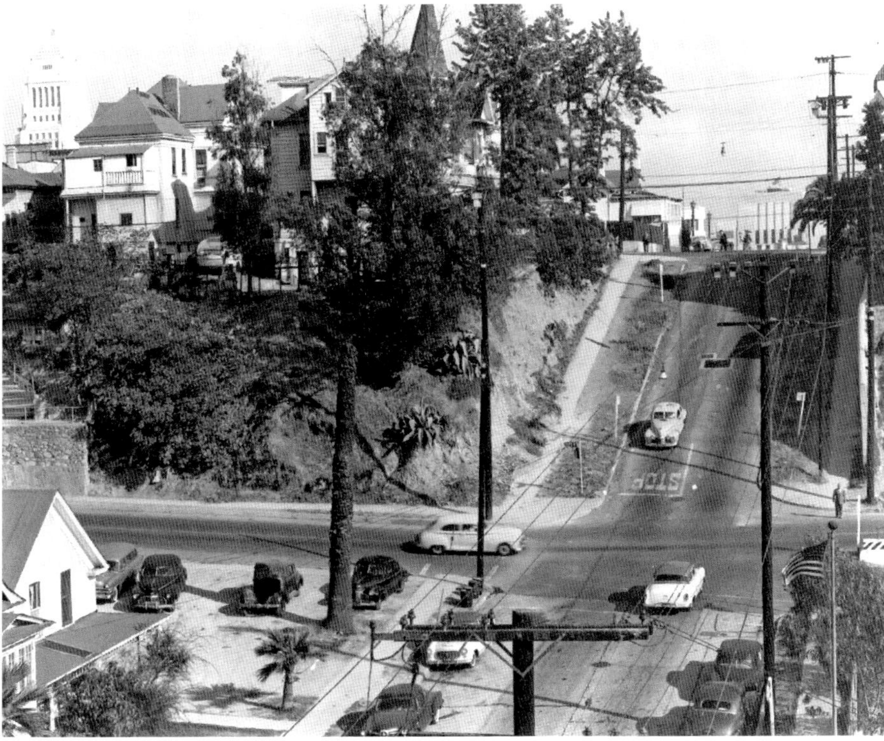

In *The Boy Who Caught a Crook* (filmed many years after this photo was taken in the early '50s), Don Beddoe's character, the Colonel, lived in the small house near the northwest corner of Hope and Second streets (lower left). On top of the steep Second Street hill, the building on the left with the pointed cupola is the Berke/Warncliffe Apartments, whose interior was used in *The Maidens of Fetish Street* (1966). The dome of the Dome Hotel Apartments at Second and Grand is visible at the top right. *Bison Archives.*

Jake, the bartender at the Angels Flight Café (veteran actor Michael Fox), tells Liz, who grew up there, "We're part of the hill, you and me." Later he grouses to Ben, "This hill, ya know. Stories? It's loaded. Nobody's ever written 'em. Now they're tearing it down." Among Liz's murder sites are the benches "at the top of the street" (at Third and Bunker Hill, across the street from where she lives) and near the bottom of the Hope Street steps at the Third Street tunnel—both of which were used a dozen years earlier in *M*. On the utility steps behind the Sunshine Apartments, Ben tells Liz he knows that her rape there five years earlier is the trigger behind her rage against men. "[Your] romantic dreams died on these steps," he tells her. She flees beneath Angels Flight and takes the stairs down to Hill Street, where she jumps on one of the railway cars and, midway up, leaps to her death.

By 1966, the big studios were phasing out the last of the B movies, whose only purpose at that point was either for television sales or closing out old contractual obligations. It's hard to tell exactly why MGM made *The Money Trap*, starring forty-nine-year-old Glenn Ford and forty-seven-year-old Rita Hayworth, neither one looking their best. (According to Peter Ford's excellent biography of his father, *Glenn Ford: A Life*, when Hayworth went to the producer to complain about her unflattering studio photos because "I look like an old whore," he reportedly answered, "Why do you think we hired you?") Some critics assumed *The Money Trap* was a twenty-year reunion of *Gilda*, the film noir classic they did together in 1946, even though they had costarred in other films since then. Ford plays a corrupt police detective, Hayworth a widow of a two-bit criminal, and they both come to bad ends. Ford's boss is Ted de Corsia, formerly the murderer in *The Naked City* and a costar in Hayworth's 1947 noir entry, *The Lady From Shanghai*. The story was written by hard-boiled novelist Lionel White, whose *Clean Break* had been the basis of Stanley Kubrick's *The Killing* ten years earlier. Cinematographer Paul Vogel, whose long career included Raymond Chandler's *Lady in the Lake* (1947), gave the movie a crisp noir patina in wide-screen black and white. *The Money Trap* was film noir to its core, even though the genre was dead in 1966.

Essentially it was made up of three stories, each with its own universe. Ford and his young wife (German actress Elke Sommer) live in a modernist Hollywood Hills home that looks like one of architectural photographer Julius Shulman's "case study houses"; all of Hayworth's scenes were shot on MGM's 1930s backlot "New York" set; Ford and his corrupt partner (Ricardo Montalban) spend their on-duty hours either rousting a mob doctor at his Beverly Hills estate or waiting outside a large, dilapidated house on Bunker Hill for a Mexican wife-murderer to show up. At least one critic, the *Los Angeles Times*'s Kevin Thomas, was upset by the back-and-forth jumps between the phony MGM streets and the real Bunker Hill locations (including Angels Flight). The house was a crumbling mansion at 238 South Bunker Hill Avenue that had been built in 1878 by attorney (later judge) Julius Brousseau and converted into apartments some time in the thirties. In 1956, when the neighborhood was still fairly intact, the house, with its off-center belvedere tower, stood conspicuously across the street from Marilyn Monroe's boardinghouse in *Bus Stop*. Half a dozen years later, artist Leo Politi lovingly painted it a couple of times for his book *Bunker Hill Los Angeles*. By 1966, when Glenn Ford and Ricardo Montalban staked out the street, the house was one of the last remaining Victorians in the neighborhood, surrounded by dirt, a broken sidewalk and a couple of straggly trees. Within days after the

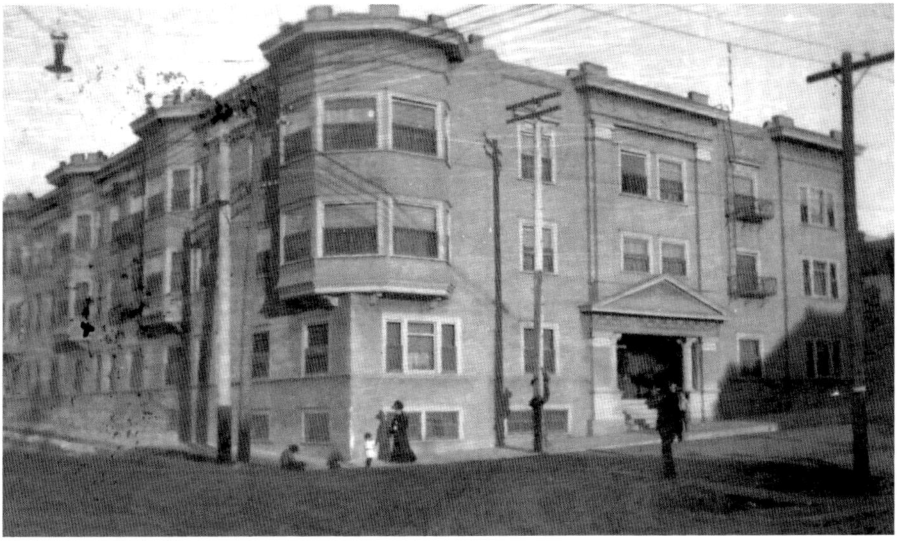

The Lovejoy Apartments stood at 529 West Third Street, at the northeast corner of Grand Avenue. Harold Lloyd used it as a background in a couple of silent comedies, including *High and Dizzy* (1920). In a long dolly shot, a camera followed Rita Moreno along the building's Second Street sidewalk in *This Rebel Breed* (1960). *Nathan Marsak.*

movie folks finished their job and packed up their gear, the Brousseau house disappeared forever.

Another wonderful old Bunker Hill Avenue structure gone to seed would make its final appearance that same year in much sleazier company, although it had already been torn down a couple of years earlier. *The Girls on F Street* (later reissued on video as *The Maidens of Fetish Street*) is an art film with bare breasts, kinky foreplay and a proud pedigree: "From the Screen Play *The Degenerates.*" Mostly it's inchoate nonsense. But in one segment, the film does capture a smog-bound Los Angeles at a time when pollution was bad enough to burn the eyes. The camera rides up to Bunker Hill on Angels Flight with a nerd named Nick (Ken McCormick). All the old buildings along the tracks are gone by now, leaving only clay and overgrown weeds. Nick spends the next ten minutes cavorting inside a large, rectangular Queen Anne overlooking Second Street but fronting at 145 South Bunker Hill Avenue, less than a block from the Brousseau house. According to the 1899 city directory, it was a furnished apartment building called the Berke, owned by Ferdinand Berke. Sometime later, it became the Warncliffe Apartments. Its interior is mostly bare and a little ratty in the early sixties when this segment was filmed, but it still retains its gaslight-era charm. The movie calls the place "the House of Fetish."

There is no dialogue, only a male narrator who strays into Ed Wood territory with profound musings. As the scene begins, he says:

> *This is the Angels Flight that ascends, descends, countless times daily, where angels fear to tread. A flight that is incapable of surmounting the plight of our human misery. For this hill has never budged and bridged the border of the ravaged slums, with all its potent, stomach-turning smells. Where each individual flight to the top of the hill never seems to leave behind his despaired hopes and disillusioned agonies. Nick is no different from all the others on his thirty-second journey of hopeless dejection. Nick wonders, as he scans the miles of horizon* [invisible because of smog], *the strange blend of peaceful serenity contrasted by distorted pulsations that seethes beneath its panoramic skylines.*

Later, when Nick has satisfied his cravings, he returns to Los Angeles below as a whirling merry-go-round cuts to an interior shot of an Angels Flight car descending. "There's no difference between a merry-go-round and a downward journey on Angels Flight…They both drop off…lower than before."

That would have been the swan song of Bunker Hill if a couple of television productions hadn't stopped by at the last minute to kill a little time with some local color. Erle Stanley Gardner's *Perry Mason*, starring film noir veteran Raymond Burr as the titular trial lawyer, had been airing in black and white since its inception in 1957, but CBS decided to take a chance by opening its September 1966 season with a color episode called "The Case of the Twice-Told Twist." The scene was practically a throwaway, designed more than anything else, it seemed, to give Angels Flight a plug during a time when preservationists were making last-ditch efforts to keep it alive. Burr and his secretary (Barbara Hale) park on the northwest corner of Third and Olive (formerly the location of the Angels Flight Café) and take the funicular down to see a client. By the time they return fifteen minutes later, juvenile delinquents have stripped their car.

The final send-off came only months before the Grim Reaper's scythe made its last pass over Bunker Hill. *The Outsider* ran for only a season, in 1968–69, on NBC, but in many ways, Darren McGavin's down-on-his-luck loner detective, David Ross, served as pulp novelist and screenwriter Roy Huggins's prototype for James Garner's more successful Jim Rockford a couple of years later. One early episode called "Through a Stained Glass Window" took advantage of the last two vestiges of old Bunker Hill: Angels Flight and the Castle, which by then had been sawed into three pieces and

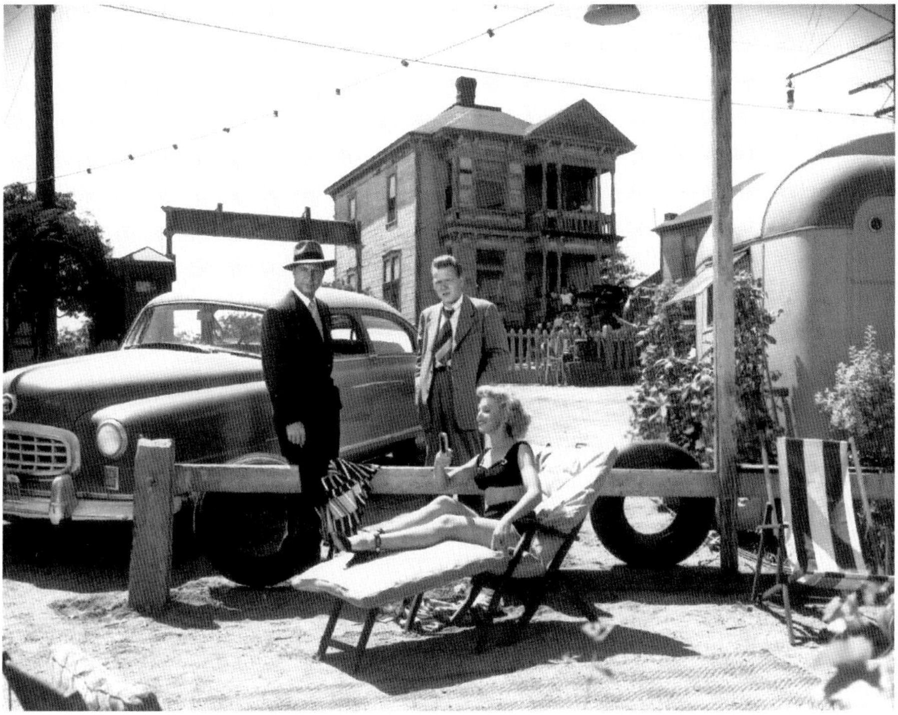

Like many other locations in *Cry Danger* (1951), the Clover Trailer Park where much of the action took place is commonly identified as being on Bunker Hill, but it was located several blocks away at 650–700 North Hill Place, north of Sunset Boulevard. The house across the street at 701 North Hill Place was the home of boxer Tommy Kansas (Lalo Rios) in *The Ring* (also 1951). *Cry Danger*'s actors above are Dick Powell, Richard Erdman and Jean Porter. *The Academy of Motion Picture Arts & Sciences.*

packed up for removal to a Highland Park neighborhood adjacent to the Pasadena Freeway. McGavin (and the camera) rides up Angels Flight, talks to the ticket man about the fate of the railway and then, with Pat Adler's paperback Bunker Hill reference book in hand, goes looking for the place where a bank robber stashed some loot. Dodging bulldozers and trucks, he wanders over to where the old house is waiting. There's nothing else left.

The next time we see Bunker Hill, it's playing itself: a post-apocalyptic wasteland in *The Omega Man* (1971), a Charlton Heston movie about earth's last living human fighting an army of vampires. A hundred years of Los Angeles history—of beautiful old homes, tourist hotels and working-class apartments, each an integral part of the growth and survival of the city as a great urban center—has been trampled in the dust.

CHAPTER 6

THERE WAS ONCE A CITY HERE

"Bunker Hill was [Fante's] *neighborhood. I lived there too before they leveled off the poor and put up high-rises. It was the best place for the poor, the best place for cabbage and fish heads, boiled carrots, the old, the insane, the young who couldn't fit into the offices down there."*
—Charles Bukowski, in a 1978 letter to Ben Pleasants

Perhaps I've overstated Bunker Hill's slide into dereliction and decrepitude. Yes, in the 1940s and '50s, film directors framed it as a grid of stairways, clapboard fleabags, dusty palms, liquor stores, dimly lit shops and desultory, irregularly patched streets. But in the eyes of local writers and artists, Bunker Hill remained a village of quirky gardens and curlicue wrought-iron fences and conversations on twilight porches. Local historian Pat Adler, in her 1964 booklet called *The Bunker Hill Story*, wrote, "The streets may be steep, but they were remote from traffic rush, with trees along the sidewalks, and a profusion of the more vigorous garden flowers—nasturtiums, hollyhocks, tough-stemmed geraniums—still thriving behind the old carriage houses." And then there was Angels Flight, a child's delight, still sliding up and down the Third Street hill even while the structures around it were being pulled down. Perhaps Hollywood's rare Technicolor exceptions, *A Star Is Born* and *Bus Stop*, had captured this Bunker Hill best, bathing its comfortable working-class residential neighborhoods on North Flower Street and South Bunker Hill Avenue in morning pastels.

Most of the buildings, like the Sunshine Apartments, were less than fifty years old during the film noir years, but the neighborhood seemed

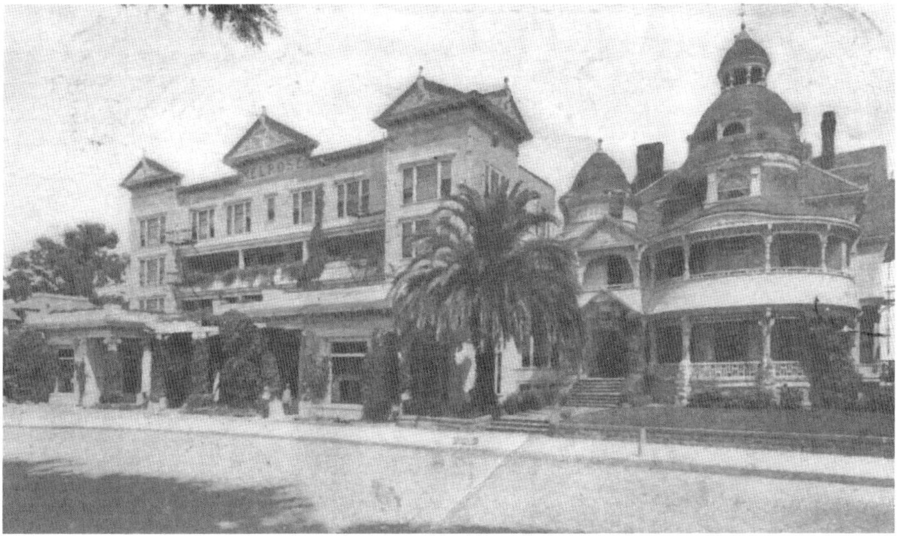

The elegant Melrose Hotel (right) was built at 130 Charity Street (later Grand Avenue) in 1881. A larger, more modern building (left) was added in 1890–91. *Jim Dawson.*

older because it hadn't kept up with the rest of restless Los Angeles. The architectural imprints on this most twentieth-century of all American cities—woodsy Craftsman homes, adobe duplexes, courtyard bungalows, modernist ranch houses, aerodynamic Googie coffee shops and drive-ins, Tiki huts, hot dog stands shaped like hot dogs, dingbats with their uppity names in 3-D lettering splayed on windowless stucco facades and the Spanish Colonial Revival homes with red-tile roofs, Southern California's premier style—were all absent from Bunker Hill. So were Beaux Arts and Art Deco, except for the termini of Angels Flight, the bone-white moderne Segrand Apartments on the northeast corner of Second and Grand and the Southern California Edison Building at Fifth and Grand.

If anyone caught in amber the vibrancy of life on this otherwise marked-for-death hilltop, it was Kent Mackenzie (1930–1980), a British-born American cinematographer studying film at the University of Southern California (USC). Though he's best known today for *The Exiles*, his 1961 neo-realist portrait of young American Indians living on Clay Street, he made his first visit a couple of years earlier to shoot a short, sixteen-millimeter film called *Bunker Hill 1956*. It documents the lives of several pensioners as they go about their quiet, self-contained lives, hoping that the city won't get around to evicting them anytime soon, despite all the newspaper articles about the hill's imminent destruction. "Every ten years it seems that somebody comes up with a scheme to demolish Bunker Hill," says one old-timer. Though we hear the voices of only three men—an elderly physician (Dr. James Green) who sees his patients in the parlor of his aging home at 232 South Grand Avenue, a nameless carpenter with a philosophical bent and a young druggist who runs the Angels Flight Pharmacy on the southeast corner of Third and Grand—Mackenzie tags along with a couple of others as they visit and shop and fill time in their little high-ceiled rooms above the city. We meet William Varney at his shoe repair shop at 510½ West Third and follow him across the street at suppertime to his home at 523 (the same house Rita Moreno later visits in *This Rebel Breed*). We amble with one pensioner to the old Melrose Hotel at 130 South Grand, with its porch bowered in vines and jacaranda, and accompany him inside to get a last glimpse of the lobby's moldy Victorian elegance. Another man lives at the Castle on Bunker Hill Avenue, where we watch the manager, Miss Olive Harp, watering the evening roses on the front lawn. The carpenter tells us that Bunker Hill's cheap rents—generally around ten dollars a month for one room with a sink and a hot plate and access to a common bathroom down the hall—allow these folks to maintain their independence and dignity in a familiar environment and that commercial avarice shouldn't take that away from them. "It's highly probable that they'll never find another Bunker Hill anywhere," he says. At dusk, as these ghostly figures disappear into the Victorian relics, the lights of the Montana Cafe at 255 South Grand, on the ground floor of the New Grand Hotel, come to life. Its affable young drinkers bring a faint hope of regeneration to the neighborhood.

Colorado-born John Fante (1909–1983) is the writer we most associate today with Bunker Hill, though he lived there only two or three months. To him, the neighborhood was a wellspring rather than a slum; a place for refugees, not hard-boiled gunsels and gumshoes. He moved into the Alta Vista Apartments at 255 South Bunker Hill Avenue in late 1933 while he was working three blocks east at two different places in the F.P. Fay Building, down in the flats at Third and Hill, across the street from Angels Flight's coral-columned gate. One job was busing tables at a saloon and hash house at 328 West Third called Marcus's Bar and Deli; the other was upstairs on the seventh floor as a reader at what he called "a crooked literary agency" that charged wannabe writers exorbitant prices to assess or edit their manuscripts.

In a December 3, 1933 letter to his mother, Fante wrote, "I have a very nice room. Papered in brown and with a number of appropriate pictures on the wall it's typically a man's room. I think of all the places I have lived in Los

Angeles it is the most satisfying, and as long as I remain here in the future I am going to stay in this hotel. I have four big brown leather chairs here in the room and three fine lamps. A rag-weave carpet covers the floor."

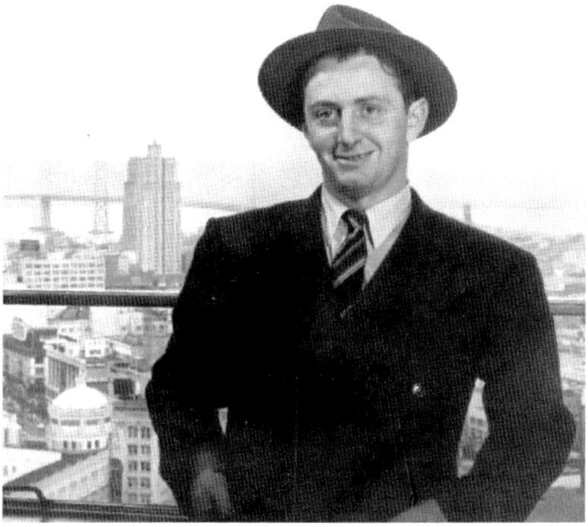

Writer John Fante turned the few months he lived on Bunker Hill into his now famous 1939 novel *Ask the Dust*. *Los Angeles Examiner/LAPL.*

(Fante didn't mention to his mother that he had taken on a roommate, a mouse he called Pedro that had his own entrance in the baseboard. Nor did he say anything about the young whore who lived across the hall or the middle-aged widow behind the lobby desk; they were minor characters in his 1939 novel, *Ask the Dust*, and he didn't reveal his sexual liaisons with them until he dictated his last novel, *Dreams From Bunker Hill*, in 1982.)

Only a month after moving into the Alta Vista, Fante was broke and living elsewhere. The reason for his sudden departure is in the opening paragraph of *Ask the Dust*:

> *One night I was sitting on the bed in my hotel room on Bunker Hill, down in the very middle of Los Angeles. It was an important night in my life, because I had to make a decision about the hotel. Either I paid up or I got out; that was what the note said, the note the landlady had put under my door.*

Fante wouldn't return to Bunker Hill until the end of the year. He wrote in a December 9, 1934 letter to his mother:

> *I am now back at the old address on Bunker Hill. The room I have is a lower one, on the bottom floor at the rear and the corner of the hotel. It is a small room with two windows, one of which overlooks a small hillside covered with deep green grass. The view from that window is superb, for I can see the Sierra mountains* [sic] *in the distance far away and the lights of west Los Angeles and Hollywood. It is a fine room, a room I know I*

> *shall always like and one where I hope to work hard and pleasantly. I pay ten dollars a month rent. That is very reasonable. I could not have found a better room at the price anywhere in the town.*

The Alta Vista was a convenient overlook at the top of the hill where Third Street dead-ended into Bunker Hill Avenue, adjacent to a small sidewalk park of green benches above a steep drop-off down to Hope Street and the gaping western terminus of the Third Street tunnel. In *Ask the Dust*, he called the Alta Vista the Alta Loma.

> *It was built on a hillside in reverse, there on the crest of Bunker Hill, built against the decline of the hill, so that the main floor was on the level with the street but the tenth floor was downstairs ten levels. If you had room 862, you got in the elevator and went down eight floors.*

That was an exaggeration. The Alta Vista was only seven stories in back (and four stories in front).

At night, the neon sign on one of the hotels down on Hope Street (he called it the St. Paul in *Ask the Dust*) threw "red and green blobs across my bed." Since he lived at the bottom of the building halfway down the hill, he wasn't restricted to just using his door. "I climbed out the window and scaled the incline to the top of Bunker Hill. A night for my nose, a feast for my nose, smelling the stars, smelling the flowers, smelling the desert, and the dust asleep, across the top of Bunker Hill. The city spread out like a Christmas tree, red and green and blue."

From his Bunker Hill Avenue aerie, Fante (and his literary alter ego, Arturo Bandini) could descend into the fascinating world of downtown Los Angeles. If he took either Olive Street or Grand Avenue down to Fifth Street, he could hang out in Pershing Square, formerly Central Park, a square block of lush banana trees, palms, benches, chess tables and a couple of statues surrounded by both the Philharmonic Auditorium—downtown's cultural nexus—and the 1923 Beaux Art–style Biltmore Hotel, with its ornate ceilings carved and painted by Vatican artist Giovanni Smeraldi. If instead he walked three blocks straight down Third Street to Angels Flight, he could ride one of the railway cars or walk down one of the two concrete stairways. "I took the steps down Angel's Flight to Hill Street; a hundred and forty steps, with tight fists, frightened of no man, but scared of the Third Street Tunnel, scared to walk through it—claustrophobia," he wrote in *Ask the Dust*. At 259 South Hill, on the northwest corner of Third, was Golden Liquors. On the

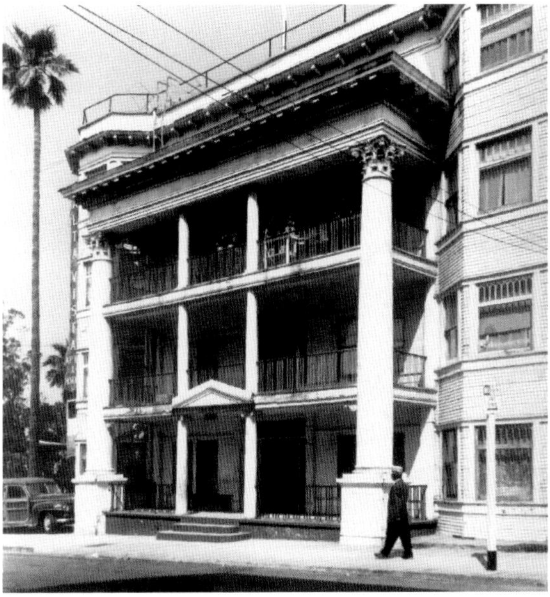

Novelist John Fante, who lived at the Alta Vista Apartments at 255 South Bunker Hill Avenue, immortalized its atmosphere and Depression-era residents in *Ask the Dust* (1939). Director Joseph Losey extensively shot the Alta Vista inside and out in *M* (1951). *Bison Archives.*

southeast corner, in the Fay Building where he worked, was the Giant Penny Store at 300 South Hill. Next door at 312 was (and still is) the Grand Central Public Market, a bustling bazaar of every type of food Los Angeles has to offer. If he kept walking east on Third instead of turning down Hill, the Million Dollar Theater was (and still is) on the next block, at the southwest corner of Broadway, along with the big department stores nearby, like the May Company, where he bought a new suit when he sold a short story. A block further was Spring Street, the financial district, where Bandini fell in love with the Mexican waitress Camilla at the Columbia Buffet. Another block further, on Main Street, were the boxing gyms, second-hand stores, burlesque houses, taxi dance halls, "honky tonks and all night picture houses" he frequented. The trip home was a fairly easy stumble if Angels Flight hadn't already shut down at midnight.

Despite his happiness at the Alta Vista, the young novelist was gone again by early January 1935 when he wrote to his mother, "I have abandoned my old room at 225 [sic] S. Bunker Hill and moved again." Apparently there had been more notes under the door. He would never return to Bunker Hill, except in his memories and in his writings.

When Black Sparrow reprinted *Ask the Dust* in 1980, poet Charles Bukowski wrote in the preface:

> *Fante was my god and I knew that gods should be left alone, one didn't bang at their door. Yet I liked to guess about where he had lived on Angel's Flight and I imagined it possible that he still lived there. Almost every day*

> *I walked by and I thought, is that the window Camilla crawled through? And, is that the hotel door? Is that the lobby? I never knew.*

But Fante didn't live near Angels Flight. A careful reading of *Ask the Dust* should have told Bukowski that he lived higher up on Third Street, above the opposite end of the tunnel. For example, early in the novel, after eating breakfast at a restaurant, Arturo Bandini "walked down the street toward Angel's Flight, wondering what I would do that day." Later, he wrote in detail about walking up the steps along Angels Flight from downtown and on up Third toward his apartment:

> *[U]p the dusty stairs of Bunker Hill, past the soot-covered frame buildings along that dark street…Dust and old buildings and old people sitting at windows, old people tottering out of doors, old people moving painfully along the dark street. The old folks from Indiana and Iowa and Illinois, from Boston and Kansas City and Des Moines, they sold their homes and their stores, and they came here by train and by automobile to the land of sunshine, to die in the sun, with just enough money to live until the sun killed them…With their bright polo shirts and sunglasses, they were in paradise, they belonged.*

Ask the Dust took over sixty-five years to reach the movie screen and would have taken longer, perhaps forever, if Robert Towne hadn't stumbled upon it in 1971 while researching his screenplay for *Chinatown*. That's why it seems such a waste that nothing about his 2006 film version of *Ask the Dust* looks or feels authentic. Rather than shoot 1930s Bunker Hill in nearby Angelino Heights or in any number of old, hilly neighborhoods north of downtown or in East Los Angeles, he built his own set on a rugby field in Cape Town, South Africa. Instead of replicating one of the Third Street blocks on top of Bunker Hill, Towne or his production designer, Dennis Gassner, inexplicably chose the 300 block *east* of Angels Flight. In other words, the movie didn't even take place *on* Bunker Hill. (They did, however, model the Alta Loma on a real Bunker Hill building: the twin-peaked Chaspeak Apartments at 512 West Second Street.) Perhaps most unforgivably, the Third Street tunnel, seen only in the background, was a replica of the Second Street tunnel, which has a wider, lower mouth and looks nothing like its neighbor. As Nathan Marsak blogged in 2008 for the L.A. history site Onbunkerhill.org, "[I]t's not so much they got it *wrong* as they got it *weird*." Towne might as well have saved himself all the hassle and shot his movie on the Paramount backlot.

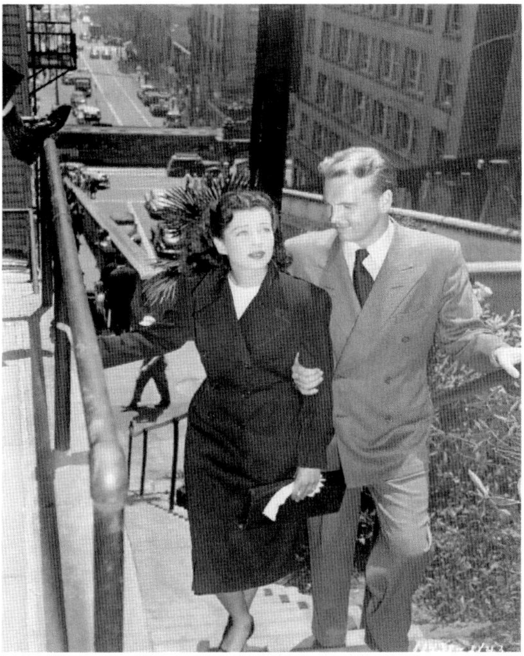

Gail Russell and John Lund wait for their cue to walk up the Third Street steps in front of the Sunshine Apartments, opposite Angels Flight, in *Night Has a Thousand Eyes* (1948). *Bison Archives.*

One of John Fante's contemporary observers of Bunker Hill was longtime *Los Angeles Times* reporter Timothy Gilman Turner (1887–1961), a Michigan native who had made his bones as a freelance journalist traveling with Pancho Villa's bandits during the 1910 Mexican revolution. He moved to Los Angeles around 1920 and eventually settled into the then-fashionable Engstrum Apartment Hotel at 623 West Fifth Street, built by O.E. Engstrum, a contractor responsible for several of Bunker Hill's early twentieth-century hotels, including the Fronteac on Grand. Turner never drove a car in Los Angeles because the streetcar came by his door. His beat was downtown. In 1942, he published a book of short stories called *Turn Off the Sunshine*, based on many of the people he'd observed around Pershing Square and Olvera Street, in the Main Street bars and in the once-fancy corner hotels dotted around the business district.

In "The Waitress Who Lost Her Sailor," Turner introduces us to Marta, a low-wage worker whom Arturo Bandini might have run into. She lives in an "old battered" room in "an old wooden boarding house" where "the bed… was of bird's-eye maple, out of vogue these forty years [and] the wallpaper was coming off there over the gas heater, exposing underneath it other wallpaper which in turn had fallen off to expose still another design of wallpaper."

Marta struggles as a hash waitress "at the foot of Bunker Hill" in a "half saloon and half restaurant" owned by a guy named Louis. (This could have been the place on Third Street where Fante had worked as a busboy in the early thirties.) On the day before her marriage to a sailor she met on the job, her tenuous world unravels. Louis fires her because business is bad, and her fiancé doesn't show up at the railway station on Main Street because his fleet has suddenly been ordered to the Atlantic and won't be back for at least six months. We last see Marta sitting on a station bench, emotionally unmoored, holding hands with a little old man, one of her customers, who happens to be sitting next to her.

If Fante captured the romance of living like a young Bohemian on Bunker Hill, Turner was probably the first to write in detail about its aging pensioners, who had been no more than dim background figures in *Ask the Dust*. In "The Old Man Who Went to the Library," we meet elderly Mr. Ross, a once successful man who now lives hand-to-mouth in one of the cheaper rooms on the top floor of an old tourist hotel "on the very highest point in Los Angeles"—probably on Bunker Hill Avenue, near the Castle and the Alta Vista. He begins his day in the bathtub, contemplating his old-fashioned surroundings.

> *Such an antique bathroom in such a new city was not so strange if you knew Bunker Hill. It rose in the very center of the old part of Los Angeles, a barrier that has annoyed motorists and city planners for two generations.*
>
> *Left on the top of the hill was a piece, caught intact, of the era when men wore stiff collars, women pinned their dresses on and children had their legs covered.*
>
> *No more perfect petrification of the '90s and early 1900s could be found in any western American city, not even San Francisco, where they cherish, even reverence, mustiness. In Los Angeles, the spanking new is reverenced, and Bunker Hill was only tolerated, for the most part ignored.*

Leaving his building, Mr. Ross "sniffed the morning fog, which had not yet lifted. He passed down a street of shade trees with its frame houses, adorned with the wooden crochet and colored glass of their period." As he approaches the concrete steps leading down to Fifth Street, across from the Central Library, he hears "the gentle rumble of a city." He gazes down at the Moorish library, at its "low walls with their perfect balance…softened to beautiful tones by the fog." Once he gets down on Fifth, however, the city is all noise and streetcars and harsh angles until he reaches his safe harbor. "He had come from the quiet haven of Bunker Hill, and now he had crossed the street and stepped into the quiet…of the library."

Foreshadowing the many nostalgic columnists, painters and student documentarians who would visit Bunker Hill in its twilight years, Turner was perhaps the first writer to address the past lives of Bunker Hill's Victorian mansions in the poignant "The Old Woman Who Came Home." In the

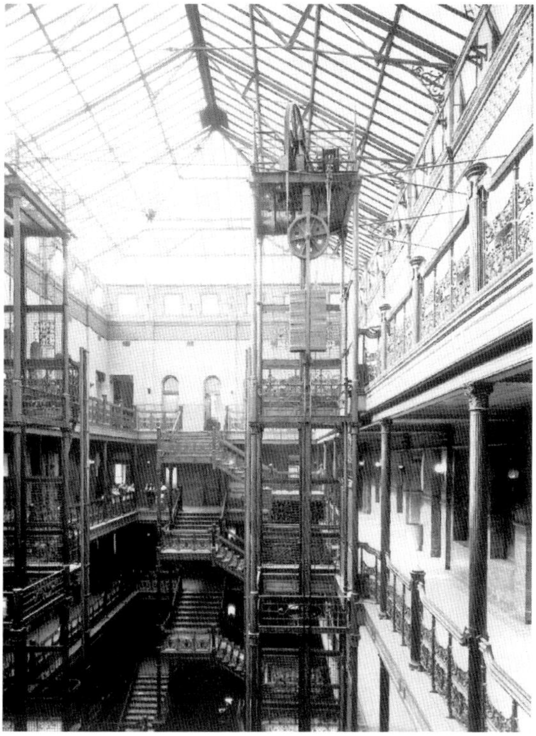

The Bradbury Building on the southeast corner of Third Street and Broadway was completed in 1893, not long after the death of Lewis Bradbury, the Bunker Hill man who commissioned it. Beginning with its use as a military hospital in the 1944 film *The White Cliffs of Dover*, the building's distinctive atrium court became a popular movie location, especially in films noirs shot downtown. The Bradbury was Lew Ayres's law office in *The Unfaithful* (1947); Cornell Wilde's parole office in *Shockproof* (1948); the place where Edmond O'Brien confronted the man who fatally poisoned him in *D.O.A.* (1949); David Wayne's hideout in *M* (1951); Mike Hammer's office in *I, the Jury* (1953); and the place where Lon Chaney Jr. tossed a victim off one of the balconies in *The Indestructible Man* (1956). An entire 1964 episode of the sci-fi TV show *The Outer Limits*, titled "Demon With a Glass Hand," was filmed within the Bradbury to take advantage of its timeless architecture. But of the more than one hundred movies and TV shows filmed inside the Bradbury, it is probably best known from its appearance in *Blade Runner* (1982). *Jim Dawson.*

early 1940s, there were still many people around who had lived on Bunker Hill during its showboat days. One afternoon a mysterious old woman named Mrs. Maynard, in a slightly shabby dress, shows up on a Bunker Hill street—most likely Flower—"looking for a house, it seemed, but the house just wasn't there. She seemed annoyed at this as if the house had promised to wait for her. She walked around the corner and back, peering between the buildings as she stood on tiptoe."

> *Finally, she was rewarded. She spied the corner of a mansard roof. It was back there on a corner of the lot that had no frontage on the street, between the laundry building and the new church. It was an old wooden pile that hadn't seen paint for a long time.*
>
> *There was a three-story apartment house on the side street with the 1900's written all over it. Perhaps the old house was connected with that.*

Mrs. Maynard's knock at the newer house brings a high school teenager named Jane to the door.

> *"I was interested in the old house there at the back," said the old woman. "Is the entrance through this place?"*
>
> *"Yes," said the girl, "you go right through into it from this hall. We run it—I mean my mother and I."*
>
> *"Do you rent rooms there?"*
>
> *"Oh, yes," replied the girl. "But they are pretty dark. We rent them mostly to people who work at night and want a quiet, cheap place."*

As they walk along the hallway, they pass "directly from the 1900's into the 1870's…At one side was an old parlor, and directly in front was the staircase. It was a nut-brown walnut staircase well patinated by the years." The old woman lovingly touches the newel post at the bottom of the steps with its mysterious hole on top and asks if the room upstairs in back of the house is vacant. Jane tells her it is.

That room is like musty rooms all over Bunker Hill, where owners have for the past several decades altered the old houses, changed their purpose, paneled over or dry-walled the old plaster walls, and covered up old doorways without any regard to the integrity or the aesthetics of the architecture.

> *The room had the original wooden blinds that folded back into the wainscoting. The wallpaper was of big flowers, and the iron bed in the corner also spoke of the 1890s. But there was still much of the preceding generation about the room besides the blinds. It had the high ceilings of that period and the woodwork, which once had been walnut, had had many a coat of ill-chosen varnish. There was one old chair in the room, a walnut one with flowers carved on the top of the back.*

Without approaching either window, the old woman tells Jane, "There should be a garden out that window to the left, and from the other window there should stretch a lawn way down past what is now Figueroa Street"— the western edge of Bunker Hill. She tells Jane that she spent her childhood in this room after her wealthy stepfather built the house. "I haven't been home—this always has been home—since I was about your age," she confesses.

> *"It was really very grand in those days. One of the wings must have been cut off. It should extend to where the laundry is now. There was a*

driveway from a road I can't locate at all that ran up through the lawn to the entrance where the new apartment house now stands. Back there was an aviary with canaries, Mexican finches, parrots, and cockatoos. My dear, I had a big St. Bernard dog, and a monkey, yes, a monkey, a cute little devil who was always kept on a chain. I also had a Shetland pony and a little cart for him."

There was also a pigtailed Chinese cook, an "apple cheeked" Irish maid, and an Irish coachman who would "take me to sail my boat in the *zanza* that watered the orchards down the dirt road that ran north. I had only servants for playmates."

But that was long ago. Her mother and stepfather had died early, leaving her an heiress. While she was off at finishing school, and traveling in Europe, and marrying badly, her guardian and her lawyer took all her money. Nowadays she's living "not far away" on county relief, after working for many years as a maid in a hotel. She and the Bunker Hill mansion, along with the neighborhood, have faded and fallen on hard times together despite their physical separation.

They went down the old nut-brown stairs slowly, for Mrs. Maynard had to run her hand along every inch of the rail.

"The curve at this landing," she said, "was the most dangerous one."

"Yes, I found it so," said Jane. "How funny, you used to slide down this railing too."

"It was much better sliding in your time than in mine," said Mrs. Maynard when they got to the bottom. "For in my time, Jane, there was a bronze Roman soldier with a gas jet on his head here on the bottom post, and you had to slow up or you would hit it and hurt yourself."

The parlor still has some of the furniture from the old woman's time in the house. She recalls the bric-a-brac and daguerreotypes that used to be in the cabinet. "I suppose they have been sold. Probably when the crash came they sold the house furnished, and down through the years things have been broken, lost, sold, and others put in their place."

When she asks Jane about her life in the house, the teenager confesses that she also grew up alone, with only her mother, an imaginary playmate and a favorite doll. When Mrs. Maynard asks her to fetch the doll, the girl brings her a familiar old toy whose eyes don't open and close anymore but remain half open. She doesn't tell Jane that it was once her doll too.

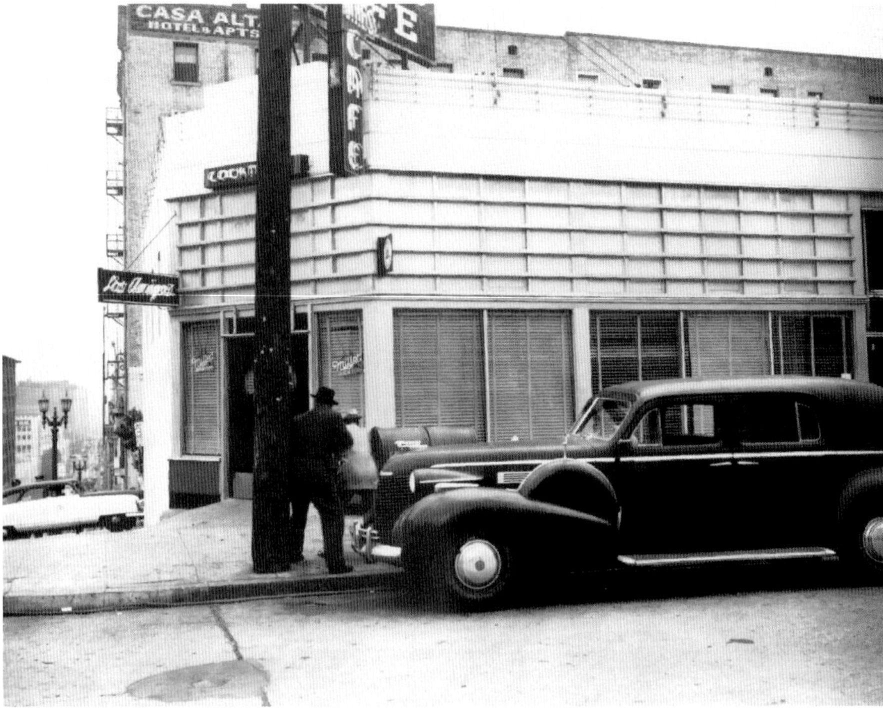

Gangsters shoot it out with L.A. cops in front of the Los Amigos Cafe at 500 West Third Street, on the southwest corner of Olive Street, in *Cry Danger* (1951). *Jim Dawson.*

At the door, with Mrs. Maynard ready to leave, the girl says:

> *"It seems that we have always known one another."*
> *"We have," said the old woman, "we have. I will tell you something. It's a secret. I have never left this house; it was only the grown-up part of me that went away."*
> *"Oh," says Jane. "Oh, I see. It was you all the time."*

One woman who would have been Mrs. Maynard's contemporary was Sarah Bixby Smith (circa 1870–1935), who spent most of her childhood in the northern part of Bunker Hill, back when Flower, Hope and Grand were called Faith, Hope and Charity, and Figueroa was Grasshopper Street. In those days, there were no hotels, no apartments and not that many houses. Her prosperous Maine family first lived at Temple and Charity in the late 1870s, moved to First Street near Olive and finally built a house on the southeast corner of Court and Hill, directly across the street from where Lewis Bradbury would soon build his mansion. In her 1926 memoir, *Adobe Days*, Bixby Smith recalled:

> *Bunker Hill was at the end of the settlement, a row of scattered houses along the ridge fringing the sky…Court Street disappeared in a hollow at Hope, where a pond was made interesting by a large flock of white ducks…In those days the hill had not been hacked away to make streets, and where now is a great gash to let First Street through there was then a breezy, open hill-top.*

She remembered the dozens of colorful varieties of wild flowers that grew everywhere on the hill, along with the many tarantulas that built their little circular trap doors in the dry soil. But her favorite memories were of the Bixby bungalow on the little spit of Court Street that dead-ended on the steep hill above Broadway, where Samuel Vandergrift would later, in 1904, build the Court Flight incline railway.

> *The level street at Court and Hill, protected on three sides by grades too steep for horses, was our safe neighborhood playground…The location of our home on the brow of the hill was chosen because of the view and the sense of air and space. Below us was the little city, the few business blocks, the homes set in gardens on tree shaded streets, the whole surrounded by orchards and vineyards. On a clear day we could see the mountains far in the east and the ocean at San Pedro, with Santa Catalina beyond.*

But those halcyon years were gone by 1900. The "little city" below had burgeoned into a sprawling commercial district, replacing the homes and gardens with office and civic buildings. Bunker Hill itself became unrecognizable to Bixby Smith, who had moved away from Court Street in her teens. A new world had replaced her bucolic paradise.

But for those who lived in that post-1890s world, the twentieth-century Bunker Hill would eventually become as worthy of nostalgia as hers had been. One artist who fell in love with Bunker Hill and captured it within his imagination was Fresno-born Leo Politi (1908–1996), a children's book writer and illustrator who settled in Los Angeles in the 1930s after studying art in Italy. He spent the rest of his life on or within walking distance of Bunker Hill, and by the 1950s, when he could see that his beloved neighborhood

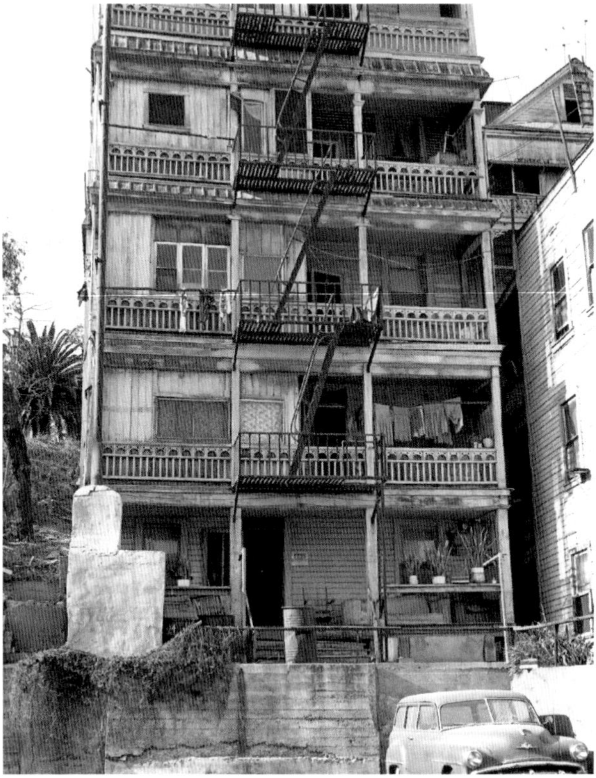

This apartment building, which fronted at 224 South Olive Street, was two stories in front and five stories in the rear. It was shabby by the time William Reagh took this photo in 1963. *The California History Room, California State Library, Sacramento.*

was entering its death throes, he routinely set up his folding chair and easel in front of many of the houses and rendered them as personal postcards to the future, usually as gaggles of local children gathered around him. One of his most popular books, published in 1964, was *Bunker Hill Los Angeles… Reminiscences of Bygone Days*, filled with twenty-six illustrations and musings about his friends who clung to what was left of their turn-of-the-century lives there. He called Bunker Hill Avenue "the most picturesque street in our city. Aside from the lovely old homes that once lined its way, another reason for its charm is that it runs so rhythmically with the contour of the Hill." Next to his painting of the twenty-room Castle at 325 South Bunker Hill Avenue, he wrote,

> *Outside, the house was tall and loaded with gingerbread scrollwork. Inside, it had an interesting hardwood stairway* [just inside the doorway]. *Bright stained-glass panels guarded the entrance. When the house was lighted at night, the stained-glass glittered with joy.*

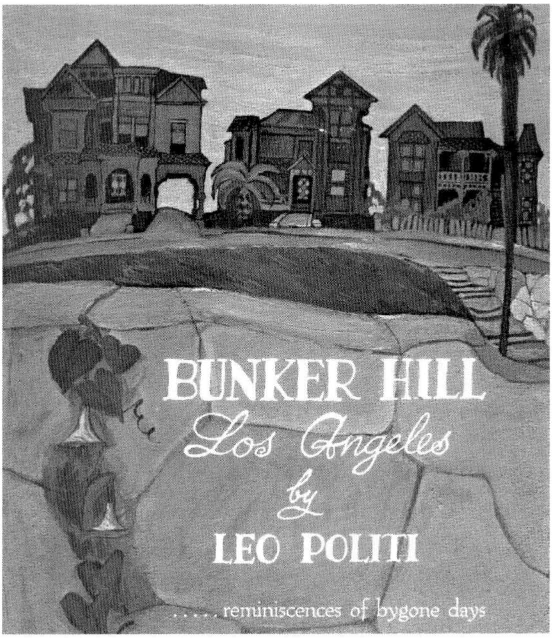

Silhouettes of the Castle, the MacDonald house and the Foss-Heindel house in the 300 block of South Bunker Hill Avenue graced the cover (in color) of Leo Politi's 1964 book of Bunker Hill paintings. *Courtesy of the Politi family.*

The man who named it the Castle was Bunker Hill's primary grading and paving contractor, Donald F. Donegan, who bought the 1882 mansion in the mid-nineties. After Donegan sold the place around 1902, the new owner kept the grand appellation but divided the place into single rooms that shared a common bathroom on each floor. By 1939, most of the tenants were pensioners over sixty-five. In December 1954, director Robert Aldrich used the front of the Castle, its stained-glass doors and its interior hardwood stairs in *Kiss Me Deadly*. For an encore, the house starred in the last location shooting on old Bunker Hill, a television show called *The Outsider*, before the last vestiges were hauled away in early 1969. By then, the huge Queen Anne had been cut into three pieces to ready it for removal to its new location in Highland Park, adjacent to the Pasadena Freeway, where it would be torched to the ground a few months later.

One of Leo Politi's friends was Anna "Nell" McKenzie, a spinster schoolteacher who had lived her entire life in the single-story Victorian that her father, Murdoch McKenzie, had built at 245 South Bunker Hill Avenue, just two doors north of the Alta Vista. The simple Eastlake-style house had already had a brief Hollywood brush in *Bus Stop* in 1956 before Politi captured it on canvas for *Bunker Hill Los Angeles*. Nell was in her eighties when she finally had to move away in the 1960s, along with the furniture that had once belonged to her parents and grandparents. "Father built a plain house because he could not afford the gingerbread ornaments," she told Politi. "At that time we owned a horse and buggy. The stable's entrance was on Hope Street below. It was reached through the garden at the rear of the house where we children used to play."

Politi himself recalled the last four children—three girls and a boy—that lived on Bunker Hill Avenue.

> *They brought life and joy; old folks liked to watch them play. When, in the summer of 1963, their grandmother's house was torn down, they moved away and Bunker Hill Avenue became as lifeless as a ghost-town street. The bulldozers came when the oleanders with their pink flowers were in full bloom.*

Another painter entranced by the fading neighborhood was Catherine "Kay" Martin, a forty-five-year-old housewife and amateur landscape painter from Springfield, Illinois, who had lived in California since the early forties. Over a period of months in 1955 and '56, she spent her days on Bunker Hill sketching what she considered to be noble survivors of a vanishing era, then drove home at night and painted her sketches in her home studio on Montecito Drive in Glendale. The old homes, with their needless, idiosyncratic detail—a sign of personal care and whimsy that seemed absent in mid-twentieth-century architecture—as well as the residents' personal touches, like "a pot of geraniums at an open window," evoked warm memories from her childhood. "I grew up in a house that could have become like these," she told the *Los Angeles Times*. Martin's two-dozen paintings are on permanent display at the Angelus Plaza, a retirement community center, at 255 South Hill Street, next to the Third Street tunnel.

Another painter was Marcel Cavalla, an Italian-born, retired pastry chef who lived at the Brousseau mansion at 238 South Bunker Hill Avenue with his many parakeets. Leo Politi, who painted a picture of his friend Cavalla in his room for *Bunker Hill Los Angeles*, said, "I believe that in his art work Marcel captured more than anyone else ever did the feeling and mood of the Hill." Politi credited Cavalla's "charming and simple sense of design and patterns" to his years decorating wedding cakes. Thanks to a patron who came looking for "the bird man of Bunker Hill," Cavalla had a successful Hollywood gallery showing that bestowed a brief celebrity upon him before his death. His paintings of Bunker Hill mansions were all sold and therefore do not exist in a collection.

Victor Czerkas (1914–2003) was an Iowa-born son of Russian immigrants who moved to Hollywood in the 1930s to get into the movies, and though he successfully worked as a commercial artist at Universal Pictures for many years, he too found himself drawn to the old downtown neighborhood, where he created many impressionist oil paintings, from the mansions (including the Brousseau) to the Hope Street steps, as Bunker Hill began to disappear. Czerkas favored many of the more rundown areas on the western side of the hill.

Many other painters and commercial artists journeyed to the picturesque neighborhood, such as Ben Abril, Frank Mapson, Jake Lee, Stan Cline, Streeter Blair and Millard Sheets. Their most popular subject was Angels Flight, the little railway that could, whose quirky charm usually inspired more kitsch than serious art.

In a 1960 paperback novel called *Angel's Flight*, Lou Cameron found the funicular an amusing anomaly:

> *A triple-gauge track ran up the slop at an impossible angle. It looked steeper than a playground slide. Running on the tracks were two dinky yellow cars attached to opposite ends of the same steel cable. At the top of the hill stood a winch house where a big steel drum pulled one car up and the other one went down, like a yo-yo. The cars were built like lopsided Toonerville Trolleys that got stepped on. They were all out of shape so that the passengers could sit upright as they rode up the hill. The floors of the cars were built like flights of stairs and gothic windows were staggered like steps up the yellow sides of the cars. I guess you might say they were quaint…*
>
> *There was a ding ding from one of the cars and it started up the slope of Angel's Flight. A girl screamed. One always did. Beside me, somebody said, "I wonder what's up there. Up there on top?" "Same thing as down here," I answered. "Couple of bars, a chili parlor, and a whorehouse."*

A year later, Los Angeles historian W.W. Robinson wrote that "even among those Angelenos who never use the little cars—and most of us are in that class—there is a feeling of nostalgia aroused by the sight or thought of Angels Flight. It is part of the present that seems to belong to the past."

Los Angeles Times columnist Art Seidenbaum waxed more lyrically in late 1964 after seeing how the destruction around Angels Flight in recent months had "opened up [the old houses] with all [their] pathetic wallpaper patches" exposed.

> *When the funicular ride was newfangled more than sixty years ago, it was framed along the route by buildings to match. For every curving metal ornament on Angels Flight, there was a wooden grace note on a building, carved on a gable, gnarled beneath an eave, patterned into lattice.*

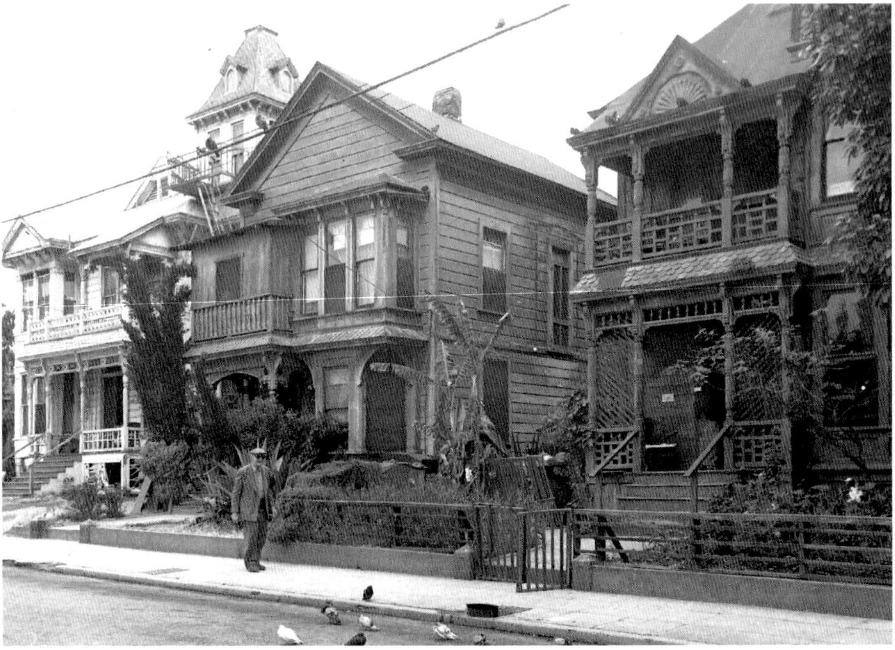

By 1960, these Bunker Hill Avenue houses were barely hanging on. The last to go would be the Julius Brousseau mansion (left) at 238 South Bunker Hill Avenue—torn down shortly after being used in the 1966 Glenn Ford film *The Money Trap*. Painter Leo Politi featured the Brousseau in his 1964 book *Bunker Hill Los Angeles*. *California History Room, California State Library, Sacramento.*

Now the other ornaments are off Bunker Hill…You can see destruction, the first step in redevelopment, as the huge wrecking balls swing into action along the tracks. Then in move the buckets with their awesome jaws, to bite, chew, and spit out the debris of what we once called elegance.

CHAPTER 7

High Crimes and Misdirections

Mike Hammer: A guy could get a heart attack walking up here.
Bunker Hill landlady: Who invited you?
—Kiss Me Deadly, *1955*

The felonies of pulp fiction and film noir are mostly on a tawdry scale. Someone betrays a lover, knocks off a bank or an armored truck or erases an inconvenience with a simple act of mayhem. The only caper that leaves a big scar is Mike Hammer's Case of the Great Whatzit—fissionable material in a lead box that's ready to blow—in the film version of *Kiss Me Deadly*, and even with the final blast, we're uncertain if Mike and his secretary Velda have found enough shelter in the Malibu surf to let them live a few more weeks before the radiation eats their red blood cells.

But as Balzac said of all great fortunes, Los Angeles was built on great crimes, and until *Chinatown*, a 1974 *film sepia*, Hollywood never bothered to expose those crimes. In the early days of Los Angeles, the Protestant Midwesterners that were lured by land speculators to its sunny climes routinely pushed non-Christians and Catholics out of their neighborhoods. In 1887, arsonists torched part of Chinatown, and the nearby municipal fire stations let it burn. In 1928, a cheaply designed Los Angeles dam in the nearby Santa Clarita Valley gave way, taking nearly four hundred Mexican lives. In the late 1930s, the city fathers, primarily *Los Angeles Times* boss Harry Chandler, transformed the original Old Plaza barrio into a tourist trap by economically starving out the residents, and then they built Union Station on the other side of Alameda Street by again letting part of Chinatown burn, this time to stem a trumped-up smallpox epidemic. In 1959, the systematic removal of a couple of tightly-knit hillside Mexican-American villages in Chavez Ravine, just north of downtown, ended with the last residents being dragged from their homes, kicking and screaming, as Caterpillars idled nearby in a cloud of diesel fumes. Los Angeles's rap sheet had no shortage of colossal crimes that made film noir's transgressions seem as trivial as beating kids out of their lunch money with loaded tiddlywinks.

Then came Bunker Hill. As Thom Andersen expressed it in *Los Angeles Plays Itself*, "The movies loved Bunker Hill. The lords of the city hated it. Rents were low, so it put the wrong kind of people too close to downtown."

In an image-conscious city like Los Angeles, built on chamber of commerce ballyhoo and Pharaonic moneymaking schemes, it's a wonder that the neighborhood lasted so long. As soon as the last of the wealthy old-line families moved out, the island of hotels, apartments, rooming houses and scrappy little shops became expendable. In 1912, according to an article

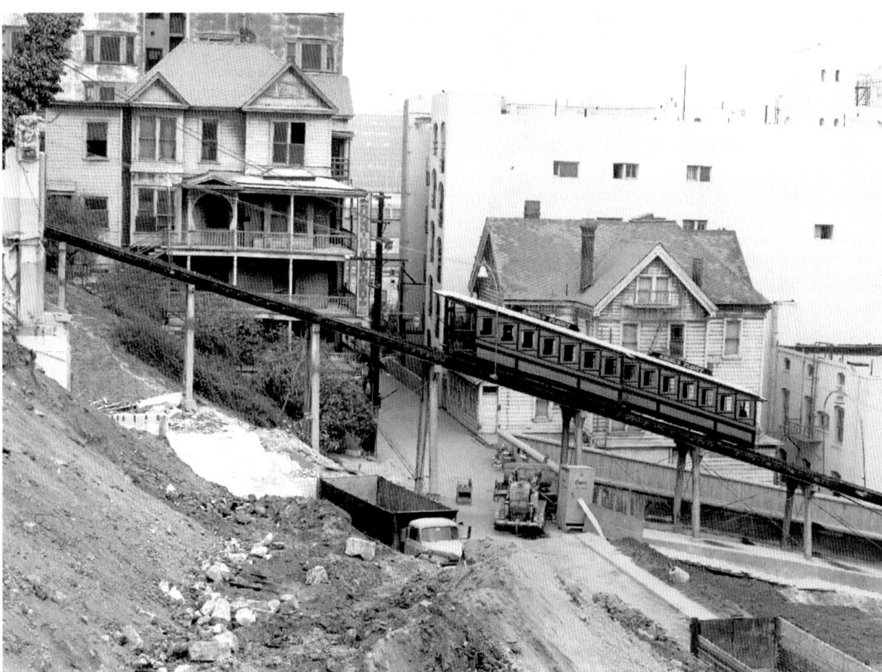

Photographer William Reagh caught one of the last images of the Sunshine Apartments (left) in 1964 before its destruction. All the buildings on the south side of Third Street are already gone. Angels Flight would continue to run for another five years. *California History Room, California State Library, Sacramento.*

in *Southwest Contractor and Manufacturer* magazine called "An Estimate of the Cost of Leveling Bunker Hill," city visionaries and land developers were already rubbing their palms together.

When New York architect Bertram Goodhue was in town ten years later to design and build the Central Library on Fifth Street, he got a bright idea. He looked northward up the slope above Fifth and imagined—as he sketched a skyline on his artist's pad—how he might transform Bunker Hill into what he called an "acropolis," a citadel where the city courthouse, the city hall and other civic amenities could be built anew and admired from miles around, just like the ancient Acropolis in Athens. Even the city library could go up there. Though nothing came of this notion, it would later inspire a different species of acropolis, with its roots in the *agora*, the marketplace.

One man ready to liquidate Bunker Hill was C.C. Bigelow, president of the Southwestern Investment Corporation and a mining baron accustomed to cutting and shaping land as it suited him. In 1928, he offered to use his own engineers and equipment to blow it up and wash it down at a bargain price of $50 million. Not long afterward, a transplanted Chicago real estate man named Henry Babcock joined Bigelow's campaign with a ninety-six-page screed called the Babcock Report that introduced a new rationale for why Bunker Hill had to be cleared out: depreciating property values had turned it into "a spoiled apple" that "threatened a bad effect" on everything around it.

> [Neighborhoods like Bunker Hill] *cannot be fenced off and left to their fate. They cannot be segregated to work out their own salvation regardless of the rest of the community. Consequently they present a problem of concern to the entire city in which they are situated. Naturally, the rehabilitation of blighted areas is governed entirely by the conditions involved.*
>
> *In the instance of Bunker Hill, the matter of topography enters largely into consideration. Admittedly, it is a traffic barrier not only for itself but for extensive and growing sections at every side of it. Architecturally, it has not kept pace with the modernly growing parts of the city. It apparently presents a striking need for rehabilitation if it is to share in the indicated improvement in realty values.*

Wall Street's collapse in October 1929 brought this budding war against Bunker Hill to a standstill, but the subsequent decade of hard times also ended any further construction or improvements. The six-story Southern

California Edison Building, erected at the very edge of Bunker Hill on the northwest corner of Fifth and Grand in 1938, would be the only, and last, significant addition.

As the Depression eased off in the late thirties, the Home Owner's Loan Corporation issued a report saying that Bunker Hill had gone past "the phases of decline" and become "thoroughly blighted," with "dilapidation and squalor everywhere in evidence." The 1940 census's revelation that only 2.2 percent of the neighborhood's 1,976 "dwelling units" were "owner occupied" empirically clarified the problem: Bunker Hill had become a transient neighborhood of absentee landlords and poor renters—in other words, a slum. The Los Angeles Regional Planning Commission came up with a solution: the rapidly growing city's need for a new transportation network. "Block after block of buildings must be cleared to make way for freeways," it suggested. "Outworn, dilapidated neighborhoods must be razed." Over the next dozen years, the Harbor Parkway (later Freeway) would take out everything along Figueroa Street and cut into Fourth Street, and the extension of the Hollywood Freeway into downtown, coupled with the construction of the new civic center, would remove the hilly neighborhoods north of First Street, including the Hill Street tunnel and everything on top of it. But when the dust settled, most of Bunker Hill stubbornly remained intact.

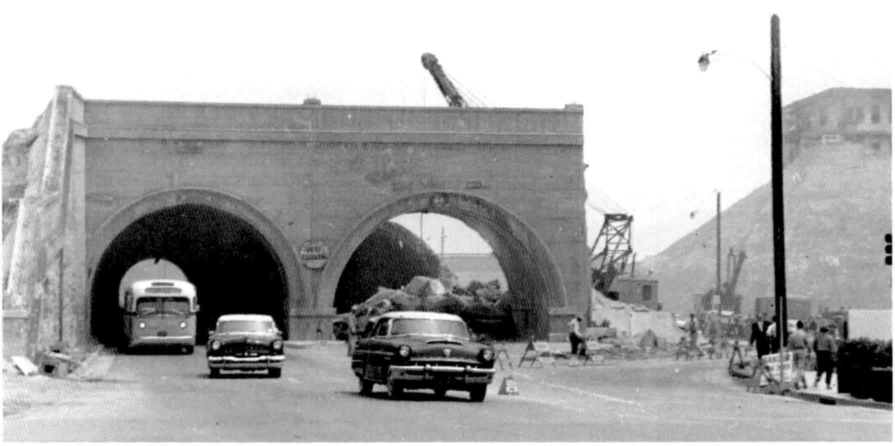

As part of the extension of the Hollywood Freeway into downtown and the construction of a new civic center, Los Angeles systematically flattened the northeastern section of Bunker Hill in the mid-'50s. Seen here from First Street in 1955, the Hill Street tunnel has already been stripped of the neighborhood above it. Within a month, the tunnel itself would be gone. *Security Pacific Collection/LAPL.*

In 1948, California created a statewide entity called the Community Redevelopment Agency, with independent offices in all the major cities. The following year a federal Housing Act gave the agency the authority to redline "blighted" areas, condemn property and force the owners to accept whatever it deemed a fair price. Pulling the strings of the Los Angeles CRA was the so-called "Committee of Twenty-five," a group of wealthy downtown mucky-mucks led by insurance magnate Asa V. Call and furniture king Neil Petree. Other members included *Los Angeles Times* owner Norman Chandler, oil baron and CRA chairman William T. Sesnon Jr. and James Lin Beebe (scion of an old Bunker Hill family) from the legacy law firm of O'Melveny and Myers. (Norman Chandler's late father, Harry, the man most responsible for creating modern Los Angeles, had already amassed a fortune by buying up cheap, arid land in the northern San Fernando Valley and then guiding Los Angeles's 1905 water diversion from northern California via an aqueduct—the inspiration for Robert Towne's *Chinatown* script nearly seventy years later.) At their meetings in Call's office on the top floor of the Corinthian-columned Pacific Mutual Insurance Building at Sixth and Grand, they masterminded the CRA's campaign against Bunker Hill into the 1950s, funding a relentless flow of charts, graphs and statistics to promulgate the hill's reputation as a Calcutta of indigent renters, cirrhotic barflies, small-time criminals, juvenile delinquents, tubercular foreigners, Bunker Hillbillies and useless geezers waiting for the Grim Reaper to darken their lonely doorways. In 1951, the committee supported Proposition C, a ballot measure that Henry Babcock, now the city's "consulting engineer," had patched together by updating his 1930 Babcock Report with plans for knocking down the "ramshackle" tenements and, with a touch of Bertram Goodhue's acropolis fantasy, turning the center of Bunker Hill into a complex of thirty-seven high-rise apartment buildings "designed for the working man and woman. Rents will be easily within their reach." Retail businesses would occupy the ground floors, and there would be enough underground garages and paved lots for easy parking.

The proposition passed, but there was still the problem that Mayor Fletcher Bowron had final say over any CRA decision. Bowron, a former judge, felt that if Bunker Hill's aging apartment houses were going to be torn down, they should be replaced by federally funded public-housing projects. The committee members responded to this New Deal "socialist housing" heresy with, at first, fits of apoplexy and then, when the 1952 election rolled around, by pulling out their checkbooks, recruiting pro-business congressman Norris Poulson as their candidate stooge and waging a victorious Red-Scare campaign against Bowron and his municipal politburo.

As soon as Poulson took office, the committee brought the rest of the city agencies on board. The Department of Building and Safety issued a report identifying 60 percent of Bunker Hill's buildings as being not simply substandard but hazardous. Police reports daily highlighted the neighborhood's considerable narcotics trade, particularly on Clay Street and in the area around Third and Flower. Health officials expressed fears of epidemics within the rotting, rat-infested tenement warrens. The assessor's office complained that the neighborhood was costing the city three times more in services than it paid in taxes. Poulson himself routinely complained about the neighborhood in his weekly radio speeches ("We want no slums in Los Angeles, and the quicker we get rid of those we have, the better," he said in 1956). And cheerleading the campaign all the way was Norman Chandler's *Los Angeles Times*, whose articles on Bunker Hill were nothing more than CRA press releases, tagged with headlines like "Bunker Hill Pictured as Crime Haunt" (July 5, 1956) and larded with such adjectives as "shabby," "wretched" and "blighted." All that stood now between Bunker Hill and its fate was the go-ahead from the city council.

The story might have ended in 1955, except for the intercession of another Babcock—apparently no relation to Henry—named Frank, the president of the Bunker Hill Property Owners Association and the proprietor of the Dome Hotel Apartments on the southwest corner of Second and Grand. According to Los Angeles preservationist Nathan Marsak, "Frank Babcock strolled down from his Dome to Superior Court and slapped the Community Redevelopment Agency with an injunction to block the development…Babcock asserted that the law was clear: the CRA could only demolish blighted areas…Bunker Hill's buildings were safe for occupancy, not conducive to ill health, transmission of disease, juvenile delinquency, infant mortality or crime." As Frank Babcock told the *Los Angeles Times*, "The only crime of which our people can be safely charged is hanging clothes to dry in a back yard."

To circumvent Frank Babcock, CRA Chairman Sesnon went before the city council to introduce an alternate plan by which the City of Los Angeles could buy Bunker Hill's mineral rights and, in return, relocate any senior-citizen owners and pay them a small royalty to assist in their new rents. But since Sesnon was an oil tycoon, Frank Babcock went back to court and derailed the idea as a conflict of interest.

After the last of the Chavez Ravine neighborhoods were scraped away in May 1959, the CRA started buying up small parcels of land on Bunker Hill, bundling them together into larger packages—usually a city block

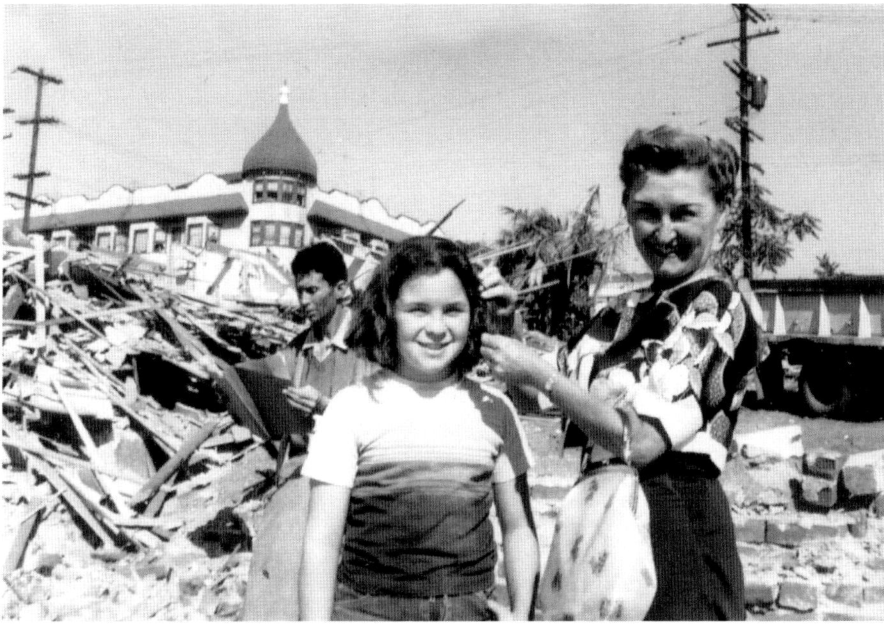

TV star Lauren Chapin of *Father Knows Best* (seen here with her mother, Meg Chapin, in the rubble of Second Street, with the Dome Hotel Apartments in the background) costarred in Bob Board's film short *The Derelict* (1957). *Courtesy of Bob Board.*

or more—and selling them to well-connected consortiums of real estate developers and insurance companies. It officially began its "urban renewal" program in 1961, the same year that Los Angeles sent its streetcars on their final ride to the scrap yard. The first victim was the Hillcrest Apartments at Olive and Third where Mike Hammer had once visited the hopeless opera singer Trivago in *Kiss Me Deadly* and back-from-the-dead Lon Chaney Jr. had stalked a lying witness in *The Indestructible Man*.

Certainly one building that belied the CRA's dire picture of blight was Frank Babcock's four-story Dome Hotel Apartments at 201 South Grand, with its distinctive onion dome and bright white stucco exterior. Inside, a long narrow skylight illuminated the balcony corridors above its lobby. The Dome had been built in 1903 as a tourist hotel called the Minnewaska—named for an area of upstate New York—and redubbed the Dome four years later. By 1959, it was a well-maintained working-class apartment building. As if to provide an Exhibit A for responsible management of Bunker Hill property, Babcock gave filmmakers Doug Wilson and Charles Davis carte blanch to shoot a low-budget film noir, *Get Outta Town*, along its corridors and within a couple of apartments. But in the early morning of July 25, 1964, a convenient if not suspicious fire destroyed part of the Dome, injuring nearly a dozen people and killing one. The damage was too extensive to repair. Frank Babcock surrendered his patch of Bunker Hill, along with his preservation crusade, and a wrecking crew took down what was left.

By then, the Dorothy Chandler Pavilion—a nearly 3,200-seat philharmonic auditorium named after its benefactor, Mrs. Norman Chandler—was nearly completed, sitting like a cenotaph atop what used to be North Bunker Hill Avenue. *Los Angeles Times* writer Julie Byrne summed up the official Chandler attitude toward the dying neighborhood around it in her caption accompanying several 1965 photos of willowy, very "mod" fashion models posing in front of two derelict Victorians. "Bunker Hill's nostalgic charm—with its now raggle-taggle gingerbread houses that were Los Angeles' pride in an earlier era—will give way to high rise architecture as our city begins to meet its space-ace potential."

In May of the following year, *Times* columnist Ray Herbert delivered what was essentially a post mortem: "After a tortuous decline, fabled Bunker Hill has finally hit bottom. Wrecking crews have stripped it almost beyond recognition, hastening the end."

In 1968, the CRA and the city council cut a $30,000 deal with the city's Cultural Heritage Board to make the Castle and the Salt Box, the last two nineteenth-century houses on Bunker Hill Avenue, the centerpieces of a "Heritage Square" adjacent to the Pasadena Freeway, a hoped-for "Victorian preserve" of mansions salvaged from all around town. In March 1969, the two houses were hauled several miles to their new resting place. Two months later, Angels Flight was packed up like a carnival ride and shipped off to a warehouse, leaving nothing behind but a hilltop of dirt.

"I was very angry at the time, and I'm still heartbroken about how the CRA handled everything," said Gordon Pattison, whose grandparents and parents had owned the Castle since the Depression. Though it had been a boardinghouse since the turn of the century, the eighty-five-year-old Queen Anne was still in relatively good shape, as was its carriage house in back. "Everything was made of redwood, which can last nearly forever," Pattison recalled in early 2012. "My grandmother had to remove the second-story porch above the front porch and the mansard roof on the turret after they were damaged in the Long Beach earthquake [in 1933], but otherwise it was still a beautiful old house that just needed tender loving care. People would walk by at night to see the light coming through the stained-glass doors."

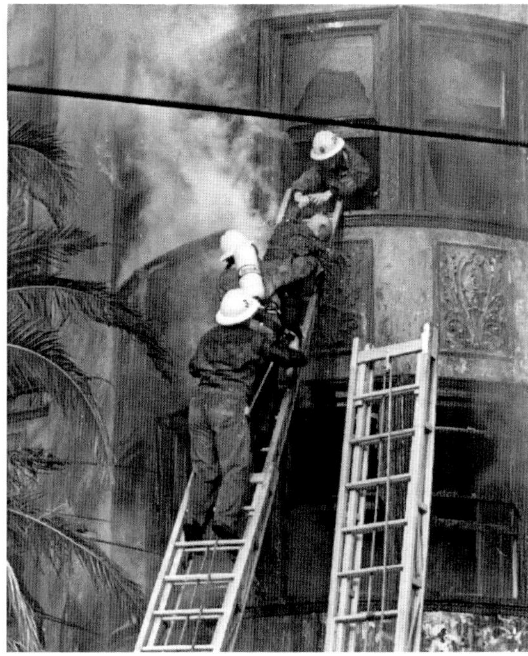

An inconvenient 1964 fire destroyed part of Frank Babcock's Dome Hotel Apartments at the corner of Second and Grand, ending his fierce opposition against the city's destruction of Bunker Hill. *Courtesy of Nathan Marsak.*

The Pattisons were more fortunate than most people on Bunker Hill. In 1964, his parents sold the Castle and the house next door to the CRA for $100,000. But he felt that the city should have protected that part of the hill where the Queen Annes were hanging on. Instead, vandals stripped them of everything, including the Castle's stained glass, and the bulldozers did the rest. Asked where the Castle would have stood in present-day Bunker Hill, he said, "In the food court of the Wells Fargo Center [at 333 South Grand], but thirty feet up, on the third floor."

Pattison remembered his father telling him about one Bunker Hill mansion in the 1930s that had not been broken up into rented rooms but rather sealed up by the family that owned it. "I'm not sure where it was, but he said he went inside and everything was still intact—the nineteenth-century furniture, the ornamental gas jets, everything just the way the family left it. I often wonder whatever happened to that house." Then, after a pause, he added, "Well, I *know* what happened. The CRA tore it down."

One of the last persons to be evicted from Bunker Hill in early June 1969 was Bunnie Burns, who lived in a small room on the eighth floor of the Northern Hotel at 420 West Second, on the southwest corner of Clay. A resident since 1952, she refused to leave when the orders came to evacuate the hotel's 180 rooms. She told a reporter, "God told me in 1964 never to set foot out of this hotel, but to keep my room like a living garden in witness to the Lord, and that people would come to me." Eventually, after her five-week stand, several people did arrive at her door—Robert G. Clayton, the CRA's property manager; two case workers; an inventory taker; a captain and three

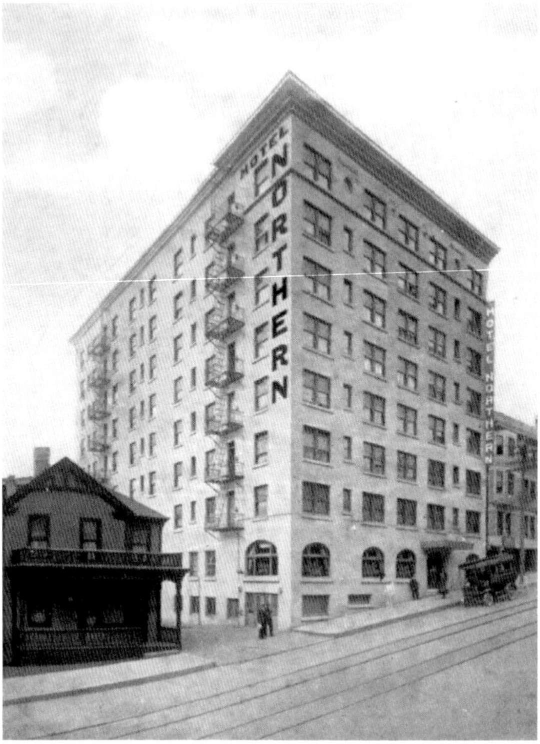

The Northern Hotel at 420 West Second Street, on the corner of Clay, once boasted of its two hundred fireproof rooms, most of them with a bath. It was among the last of Bunker Hill's hotels to be torn down in 1969. *Jim Dawson.*

deputies from the county sheriff's department; and a little old blind man whom Bunnie knew and trusted. She decided "to go peaceably" and let them relocate her a block away at the Astor Hotel on Hill and Second. "I'm so lonely here," she lamented after moving into her new room.

Most practical people would say that when all was said and done, the CRA served the greater good. True, eight or nine thousand people's lives were upended. The move was most painful for the elderly poor, especially the ones who had grown old on Bunker Hill and would never feel at home anywhere else. But they are all gone now, as obliterated by time as old Bunker Hill itself. The children who lived there and still remember, like Gordon Pattison, have had a half-century to get over it.

Had Bunker Hill not been torn down, it probably would have been the destination of the Central American civil war refugees who teemed into the Pico-Union neighborhood west of the Harbor Freeway in the late 1970s and early eighties. Certainly the turn-of-the-century rooming houses, built as rooming houses and nothing more, had no other purpose than to warehouse lots of poor people. But the garden districts along Bunker Hill Avenue and parts of Flower, Hope and Grand—once Faith, Hope and Charity Streets—likely would have caught the gentrification wave that soon swept into other vintage neighborhoods like nearby Angelino Heights, just north of the Hollywood Freeway. By the 1970s, a younger generation had discovered the haunting beauty of Victorian architecture, now fading fast. Romantics with more money than good sense bought up battered old houses, stripped away all the add-ons and ugly plywood of the previous generations and rehabilitated them back into what they imagined to be elegant Gilded Age homes with vivid paint jobs.

But all of Bunker Hill's Victorian traces disappeared beneath an industrial park for corporate executives, divided not by lots but by whole blocks, on a scale the old inhabitants would have considered cold and alien. Without Bunker Hill's thousands of residents, downtown L.A. became a ghost town after dark, and despite many attempts over the last half-century to revitalized its soul, nothing has really worked.

In his 1964 book of Bunker Hill paintings, Leo Politi wished "that some of the old homes could have been preserved. Or, even that the streets which ran so rhythmically with the contour of the Hill could have remained as they were, and the new built to adjust to the old. By so doing we could have retained some of the city's heritage in this delightful area." Perhaps a modern downtown "could have been built elsewhere on level ground…But the city planners had decided otherwise. They had no use for the old in their new plans."

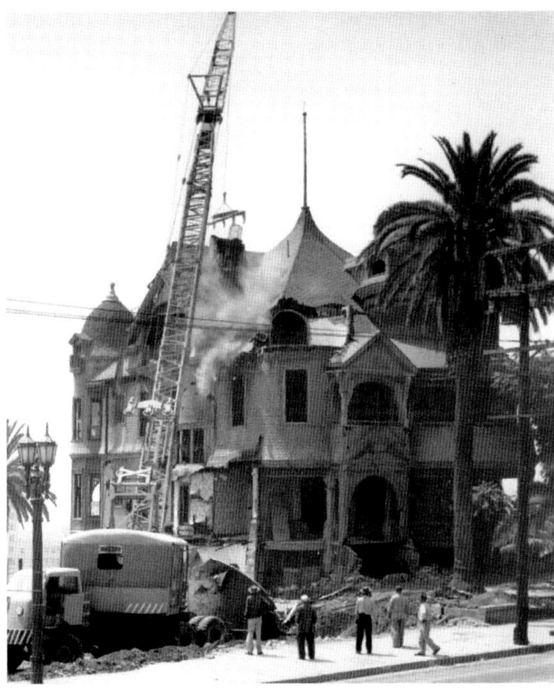

On July 9, 1957, the Community Redevelopment Agency took only eight hours to raze the once-posh 1881 Melrose Hotel at 130 South Grand Avenue, where President William McKinley once spoke to a crowd from the front porch. *Bob Board.*

Gordon Pattison agreed. "I don't know why the city didn't spare one or two blocks of those wonderful old houses. There was something timeless and mysterious about them. Even after we moved away, I'd go back sometimes and walk along the streets. Bunker Hill was a tranquil oasis. You'd always hear the gentle cooing of pigeons—there were pigeons everywhere. It saddens me just to think about it."

CHAPTER 8

A Selective List of Films Shot on Bunker Hill

We'll never know how many films were shot on Bunker Hill, so I can only say that my list is incomplete. Most of these movies are accessible in one form or another. Some turn up on the Turner Classic Movie channel. Some are available from companies like Netflix. Many are available on videotape or DVD/Blu-ray. The rest will mostly become available over the next few years because of restoration programs by various Hollywood film studios, the UCLA and USC film departments, Martin Scorsese's Film Foundation, Eddie Muller's Film Noir Foundation, the Academy of Motion Picture Arts and Sciences, the American Film Institute, the Library of Congress and other cinema-friendly institutions.

Act of Violence (MGM, 1949)

An upstanding suburban businessman (Van Heflin) is stalked by a fellow ex-soldier (Robert Ryan) he betrayed when they were POWs in Nazi Germany. Slipping away from a convention at a Los Angeles hotel, Heflin runs through a montage of Bunker Hill locations, including the Hill Street terrace near First Street, overlooking the Los Angeles Times building and L.A. City Hall; the Third Street steps from Olive down to Clay; and under Angels Flight as the railway cars cross each other above him. He also runs through the Third Street tunnel. (WarnerVideo.com)

All Jazzed Up (Christie Film Co., 1920)

Much of this silent two-reeler about honeymooners Bobby Vernon and Helen Darling in the big city was shot at the bottom of Angels Flight at Hill and Third, on the two railway cars themselves and at the Angels Flight station platform at the top (300 South Olive Street). At one point, Vernon leaps from one car to the other directly above Clay Street to unite with his bride. (UnknownVideo.com)

And Ten Thousand More (Los Angeles City Housing Authority, 1951)

In 1949, the City of Los Angeles commissioned this twelve-minute, pro-public housing film by Algernon G. Walker and Gene Peterson, grad students at USC's Department of Cinema. A reporter (Harold Hillhouse, with a voice-over by Chet Huntley) visits some of the tenement slums where, according to the 1940 census, fifty-eight thousand Los Angeles residents lived. The only Bunker Hill coverage is a hilly area around Hope Street and what looks like an alleyway with stacked back porches near Cinnabar Street where Jack Palance chased Joan Crawford in *Sudden Fear* (1952). (Hugh M. Hefner Moving Image Archive, USC School of Cinematic Arts)

Angel's Flight, reissued as *Angel's Flight Railway* (1964, 1997)

Edmund Penney filmed this lyrical fifteen-minute documentary about the waning days of the Bunker Hill funicular—beginning just before the wrecking balls and bulldozers took down all the buildings around it and ending with the little cars going up and down a desolate hillside, seemingly for no purpose. (Chiptaylor.com)

Angel's Flight (Independent, 1965)

A stripper named Liz (Indus Arthur) avenges an early rape behind the Sunshine Apartments by murdering handsome men with a straight razor. Shot all over Bunker Hill in 1962 and '63, it has several Angels Flight

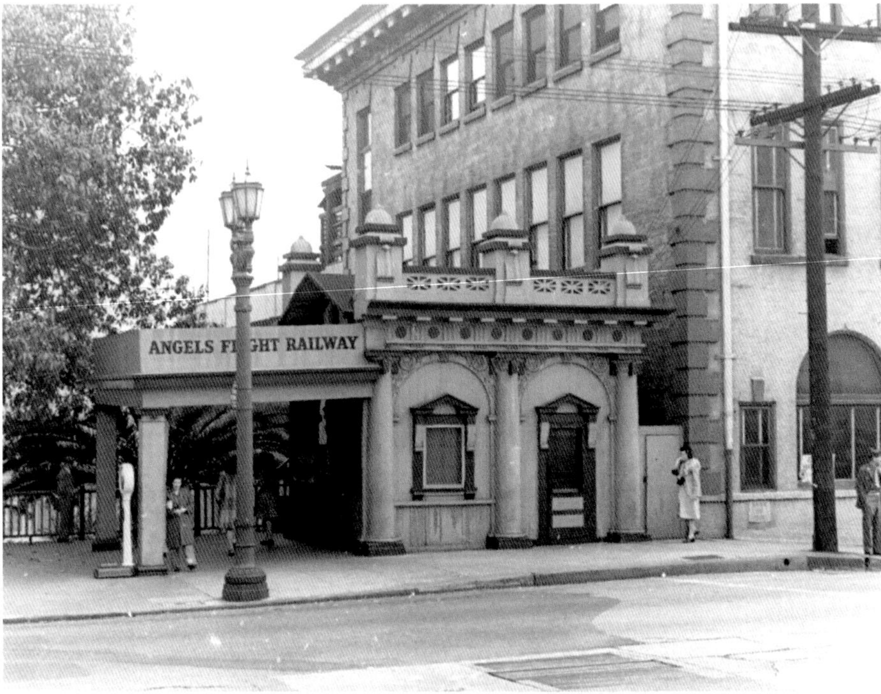

The Royal Building at 300 South Olive Street (right), formerly the Elks Hall, was built in 1909 next to the Angels Flight station. By 1960, it was a hotel, men's dormitory and gymnasium owned by the Moose Lodge. Its exterior, interior stairways, corridors and a corner apartment—not to mention Angels Flight's station—were used extensively in the 1965 noir-slasher film *Angel's Flight*. *Bison Archives.*

scenes, from the corner of Third and Hill to the Olive Street station at the top. There are also exteriors of the Angels Flight Café on the northwest corner of Third and Olive (the interiors were shot on a soundstage), as well as the Royal Apartments (formerly the Elks Lodge) on the southeast corner, adjacent to the Angels Flight station, where a broken-down reporter (William Thourlby) lives. Liz and her wacky landlady live in the McBurney rooming house at 256 South Bunker Hill Avenue, on the northeast corner of Third Street, across from the benches above the western terminus of the Third Street tunnel where she slits one victim's throat—referred to in the script as "the green benches at the top of the street." (These same benches were used in *M*.) There is also a scene where cops canvass Hill Street from the Belmont Hotel at 251 South Hill to the liquor store at the northwest corner of Third, next to the tunnel's east end, and at the New Grand Hotel and its corner delicatessen at Third and Grand. One of the murders occurs at the foot of the Hope Street stairs at the west entrance of the Third Street tunnel. One scene also takes place nearby at Bob's Café at 708 West Third, between Hope and Flower, where the reporter runs into barfly Rue McClanahan. The film's last scene begins on the utility steps behind the Sunshine Apartments. From there, Liz flees south on Clay Street beneath Angels Flight and then takes the stairs down to Hill Street, where she hops on one of the funicular cars. Bunker Hill is often referred to by name or simply called "the Hill" throughout *Angel's Flight*, and there are references to its ongoing destruction. However, the Bunker Hill strip club where Liz works was actually located in the San Gabriel Valley northeast of Los Angeles. A thirty-five-millimeter negative and a bootleg DVD exist, but no print has been struck at this writing; some footage is missing, so the title sequence is repeated at the end.

Armored Car Robbery (RKO, 1950)

Charles McGraw and William Tallman star in this efficient police procedural whose story is explained in the title. The robbery occurs at the entrance of the old Wrigley Field stadium at 435 Forty-second Street, at the corner of Avalon, and from there, the action plays out all over Los Angeles, from the Slausen Avenue river bridge to Los Angeles Harbor to a motor court in the San Fernando Valley. During the police response to the robbery, there's a montage that includes a pan from the City Library at Fifth Street down Grand Avenue and a pan of police cars driving south down Hope Street and turning east into the Second Street tunnel. (WarnerVideo.com)

The Asphalt Jungle (MGM, 1950)

Though this tale of a jewel heist gone wrong was filmed in Cincinnati and nearby Lexington, Kentucky, the twelve-second pan shot following the opening credits was a drop-in clip filmed on Bunker Hill. As the camera looks east on First Street from Grand Avenue, a police prowl car turns west onto First from Olive Street and cruises slowly along the storefronts. The Seymour Apartments at the southwest corner of First and Olive, with its open cupola, is clearly visible, as is the Los Angeles Times building a couple of blocks away. (The Criterion Collection)

BACKFIRE (WARNER BROTHERS, 1950)

After recovering from war injuries, Gordon McCrae discovers that his buddy Edmond O'Brien is wanted for murder. There are several scenes outside the main doors and corner steps of the Fremont Hotel at the southwest corner of Fourth and Olive. (WarnerVideo.com)

THE BIGAMIST (INDEPENDENT, 1953)

Ida Lupino directed and starred in this B film about a salesman (Edmond O'Brien) who maintains two lives—and two wives—in San Francisco (Joan Fontaine) and Los Angeles (Lupino). Among its various Los Angeles locations is a wide shot down the hilly 400 block of Grand Avenue from Fourth Street, with the Southern California Edison Building and the intersection of Fifth Street in the background, as O'Brien walks up the sidewalk on the east side of the street toward Lupino's apartment. (Critics Choice/Classic Movie Collection)

BLISS (ROLIN, 1917)

Harold Lloyd pretends to be a count in order to impress Bebe Daniels's father in this film short from the Roach-Linthicum (Rolin) Studio located in the Bradbury mansion at 139 North Hill Street, at the corner of Court Street, in the Court Hill section of Bunker Hill. There is a flirtation between the leads in front of a house at 425 Court. Most of Harold Lloyd's early film shorts (many of which have been lost) were filmed for Hal Roach in the vicinity of the Bradbury house and on Bunker Hill. (*American Slapstick Vol. 2*)

THE BOY WHO CAUGHT A CROOK (UNITED ARTISTS, 1961)

A young boy (Roger Mobley) with a newspaper route on Bunker Hill Avenue and his friend, a local bum named "Colonel" (Don Beddoe) who lives at a house at 711 West Second Street near the northwest corner of Hope, find a briefcase that bank robber Johnny Seven tossed out of his car during a police chase. Local footage includes an opening shot, taken from the corner

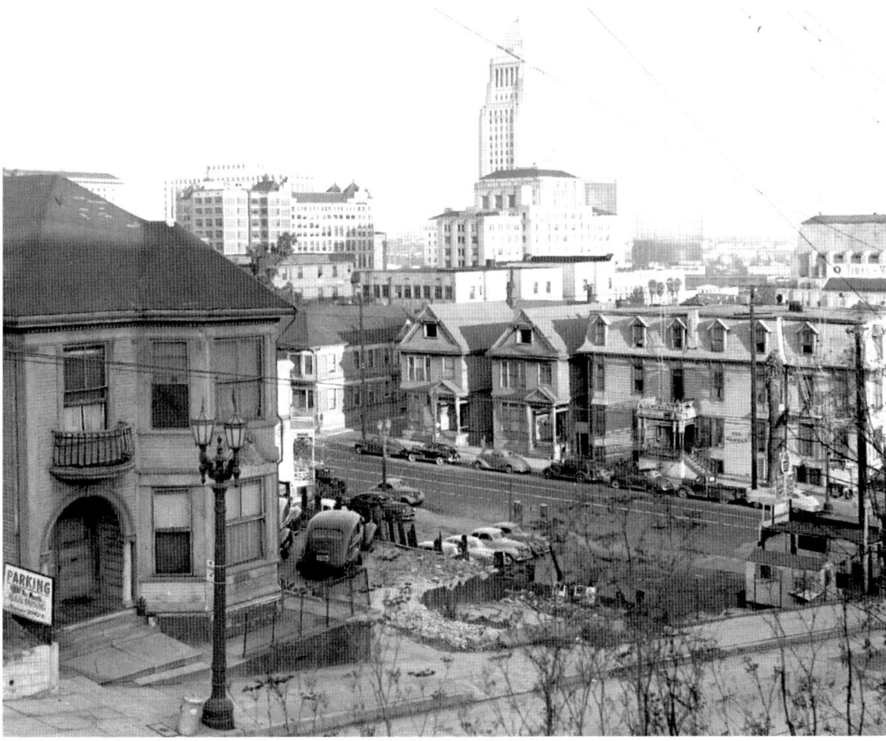

In Arnold Hylen's 1950 photo, above, the Koster House is on the left at 507 West Second Street and the Argyle Apartments on the right at 138 South Olive Street, as Los Angeles City Hall stands four blocks away on Spring Street. *The California History Room, California State Library, Sacramento.*

of Second Street and Bunker Hill Avenue, that begins with a view of Los Angeles City Hall several blocks distant and pans southward down Bunker Hill Avenue. When the boy and Colonel find the briefcase in a field just north of First Street, between Figueroa and the Harbor Freeway, they take it to a nearby gas station at 117 North Figueroa. The crook avoids the police by pulling onto what looks like the 100 block of either North Grand or North Bunker Hill avenues and parking between two apartment houses. Piles of dirt and stranded houses are often glimpsed in the background, and the various characters mention how the neighborhood is systematically being torn down. Unfortunately, the main action on the boy's street and in his house were shot on a backlot; at different times his address is given as being in both the 600 and 900 blocks of Bunker Hill Avenue, neither of which existed on Bunker Hill.

The Brasher Doubloon (Twentieth Century Fox, 1947)

Philip Marlowe (George Montgomery) is hired to retrieve a valuable coin in this fourth film adaptation of Raymond Chandler's novels (in this case *The High Window*), each done by a different studio with a different lead. Marlowe drives up First Street (with the L.A. City Building in the background), turns onto Olive Street and parks on the west side of the street opposite the Gladden Apartments (formerly the Cecil Hotel) on the southeast corner at 100 Olive Street, where Raymond Chandler himself actually lived in 1916. When Marlowe goes into the Gladden, several scenes appear to have been shot in the corridors inside. A *Los Angeles Times* reviewer (June 2, 1947) noted the film's "breath-taking street view of a Los Angeles rooming house."

Bumping Into Broadway (Rolin, 1919)

In one of Harold Lloyd's earliest two-reel comedies, he hops into a trash cart and grabs the back of a car at the corner of Third and Grand, in front of the Lovejoy Apartments on the northeast corner. (Newline.com)

Bunker Hill 1956 (University of Southern California, 1956)

USC film student Kent Mackenzie made this poignant eighteen-minute documentary about retirees living out their lives in Bunker Hill's "small town atmosphere," knowing that the city is planning to evict them sometime soon. Accompanied by voiceovers of a pharmacist, an elderly physician (Dr. James Green) and a carpenter, the film includes intimate shots of the Grand Central Market on Hill Street between Third and Fourth, Angels Flight, the 400 block of Grand Avenue, the Castle at 325 South Bunker Hill Avenue, the benches at Third and Grand, the old Melrose Hotel (exterior and interiors) at 130 South Grand, Dr. Green's home office in the parlor of his Victorian house at 232 South Grand, shoemaker William Varney's house at 523 West Third Street (which also turns up a couple of years later in *This Rebel Breed*) and Bunker Hill's small business district, including the Angels Flight Pharmacy on the southeast corner of Third and Grand, both the Delicatessen and the Montana Club on the ground floor of the New Grand

Hotel on the northwest corner and Varney's Custom Made Shoes at 510$^1/_2$ West Third. Though *Bunker Hill 1956* was screened at the Edinburgh Film Festival in Scotland, it disappeared until its revival at a 2004 UCLA film festival. (Available on Milestone's *The Exiles* DVD, Milestonefilms.com)

Bunker Hill: A Tale of Urban Renewal (Independent, 2009)

Greg Kimble directed and narrated this twenty-two-minute documentary about the founding and the eventual destruction of Bunker Hill. Its most compelling segment is roughly seven minutes of black and white film footage called "A Day on Bunker Hill" (circa 1948) that a Hollywood production designer named Eugene Laurié (la-*ray*) shot on a leisurely afternoon stroll. Following mostly a group of poor children, he visits the slums in the area of Olive Street between Temple and First Street and includes added shots of Clay Street and the busy corner of Third and Olive at the top of Angels Flight. (Available on Milestone's *The Exiles* DVD, Milestonefilms.com)

Bunker Hill Los Angeles (The Criterion Collection, 2011)

This seven-minute film of two-dozen Bunker Hill photos and *Kiss Me Deadly* film clips, accompanied by Don Bajema's reading of Jim Dawson's script, is an added feature of the 2011 Blu-ray/DVD restoration of the 1955 film noir classic. It's accompanied by a two-minute feature showing how *Kiss Me Deadly*'s Bunker Hill locations look today. (Available on the Criterion Collection's *Kiss Me Deadly*.)

Bus Stop (Twentieth Century Fox, 1956)

An obnoxious rodeo cowboy (Don Murray) falls in love with a Phoenix showgirl (Marilyn Monroe) and insists that she return with him to his Idaho ranch. The non-rodeo Phoenix exteriors were shot on Bunker Hill. When Murray and Arthur O'Connell arrive in the city and get off the bus, they're at Third and Grand (with a fake street sign on Third that says Mountainview). The New Grand Hotel's delicatessen is plainly visible on the northwest corner. When

Murray later visits Monroe at the Thompson house at 237 South Bunker Hill Avenue, the large, distinctive Brousseau mansion at 238 South Bunker Hill across the street fills the background of the frame. (A more dilapidated Brousseau house, minus its neighbors, would have a more starring role ten years later in *The Money Trap*). In another scene, a dolly shot follows Murray and O'Connell along the fronts of several houses on the west side of the street, beginning with the Earlcliffe Apartments at 231 S. Bunker Hill, then past the houses at 237 and 241. This is one of the most flattering portraits of Bunker Hill on film because it reveals well-tended working-class homes bathed in Technicolor pastels. You can almost smell the honeysuckle. But the otherwise continuous take has an awkward edit in which a brief encounter between Murray and a blonde actress named Lucille Knox has been excised, leaving only a glimpse of the back of her legs as she goes into the David Sterling house at 241 South Bunker Hill. The jump occurs in the middle of Arthur O'Connell's line: "Look, if you'll go to the ro(*cut*)deo, I promise I'll find her and hold her for you." (WarnerVideo.com)

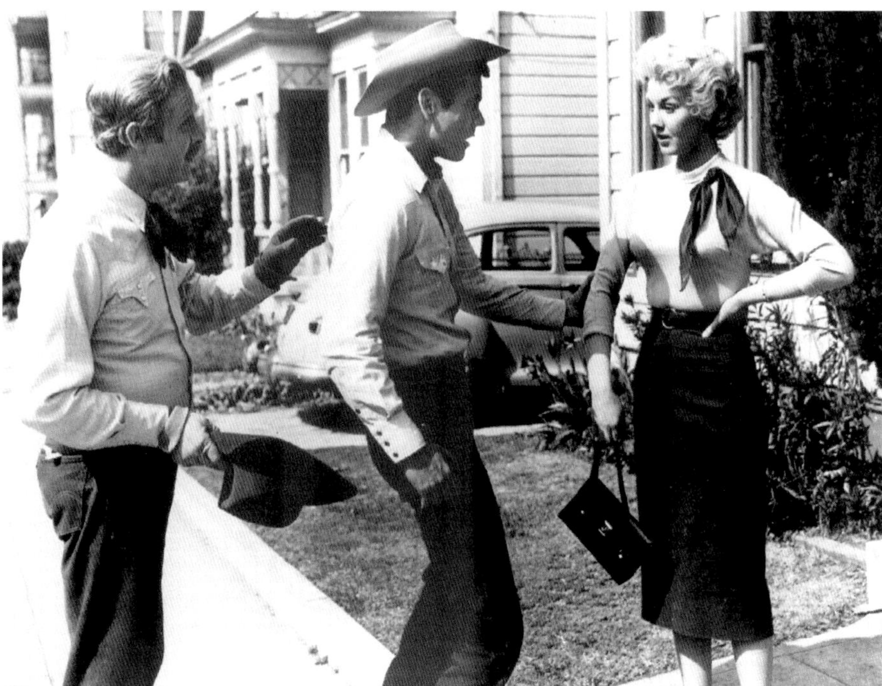

In a scene that was cut from the 1956 movie *Bus Stop*, Arthur O'Connell tries to stop Don Murray from pestering Lucille Knox in front of 241 South Bunker Hill Avenue. To the left is Anna "Nell" McKenzie's house at 245, which later appeared in artist Leo Politi's *1964 Bunker Hill Los Angeles*. At the corner is the columned Alta Vista at 255. *Jim Dawson.*

Criss Cross (Universal Pictures, 1949)

In this Robert Siodmak classic, armored car driver Burt Lancaster pulls an inside job with local gangster Dan Duryea, but everything unravels when a guard is murdered. There are several exterior and interior scenes at Lancaster's mother's white hillside home at 215 North Hill Street, which stood on the terrace above the Hill Street tunnel near Temple Street; in an early scene Lancaster gets off a streetcar there and walks up the stairs to the house. (The Hill Street tunnel ran north and south beneath Hill Street from First to Temple.) For the scenes where Lancaster and his cronies plan the heist, Siodmak used the exterior and some hallway interiors of the Sunshine Apartments at 421 Third Street, opposite Angels Flight. (UniversalStudios.com/home)

Cry Danger (Republic/RKO/Paramount, 1951)

Released from prison for a robbery he didn't commit, Dick Powell returns to Los Angeles to confront the people who framed him. There's a scene inside and outside of a Bunker Hill bar called Los Amigos at 500 Third Street on the southwest corner of Olive Street (across the street from both the Angels Flight Station and—on the northwest corner—the Angels Flight Café, which is glimpsed during a police shootout near the end of the film). A couple of scenes are also shot outside and inside the New Grand Hotel

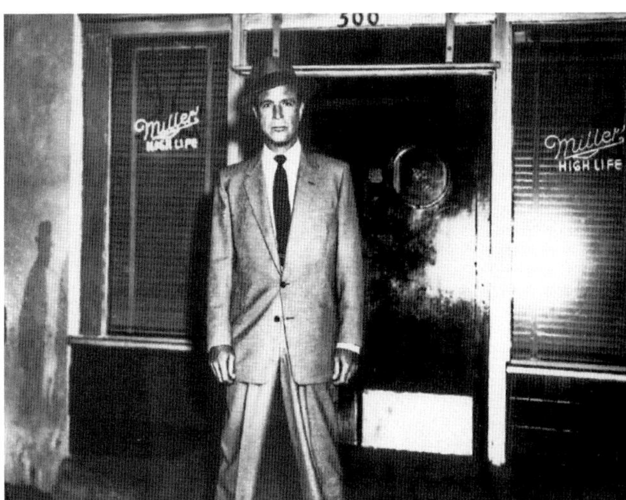

Dick Powell stands in front of the Los Amigos at 500 West Third Street, on the corner of Olive, in *Cry Danger* (1951). *Jim Dawson.*

(called the Crosley Hotel in the film) at 257 South Grand Avenue on the northwest corner of Third Street. However, the "Clover Trailer Park" where the principals live was actually shot several blocks north of Bunker Hill at 650–700 North Hill Place, just off Sunset Boulevard (now Cesar E. Chavez) on a hill above Chinatown.

Cry of the Hunted (MGM, 1953)

Prisoner Vittorio Gassman eludes the police in Los Angeles and heads for the bayous of Louisiana. Escaping from detective William Conrad after a car crash in the Third Street tunnel, Gassman runs out of the tunnel's east end, chases one of the Angels Flight cars up the tracks and climbs on. Conrad runs out of the tunnel and goes up the opposite stairway on the north side of Third Street. The scene ends at Olive Street, with the Angels Flight Café on the northwest corner, the Hillcrest Hotel on the northeast corner and other buildings clearly visible.

The Derelict (Independent, 1957)

Bob Board directed this fifteen-minute short about a hobo (Neil Morrow) who hops off a train in downtown Los Angeles and roams the streets (where he runs into cameo players Richard Basehart and his wife, Valentina Cortese). Leaving the Union Mission on Main Street, he takes Angels Flight up to Bunker Hill, where buildings along Second Street across from the Dome Hotel Apartments are being torn down. He eventually hops another boxcar out of town, just as another hobo is coming in on another train. (Currently not available on DVD.)

Dime With a Halo (MGM, 1963)

In this black and white studio B movie filmed by TV director Boris Sagal, several street urchins try to find a trustworthy adult to cash in their winning racetrack ticket in Tijuana. The film opens on Bunker Hill as a woman (Barbara Luna) and her kid brother (*The Boy Who Caught a Crook* star Roger Mobley) drive west up Second Street. They pass the twin-towered Chaspeak Apartments and the Dome Hotel Apartments and turn left and park in front of the corner house at 201 South Bunker Hill Avenue (which had been used previously in *This Rebel Breed*). Several vista shots reveal that nearly everything on Bunker Hill north of Second Street had been razed by that time.

Down Three Dark Streets (United Artists, 1954)

This Broderick Crawford police procedural, which tracks three cases left behind by a slain detective in order to find his murderer, was shot all over Los Angeles, including the 1925 subway station beneath the Pacific Electric Terminal Building at 437 South Hill Street. The film ends dramatically at the Hollywood sign.

A Drive Through Bunker Hill (Columbia, 1948)

Throughout most of Hollywood history, actors sitting inside automobiles were shot in studio mock-ups, as previously filmed footage of a street or road was projected on a screen behind them. It was called a "process shot," and the film was a "process plate." For the 1949 film *Shockproof* (see below), a second-unit director in summer 1948 shot several minutes of film from the back of a camera car to match a scene in which Cornell Wilde picks up Patricia Knight at the Koster house at 507 West Second Street. Beginning on Second Street just above Olive (with the balustrade above the Second Street tunnel in the frame), the film tours Bunker Hill. We go up Second and turn south on Grand Avenue, showing the white, modern Segrand Apartments on the northeast corner. We pass the Frontenac Apartments at 212 South Grand, built in 1905 and once one of the finer hotels on the hill. We pass Third Street, with the Angels Flight Pharmacy on the right, and then Fourth. At Fifth Street, we turn west, drive a long block and turn right on Flower. Just north of the corner of Fifth and Flower is a billboard for RCA Victor televisions showing a cartoon donkey and elephant wearing boxing gloves, with a caption saying, "Pick a sure winner!"—TV was brand new, and 1948 was an election year. The camera then goes back and shoots the same sequence from a different angle, for side shots in the car. This clip can be viewed at several online sites, including http://onbunkerhill.org/adrivethroughbunkerhill and YouTube, as "A Drive Through Bunker Hill."

An Eastern Westerner (Rolin, 1920)

In this twenty-four-minute silent short, Harold Lloyd's father decides to toughen up his dissolute son by sending him out West. Early in the movie, when Lloyd is thrown out of a speakeasy, he shakes off two bouncers by leading them into a taxi cab parked on the east side of Grand Avenue and then stepping out the other side as it pulls away from the curb toward Third Street. The scene takes in the Angels Flight Pharmacy on the southeast corner of Third, the Lovejoy Apartments on the far corner and the Dome Hotel up the street on the northwest corner of Second. (Newline.com)

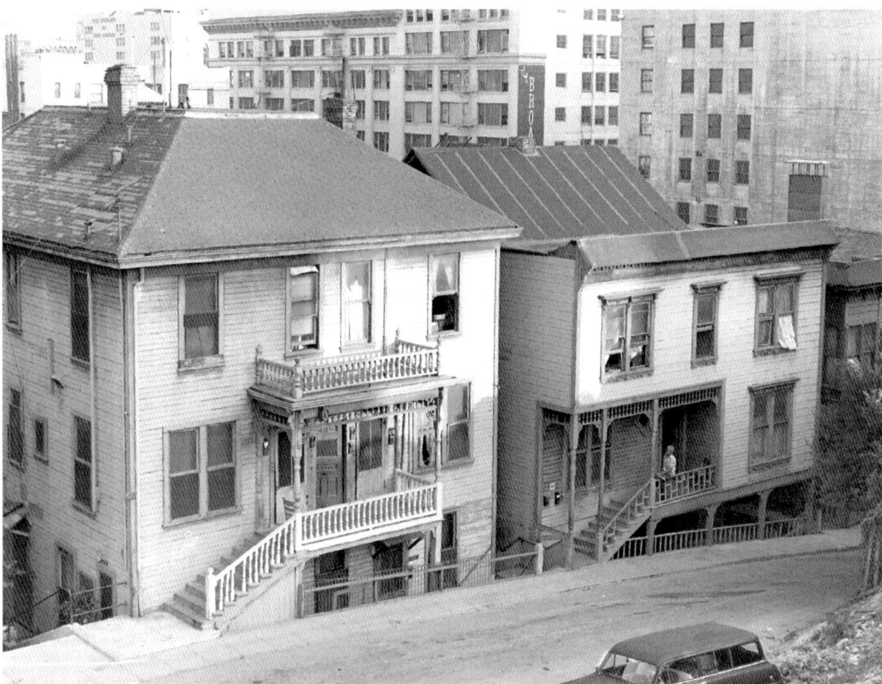

Yvonne and Homer, the Native American couple in *The Exiles* (1961), lived in a rear apartment at 334 Clay Street (left), where a lengthy scene was filmed. In the 1955 noir programmer *Finger Man*, henchman Timothy Carey lived in the basement apartment at 338 Clay Street (right). Frank Lovejoy pounded a murder confession out of him on the porch beneath the sidewalk. Painter Leo Politi later featured this building in *Bunker Hill Los Angeles*. *California History Room, California State Library, Sacramento.*

The Exiles (Independent, 1961; Milestone Films)

Using non-actors, filmmaker Kent Mackenzie (see *Bunker Hill 1956*) shot this compelling neo-realist drama that takes place over fourteen or fifteen hours in the lives of a group of dislocated American Indians living on Bunker Hill in 1958. There are numerous shots of Broadway and Hill Streets (including the Roxie Theater at 518 Broadway and the Grand Central Market that fronts on both Broadway and Hill), as well as a couple of real "Indian bars" (the Columbine Beer Room at 263 South Main and the Ritz Club cattycorner across the street at 312 South Main). But much of the story takes place on and around Bunker Hill: Angels Flight, the clapboard apartment buildings on Third Street opposite Angels Flight, the Third Street tunnel and Clay Street. Two of the principals, Homer and Yvonne, live at 334 South Clay, half a block south of Angels Flight, where they and their friends begin the evening, but Yvonne ends up spending the night with a girlfriend at the Sunshine Apartments at 421 West Third (filmed inside and out). There is a tribal scene of Indians gathering late at night on a hilltop near the recently stripped Chavez Ravine, as downtown L.A. sparkles in the background. Shot in 1958 in sixteen-millimeter under the original title *The Trail of the Thunderbird*, the film was restored forty-five years later at UCLA's Film and Television Archives. The DVD includes Mackenzie's eighteen-minute *Bunker Hill 1956* documentary, Robert Kirste's three-minute home movie called *Last Day of Angels Flight*, and Greg Kimble's twenty-two-minute *Bunker Hill: A Tale of Urban Renewal*. (Milestonefilms.com)

Finger Man (Allied Artists, 1955)

Frank Lovejoy stars in this routine, hour-long B movie, originally called *Dark Venture*, about a small-time crook forced to bargain his way out of an arrest by setting up a mobster for the local feds. Lovejoy lives at the Auburn Apartments at 703 West First Street, on the northwest corner of Hope. When Peggy Castle leaves his place before she's murdered by Timothy Carey, she walks across First Street (where we see a column of the Lima Apartments on the southwest corner) and then across Hope Street toward George's Market at 644 West First. There are a couple of scenes at the Pacific Electric Terminal Building at 437 South Hill Street: one at the magazine stands in the foyer, the other down below in the subway station. Another scene takes place at 338 South Clay Street, where Lovejoy waits for Carey to arrive at the sunken porch beneath the sidewalk and beats him into submission. (Republic Video)

For Heaven's Sake (Harold Lloyd Corporation, 1926)

In this fifty-eight-minute comedy, a millionaire (Harold Lloyd) tries to impress an attractive volunteer at the local skid row mission by bringing in all the neighborhood ne'er-do-wells to be saved. A runaway double-decker bus sequence takes place on both the 300 block of Clay Street and on the 500 and 600 blocks of Third Street. (Newline.com)

Gangster's Revenge (Independent, 1960)

(see *Get Outta Town*)

Get Outta Town (Independent, 1960)

Actor Doug Wilson and director Charlie Davis produced this snappy, better-than-average low-budget black and white film about an ex-safecracker who returns to Los Angeles for his brother's funeral. There is an extended scene on the Spring Street side of City Hall and a couple of quick shots at Second and Olive, on Second Street between Olive and Grand, and on the 200 block of Grand. But most of the film's location work was done inside the Dome Hotel Apartments at Second and Grand, giving a good sense of its layout, its small apartments, its corridors, its narrow balconies and stairways and the long skylight above the lobby. Sterling World Distributors released the film in 1960, and Beckman Film Corp. reissued it as *Gangster's Revenge* a couple years later, but distribution was always limited. The film was released on video/DVD as *Get Outta Town*.

Girl Shy (Harold Lloyd Corporation, 1924)

In this feature-length silent comedy, shy, stuttering bachelor Harold Lloyd falls in love with a rich girl and tries to save her from marrying a bigamist. During a headlong rush to the wedding aboard a horse-drawn wagon, he rides west on Third Street through the intersection at Grand. (Newline.com)

The Girls of F Street

(see *The Maidens of Fetish Street*)

The Glenn Miller Story (Universal Pictures, 1953)

Jimmy Stewart stars in this biopic of the famous 1930s big band leader who perished in World War II. Shot in color, the film begins with Stewart getting his trombone out of hock from a pawnshop on Clay Street, at the top of the lower section of the Third Street steps. The shop was a façade that covered part of a clapboard building (formerly the Rose McCoy house) and was designed so that the camera could see the orange Angels Flight cars (rarely seen in full color in a Hollywood film before now) through the front and side windows. During the first ten minutes of the film, Stewart visits the shop three times, with the funicular cars crossing above Clay Street each time. The camera also captures the 200 block of Clay Street going north. (UniversalStudios.com/home)

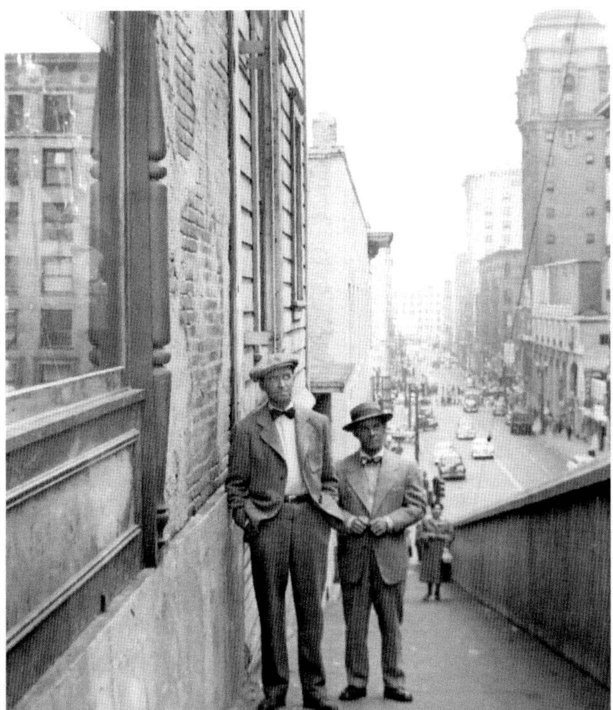

Jimmy Stewart and Harry Morgan stand on the Third Street ramp leading up to Clay Street in *The Glenn Miller Story* (1953). The mock-up exterior of the pawnshop where Stewart's title character hocked his trombone is on the left; the pawnshop's interior was a studio set. *Bison Archives.*

Good Night, Nurse (Nestor Films, 1916)

In this silent, one-reel comedy (not to be confused with a couple of other early movies with the same title) a love-struck young man (Neal Burns) feigns sickness to gain admittance to the hospital where the object of his obsession is a nurse. A chase scene includes a roughly thirty-second sequence on Angels Flight.

Haunted Spooks (Rolin, 1920)

A lawyer hires a stooge (Harold Lloyd) to be a groom for his client (Mildred Davis) in order that she can inherit a mansion (the Bradbury house at the corner of Hill and Court Streets). Most of this comedy short was filmed inside the house itself. (Newline.com)

High and Dizzy (Rolin, 1920)

In this twenty-six-minute comedy, Harold Lloyd accidentally gets high on illegal booze and, through a series of improbable events, meets the girl of his dreams, a sleepwalker (Mildred Davis), on the eleventh-floor ledge of the Citizens National Bank Building at the northwest corner of Fifth and Spring. After an establishing long shot of Lloyd on the ledge of the real building, the film switches to a mock-up of the ledge and eleventh floor windows that was built above the south end of the Hill Street tunnel, so that the 100 block of South Hill Street and beyond looked far below. There is also a scene with a policeman in front of the Lovejoy Apartments on the northeast corner of Third and Grand. (Newline.com)

Hollow Triumph, aka *The Scar* (Eagle-Lion, 1948)

Gangster Paul Henreid tries to avoid a mob hit by murdering a look-alike psychiatrist and assuming his identity. At one point, he evades two henchmen (including Jack Webb) at Third and Hill by hopping on one of Angels Flight's cars and kicking one of his pursuers out the door. The most available reissue is of the British version, called *The Scar*, on Alpha Video's public domain series. (Alpha Video; Oldies.com)

Hop to It! (Cumberland Productions, 1925)

Oliver Hardy and Bobby Ray are incompetent bellhops in this silent short. During one scene, they pass beneath Angels Flight on Clay Street.

Hot Water (Harold Lloyd Corporation, 1924)

In this hour-long comedy, a hardworking husband (Harold Lloyd) is bedeviled by his imperious and indolent in-laws. At one point, when he pushes his car out of a traffic jam at the corner of Third and Grand, there's a sudden cut to the car rolling away from him a block away on the hilly intersection of Third and Olive, just a few feet away from the Angels Flight station. Lloyd chases his car down Olive toward Fourth Street, past the Palace Hotel, the Ems and the Olive Inn at 317, 321 and 337 South Olive Street, respectively. (Newline.com)

The Impatient Maiden (Universal Pictures, 1932)

Fresh from making the classic *Frankenstein*, James Whale directed this odd story about a legal secretary and a ditzy flapper (Mae Clarke and Una Merkel) and their on-again-off-again relationships with a young doctor and his ambulance assistant (Lew Ayres and Andy Devine). The old-fashioned title comes compliments of the Hollywood censors, who took issue with the original *The Impatient Virgin*. The film opens as the camera looks up Angels Flight from Hill Street and pans over to the Sunshine Apartments where the girls live. In closer shots, they step off the Sunshine's porch and walk up the Third Street steps to the Angels Flight station; then the camera rides with them on one of the Angels Flight cars (actually a studio mockup with process shots) down to the bottom. Later, the ambulance crew parks on Clay Street beneath the Sunshine and carries a stretcher up the back utility steps.

Incredibly Strange People Who Stopped Living and Became Mixed-Up Zombies!!? (1964)

Ray Dennis Steckler directed and starred in (under the name Cash Flagg) this nutty movie about a Long Beach carnival where a fortune-telling Gypsy hypnotizes a guy (Flagg) and makes him murder strippers. At one point, he climbs up the steps on the south side of Third Street to Clay Street and stares down at the opening of the Third Street tunnel, while the camera dollies up and down the hill above him aboard Angels Flight, showing Third Street when all the buildings on the south side of the funicular have already been torn down. Then he walks down the steps on the north side of Third Street.

The Indestructible Man (1956)

After a prisoner (Lon Chaney Jr.) is executed, scientists revive his body by "increas[ing] his cellular structure," which makes him impervious to bullets. At one point in his search for revenge against the people who turned state's evidence against him, he crosses Hill Street in a long pan shot and climbs on one of the Angels Flight cars. From the Olive Street station, he walks over to the Hillcrest Hotel (258 South Olive Street) and goes inside. The man he's looking for hears him coming and climbs down the fire escape to the Third Street steps. Meanwhile, when Chaney's ex-girlfriend (Marion Carr) sees another of his accomplices on crutches at the bottom of Third Street, she hurriedly takes Angels Flight down to warn him (with the camera inside the car along with her, panning over to the lower part of the steps). But she's too late to catch him, and the man climbs the hill and meets Chaney on the Hillcrest porch. He tries to escape by hobbling around the corner to Olive Street and past several shops. But Chaney grabs him at the top of the concrete utility stairway behind the Hillcrest, and tosses him down the steps toward Clay Street. (Ralph Meeker parked at the bottom of these same steps to go up and see an opera-singing witness at the Hillcrest Hotel in *Kiss Me Deadly* a year earlier.) This entire segment lasts nearly four minutes. Chaney later throws a man off one of the balconies of the Bradbury Building. (Available on various low-budget DVDs.)

Just Neighbors (Rolin, 1919)

In this silent short filmed mostly around Court and Olive Streets, neighbors Harold Lloyd and Snub Pollard create havoc when they try to build a garden shed. Several scenes take place in front of a house at 201 South Olive.

Just Nuts (Rolin, 1915)

This short film was part of Harold Lloyd's early Willie Work series, most of which has been lost. There are scenes on Clay Street, on Court Street near Olive and in front of the Bradbury mansion at the corner of North Hill and Court.

The Killing (United Artists, 1956)

Stanley Kubrick produced and directed this adaptation of novelist Lionel White's *Clean Break*, with extra dialogue written by pulp icon Jim Thompson. Johnny Clay (Sterling Hayden) puts together what looks like a foolproof racetrack robbery with a gang of colorful hoods played by top-notch character actors. They make their plans at the Mission Apartments at 504 West Second Street, though the address is given as "504 W. Olive." (The Mission was on the southwest corner of Second and Olive, so the address might have been a mistake by the prop department, since it was never spoken but rather written on racing stubs, and the glass above the Mission's arched doorway simply said 504.) The camera looks east down Second Street toward the Second Street tunnel and downtown, first at night after the planning and later during the day after everything has gone wrong inside. At one point Hayden leaves a bus station key in a conspirator's mailbox at

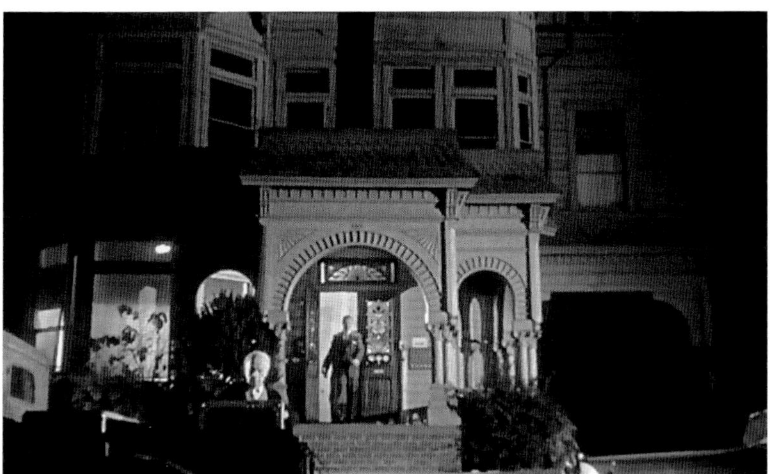

Mike Hammer (Ralph Meeker) leaves the Castle at 325 South Bunker Hill Avenue in 1955's *Kiss Me Deadly*. *Criterion Collection.*

the New Grand Hotel at 257 South Grand Avenue. There's also a rooftop shot looking down on Grand as a police car turns north from Third Street heading toward Second. (MGM.com/dvd)

Kiss Me Deadly (1955)

Playing Mike Hammer—Mickey Spillaine's classic detective—Ralph Meeker stumbles into a heist of nuclear material and wanders all over Los Angeles, from a gas station at 4807 Las Virgenes in Calabasas to his apartment building at 10401 Wilshire Boulevard (at Beverly Glen) to a rich criminal's house in Beverly Hills and a beach house in Point Dune. There are also scenes at Bunker Hill locations, including the Hillcrest Hotel at 258 South Olive Street, where Hammer intimidates an opera-loving Mr. Trivago by breaking one of his Caruso records, and the Castle at 325 South Bunker Hill, where he visits the apartment of Christina Bailey (Cloris Leachman), whose death drives the plot. Meeker also drives beneath Angels Flight and parks on Clay Street at the bottom of the long utility steps behind the Hillcrest Hotel and Sunshine Apartments. But other locations stand in for Bunker Hill, including a large Queen Anne home at 601½ Sunset Boulevard (now Cesar E. Chavez) on the corner of Hill Place where Meeker visits Ray Diker (though the script identifies the street as 121 Flower), the rambling Jalisco Hotel at 616½ North Spring Street in Chinatown where Lily Carver (Gaby Rodgers) is hiding out and on the 2600 block of Temple Street where Hammer is followed by a man with a switchblade. Hammer beats him up mid-block at the mouth of an alley called Dryden Place, and then the film cuts back to Bunker Hill as Hammer sends him tumbling down the Hope Street stairs at the western end of the Third Street tunnel. (The Criterion Collection)

L.A. Noire (Rockstar Games, 2011)

In this video game for PlayStation, Xbox 360 and Microsoft Windows, the player is a Los Angeles detective loose in the city in 1947, investigating several cases based on classic film noir themes. The designers have created an amazing likeness of the postwar city using thousands of maps, photos and film clips. However, Bunker Hill is not as complete as many aficionados might have wished. According to *L.A. Noire* gameboy Nathan Marsak, Bunker Hill Avenue and its mansions are missing, along with the buildings at the corner of Grand and Third (the Angels Flight Pharmacy, the Lovejoy Apartments and the New Grand Hotel, which was being called the Nugent in 1947), the Astoria Hotel and other landmarks. Part of Second Street above Hill has been replaced by stairs, and worst of all, Angels Flight is stationary. How can you visit 1947 Los Angeles without riding Angels Flight?

The Last Day of Angels Flight (Home movie, 1969)

Also called *Richard Kirste's Last Day of Angels Flight*, this is a two-and-a-half-minute color home movie. With his eight-millimeter camera running, Kirste rides down Angels Flight for the last time on a day in May 1969. He also shows the lines of people on Hill Street at the bottom and at the Olive Street station at the top. In a narration voiceover, Kirste remembers his childhood visits to Bunker Hill and other local landmarks, such as the Grand Central Market. (Available on Milestone's *The Exiles* DVD, Milestonefilms.com)

The Little Shop of Horrors (Independent, 1960)

In this ultra-low-budget Roger Corman quickie, an employee (Jonathan Haze) at a florist shop cultivates a mutant Venus flytrap that eats people. His mother's home is the Rochester house at 1210 West Temple Street, just west of Bunker Hill but looking like it belonged there. Near the film's end, he goes up to Bunker Hill late at night and meets a hooker at the Angels Flight station. There are also shots across the street at the Angels Flight Café at 501 West Third and at the little park of benches at Third and Bunker Hill Avenue that was used earlier in *M* and later in *Angel's Flight*.

Look Out Below (Rolin, 1919)

Harold Lloyd woos Bebe Daniels in one of the first of his so-called "thrill comedies," which culminated four years later with his most famous performance, hanging from a clock on the side of a tall building in *Safety Last* (1923). In *Look Out Below*, he perfected the use of facades on elevated platforms, namely the terrace above the southern end of the Hill Street tunnel, to give the illusion of height above the streets of Los Angeles. For the clock scene in *Safety Last*, he built a similar facade on the roof of 908 South Broadway, on the southeast corner of Ninth (which is still there). A couple of short clips from *Look Out Below* are on the Internet but the only extant thirty-five-millimeter print is in the National Archives of the British Film Institute.

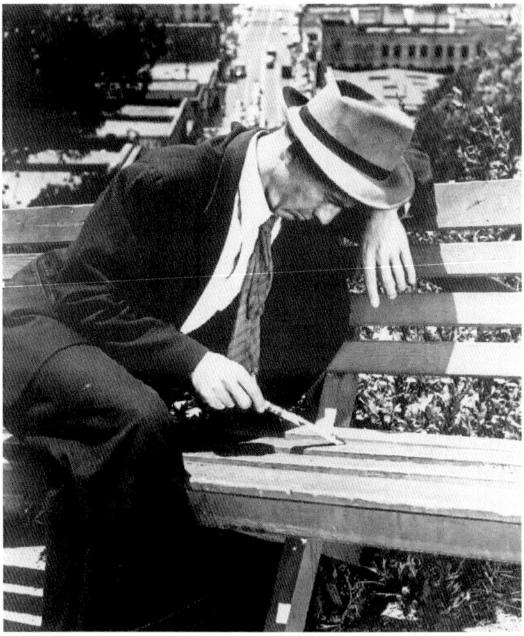

David Wayne etches with his knife into one of the benches on Bunker Hill Avenue at the top of Third Street in *M* (1951). The benches later appeared in *Bunker Hill 1956* (1956), *The Little Shop of Horrors* (1960), *This Rebel Breed* (1961), and *Angel's Flight* (1965). *Bison Archives.*

M (Columbia, 1951)

Bunker Hill replaces Weimar-era Berlin in Joseph Losey's remake of Fritz Lang's German classic (from the same script, with the same producer). Both the cops and the criminals are looking for a child murderer (David Wayne effectively playing the Peter Lorre role). Most of the film is shot on location around Los Angeles, primarily on the streets of Bunker Hill (including an opening shot aboard Angels Flight) and at Santa Monica's Ocean Park Pier (edited together to seem only minutes apart instead of nearly twenty miles). Wayne's character lives in an upstairs apartment in the old Foss-Heindel house at 315 South Bunker Hill Avenue. The killer's first victim and her mother (1930s star Karen Morley) live at the Alta Vista Apartments (where their apartment and the hallway interiors and side stairway exteriors were shot) at 255 South Bunker Hill, at the top of Third Street. The child's balloon floats above the Sunshine Apartments and the Hillcrest Hotel on Third Street. When Wayne tries to kidnap another girl at the corner store of the Nugent/New Grand Hotel at Grand Avenue and Third, her mother arrives just in time to scare him off. After successfully luring away a third girl, he's recognized as the killer and chased down the Hope Street steps adjacent to the western end of the Third Street tunnel (which was also used later in *Kiss Me Deadly*). Reaching Third Street at the bottom, he runs through the

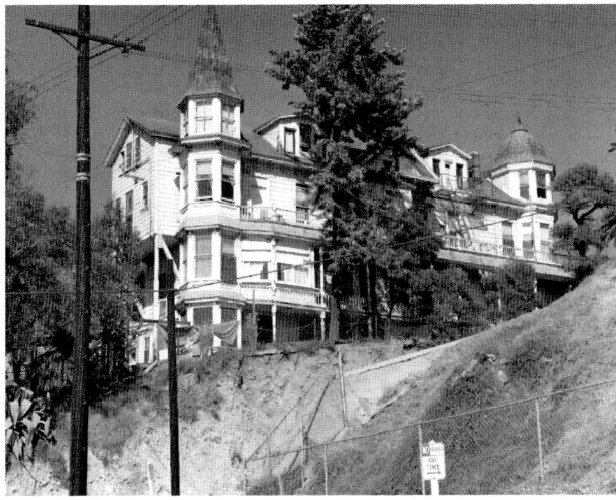

The Berke/Warncliffe Apartments, seen here from Hope Street near the corner of Second in 1956, fronted at 145 South Bunker Hill Avenue. Its interior was used in the Bunker Hill segment of *The Maidens of Fetish Street*, an arty 1966 porn film. *California History Room, California State Library, Sacramento.*

tunnel with the girl and comes out at the foot of Angels Flight on Hill Street. From there, he leads her to the Bradbury Building at 304 South Broadway, where a lengthy search by street criminals takes the viewer literally from the basement to the roof. The final scene is in a downtown underground parking garage.

The Maidens of Fetish Street, aka *The Girls of F Street* (Cameo Productions, 1966)

An incoherent mish-mash of film noir, soft porn and art-house pretentiousness barely held together by a voice-over narrator, director-producer Saul Resnick's ultra-low budget boobs 'n' buns fest features a half-hour segment in which a lonely man (Ken McCormick) visits "the House of Fetish" on Bunker Hill. The scene, probably filmed in 1962 or '63, opens on a trip up Angels Flight and segues to a rooftop panorama of houses on Bunker Hill Avenue. Most of the action takes place within a large, rectangular Queen Anne at 145 South Bunker Hill, at the northwest corner of Second Street, providing one of the few extensive "tours" inside a Bunker Hill Victorian before it was torn down. Owned in the late nineteenth century by the Berke family, the building had already been broken up into furnished rooms by 1899 and was listed in the city directory as The Berke. By 1936, the place was called the Warncliffe Apartments. (Something Weird Video)

Making a Living (Keystone Film Company, 1914)

Charlie Chaplin steals reporter Henry Lehrman's camera and uses the photos to get himself hired at Lehrman's newspaper. They get into a fistfight in the middle of Fourth and Grand.

The Money Trap (MGM, 1966)

Glenn Ford is a police detective gone bad in this late film noir, one of MGM's last B movies before the theaters abandoned double bills. Directed by television veteran Burt Kennedy, the film was perhaps made to keep its MGM stars—Ford, Rita Hayworth, Joseph Cotten and Ricardo Montalban—busy or to fulfill their contracts. The film begins with the murder of a prostitute by her Mexican husband. Ford and partner Montalban question and later keep watch on the suspect's sister at the rundown Brousseau mansion at 238 South Bunker Hill Avenue, which also appears across the street from Marilyn Monroe's boardinghouse in *Bus Stop* (1956). By 1966, redevelopment had already cleared most of Bunker Hill, and the Brousseau house was one of the few remaining Victorians, surrounded by bare dirt and a couple trees. Built in 1878 by Judge Julius Brousseau, it had been converted to a rooming house by the 1940s and was torn down shortly after *The Money Trap* was shot there. Glenn Ford also follows the killer's sister to Olive and Third streets, gets on Angels Flight and rides down the hill with her.

My Gun Is Quick (United Artists, 1957)

Robert Bray plays Mike Hammer in this low-budget adaptation of Mickey Spillane's best-selling novel of the same title. A chance meeting with a young hooker just before she's murdered puts the hard-boiled peeper on a search for a stash of Nazi diamonds. In a nice set piece, the camera pans with Hammer as he drives north on Olive Street past the Casa Alta Hotel and the Angels Flight Café at the corner of Third, then parks in front of the Astoria Hotel at 248 South Olive, where he plans to talk to a suspect. The shot takes in the hotels on the west side of the street. As Hammer gets out of his car, he's diverted by activity down at the bottom of the utility steps going down to Clay Street between the Astoria and the rear of both the Hillcrest Hotel and the Sunshine Apartments—the same stairway seen in *The Indestructible Man*

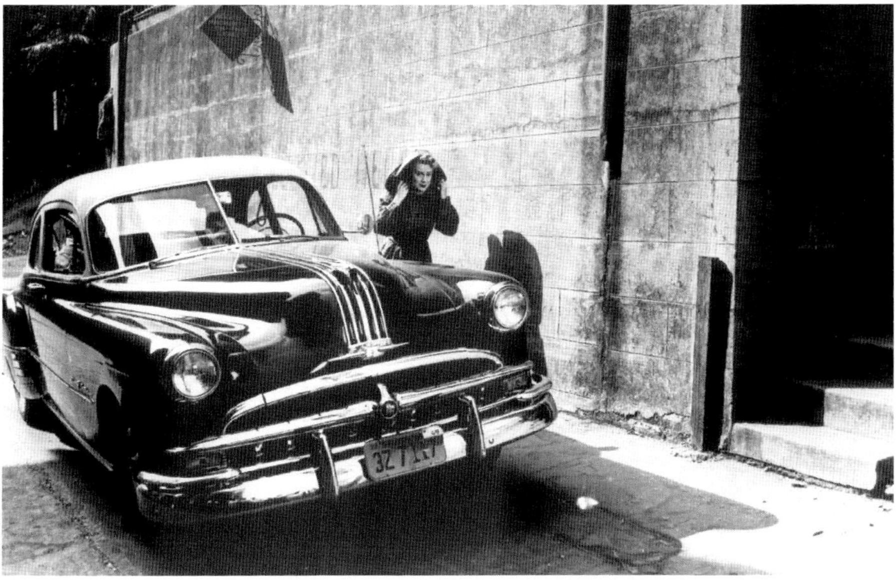

June Havoc parks on Clay Street beneath the Sunshine Apartments, next to the utility stairway leading up to Olive Street, in *Once a Thief* (1950). *Jim Dawson.*

and *Once a Thief*. He runs all the way down the steps to where a crowd has gathered on Clay and sees that his suspect has been thrown from a window. (At this point he's standing almost exactly where Ralph Meeker's Mike Hammer parked and began his walk up those same steps in *Kiss Me Deadly* two years earlier.) We see not only the Sunshine Apartments behind Hammer but also the apartment building's wooden back stairs (adjacent to the concrete steps), which were used twenty-five years earlier in *The Impatient Maiden*. When Hammer spots the killer watching them from Olive Street, he runs back up the steps in pursuit, jumps in his Ford convertible, does a U-turn and swerves west onto Third Street. Then we cut to a wide-vista shot of Bunker Hill and the Monarch Hotel at 905 Fifth Street, taken from the Sixth Street overpass of the Harbor Freeway. The camera pans left as Hammer crosses above the freeway on the Fifth Street overpass leading to the Harbor's southbound lane.

Never Weaken (Rolin, 1921)

In his final two-reel comedy (twenty-nine minutes), Harold Lloyd uses questionable tactics to drum up business for his girlfriend's employer, a doctor who specializes in setting broken or dislocated bones. At one point,

Lloyd fills the intersection of Third and Grand outside the Angels Flight Pharmacy with powdered soap, just before a passing water wagon turns it into a slippery mess that fills the screen with pratfalls. There's also a scene with Lloyd aboard a swinging girder on a fake building atop the southern entrance of the Hill Street tunnel. (Newline.com)

Night Has a Thousand Eyes (Paramount, 1948)

In this Cornell Woolrich story directed by John Farrow, Edward G. Robinson is mentalist con man John Triton hiding out on Bunker Hill in the rambling Sunshine Apartments at 421 West Third Street. "It was an odd part of the city," Robinson says in voiceover. "It was strictly a no-questions-asked area." An establishing 180-degree shot—taken from halfway up the Third Street steps—begins by looking down toward Hill Street, then follows one of the Angels Flight cars up the hill, pans across the top of the hill to Robinson's character (a stand-in) coming down the steps on the north side of the street and follows him up onto the porch and to the door of the boardinghouse. Another shot shows John Lund and Gail Russell coming up the steps to the Sunshine Apartments' porch.

Non-Skid Kid (1922)

In this silent two-reeler, future *Our Gang* kid Ernie "Sunshine Sammy" Morrison helps Eddie Boland get his broken-down car to the local mechanics, who happen to be girls. One scene is shot on the 200 block of Grand Avenue with the Dome Hotel in the background. (*American Slapstick*)

Not Wanted (Emerald Productions, 1949)

In this sensitive if culturally dated film by writer-producer-uncredited director Ida Lupino, a pretty but naïve small-town girl (Sally Forrest) gets knocked up by a footloose jazz pianist (Leo Penn) and decides to have the baby in an unwed mothers' home. The film was later rereleased under the title *The Wrong Rut*, with color footage of a C-section birth inserted into the otherwise black and white film. The movie opens on Second Street, as a distraught Forrest walks up the sidewalk from Hill Street toward the camera,

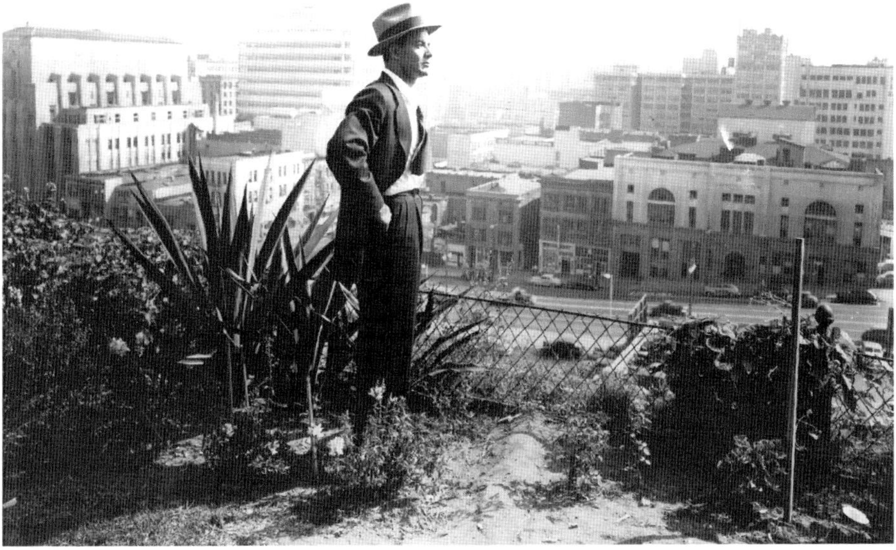

Cornell Wilde stands outside his character's mother's house at 134 North Hill Street, on the terrace above the Hill Street tunnel, in *Shockproof* (1949). The building with the arched windows (right) is the Central Division Police Station at 318 West First Street, which was used in *A Star Is Born* (1954). *Bison Archives.*

sees a crying baby in front of the grocery at 427 West Second beneath the Argyle Apartments and tries to take it. Near the end of the film, she's chased by Keefe Brasselle in a scene that begins at the Texaco station at the southwest corner of Hill and First (with the rear of the Gladden Apartments in the background). She runs toward the Hill Street tunnel, runs up the steps to the balustrade and tries to jump into the traffic going into the tunnel below. When Brasselle stops her, she breaks away and climbs the steps up to the top of the hill. There are also a couple of other scenes that look like they were shot at Bunker Hill houses. (Kino.com)

Once a Thief (United Artists, 1950)

Reformed jewel thief June Havoc falls under the sway of sleazy gigolo Cesar Romero in this hard-hearted tale directed by Billy Wilder's brother, W. Lee Wilder. There are several scenes shot on Bunker Hill. Romero's bookie joint/dry cleaners is in the shabby storefront on the Second Street side of the Argyle Hotel at Second and Olive; a scene in *The Turning Point* was also shot there. When Havoc drives up to the place, the entire south side of the 500 block of Second Street is in the background, with the Mission Apartments, the Shirley Apartments, the twin-towered Chaspeak Apartments and the Dome Hotel Apartments farther up. In another scene, on Clay Street, Havoc drives under Angels Flight and parks at the Sunshine Apartments' retaining wall, then runs up the long stairway between the rear of the Sunshine Apartments and the south side of the Astoria Hotel that fronts at 248 South Olive Street—the same stairway used in *The Indestructible Man*, *Kiss Me Deadly* and *My Gun Is Quick*. "The occasional location shots of Los Angeles landmarks lend a minor note of authenticity to this feeble, far-fetched melodrama," wrote reviewer Ezra Goodman on December 18, 1950.

The Savage Eye (1960)

In writer-director Ben Maddow's experimental movie of documentary film clips intercut with set-up shots of actress Barbara Baxley, all overlaid with a silly narration by Gary Merrill, a desperate divorcee travels around Los Angeles trying to make sense of her life. At one point she walks through the Second Street tunnel.

The Scar

See *Hollow Triumph*.

The Set-Up (RKO, 1949)

In this real-time boxing drama, Robert Ryan is a nearly washed-up fighter who hasn't been told he's supposed to take a fall in a tank town called Paradise City (an unconvincing set on RKO's Culver City lot). At one point, director Robert Wise moves the action to downtown L.A., on the terrace above the Hill Street tunnel: Ryan's wife, Audrey Totter, takes a night stroll down the steps to the balustrade at the top of the southern end of the tunnel near First Street, where streetcars and buses pass beneath her. The Los Angeles Times building is briefly visible in the background. (The same steps were used in a chase scene that same year in *Not Wanted* and as a murder scene at the beginning of *Woman on the Run* in 1950.) (WarnerVideo.com)

Shockproof (Columbia, 1949)

In this film written by Sam Fuller (under the title *The Lovers*) and directed by Douglas Sirk, parole officer Cornell Wilde falls for one of his charges, a paroled murderess (Patricia Knight), the moment she shows up at his office in the Bradbury Building. At first, he gets her a room at the Koster house at 507 West Second Street, between Grand and Olive. Later, when he's driving her to his mother's house in the 100 block of North Hill Street, he picks up his kid brother on Court Street, just above where the Court Flight funicular used to be. The film footage that was shot for the rear-projection in the scene when Wilde picks her up on Second Street is available for viewing at http://onbunkerhill.org/adrivethroughbunkerhill or on YouTube under "A Drive Through Bunker Hill."

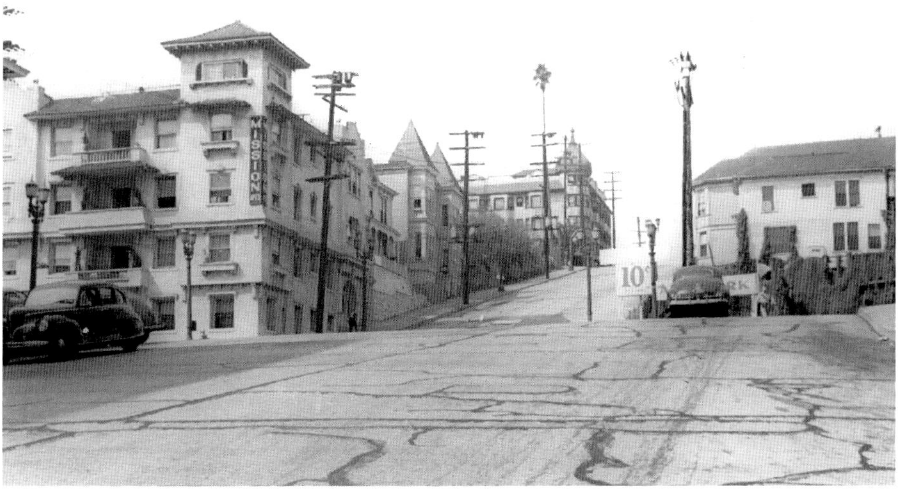

Second Street above Olive, seen here in 1945, was a popular filming spot. From left to right: Jack Palance's car ran down Gloria Grahame on the Second Street sidewalk in front of the Mission Apartments in *Sudden Fear* (1952); Sterling Hayden's gang planned their racetrack robbery at the Mission (using the arched doorway at 504 West Second) in Stanley Kubrick's *The Killing* (1955); a truck barreling down the hill almost hit John Hodiak in front of the pointy-roofed Chaspeak Apartments in *Somewhere in the Night* (1946); the onion-domed Dome Hotel Apartments at the corner of Second and Grand provided interiors and exteriors for *Get Outta Town* (1960); and Cornell Wilde picked up Patricia Knight at the Koster house (right) in *Shockproof* (1949). *Bison Archives.*

The Sniper (Columbia, 1952)

Stanley Kramer produced this psychological study cum police procedural about an emotionally disturbed laundry deliveryman (Arthur Franz) who kills attractive young brunettes with his sniper-scoped U.S. Army carbine. The film makes good use of San Francisco's hilly neighborhoods and spectacular vistas, but the director shot at least one pickup scene in downtown Los Angeles, at the top of the Hill Street terrace. Franz walks along Court Street just above where Court Flight used to be, with part of L.A.'s off-center Hall of Records on Broadway visible through the trees in the background. He approaches a group of kids playing stickball near the end of the pavement in front of the Harmonia and Stevens apartment buildings at 138 and 140 North Hill Street, before the hill leads down to the balustrade above the tunnel's south end. Downtown Hill Street is visible in the background.

Somewhere in the Night (Twentieth Century Fox, 1946)

An amnesiac (John Hodiak) newly discharged from the marines tries to discover his identity in Los Angeles. There is a street scene that ostensibly takes place in San Pedro, near Los Angeles harbor, that could have been shot in Bunker Hill, perhaps around Hope or Flower Streets. But a more poignant scene in which Hodiak visits a lonely, wistful woman (Josephine Hutchins) was shot at the Chaspeak Apartments at 512 West Second Street, directly across from the Koster house used in *Shockproof*. When Hodiak leaves the house, a truck nearly runs him down as it barrels on down Second past the Mission Apartments at Olive—the same spot where Jack Palance would later run down Gloria Grahame near the end of *Sudden Fear* (1952).

Southside 1–1000 (Allied Artists, 1950)

In this semi-documentary film reminiscent of 1947's influential *T-Men*, Treasury agent Don DeFoe goes underground to break up a Los Angeles counterfeiting ring led by the daughter of the funny money's imprisoned engraver. Along with scenes shot all over downtown Los Angeles, there is an episode in which DeFoe and thug Paul Tobias ride up Angels Flight to evade the agents tailing them and jump into an awaiting car at the corner of Olive and Third.

A Star Is Born (Warner Brothers, 1954)

In George Cukor's expensive remake of the classic 1937 film, fading matinee idol Norman Main (James Mason) falls in love with a wide-eyed ingénue (Judy Garland) on her way up. In a scene that was excised from the release in 1954 but reinserted during the film's 1983 restoration, Garland, thinking her career is going nowhere, moves to the Lancaster Apartments at 121 North Flower Street. When Mason discovers where she lives, he drives his roadster up the First Street hill from Hope Street, turns left on Flower, parks on the east side of the street and runs across Flower and up the front steps of the apartment—all in glorious Technicolor CinemaScope with panoramic shots of the neighborhood in the background. Garland shouts down to him from the rooftop where she's sunning herself, and he joins her there. (WarnerVideo.com)

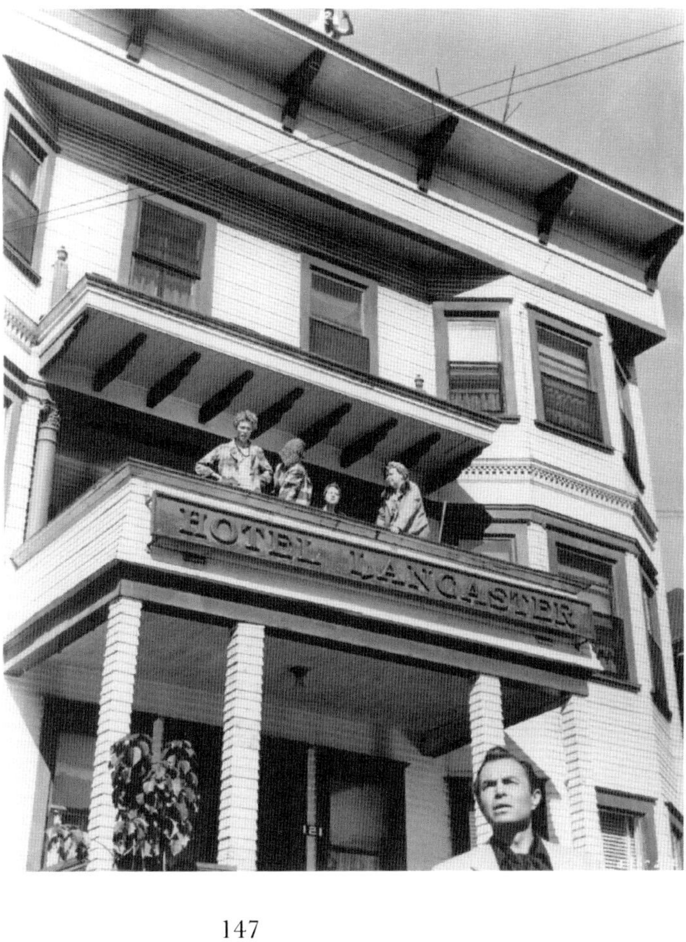

Judy Garland shouts down to James Mason from the roof of the Hotel Lancaster at 121 North Flower Street in *A Star Is Born* (1954). *Bison Archives.*

Sudden Fear (Independent, 1952)

Bunker Hill is a stand-in for a seedy part of San Francisco in this melodrama about an heiress playwright (Joan Crawford) whose younger husband (Jack Palance) is plotting to kill her. San Francisco's famous Lombard Street gets its close-up through parts of the film, but when Palance U-turns his car and begins chasing Crawford through the night streets, we cut from the Bay Area to Third Street on Bunker Hill. Palance turns right (north) onto Cinnebar Street, then quickly turns left into a narrow driveway running behind the Rangeley Apartments (723 West Third), parks and goes after Crawford on foot. After running through porches and alleyways and down the long utility stairs between Olive and Clay behind Third Street's Hillcrest Hotel and Sunshine Apartments, Crawford comes to a locked alley door behind the Mission Apartments at 504 West Second Street. Meanwhile, Palance, now back in his car, turns east on Second from Grand Avenue (we see the Dome Hotel Apartments behind him) and mistakenly runs down his co-conspirator, Gloria Grahame, in front of the Mission Apartments. (However, the final scene in which his car is lying on its side was shot in front of another corner apartment building altogether, possibly in San Francisco.) Director David Miller shot on at least seven different Bunker Hill locations within two or three blocks of each other, many of them unidentifiable, and juxtaposed them into a disorienting nightmare sequence in which scenes don't always match up, thus magnifying the overall disorientation. (Kino.com)

Target Earth (Aptcon Pictures, 1954)

In this low-budget science fiction flick with a dash of film noir, a group of people, including Richard Dinning and Pat Crowley, is held hostage by a smalltime gangster in a city under attack by a robot army from Venus. Early in the film, Crowley walks down Fifth Street in front of the Engstrum Apartments (623 West Fifth) and the art deco Southern California Edison Building (601), directly across the street from the Central Los Angeles Public Library, which is seen in a pan shot. Another shot looks south down an empty Grand Avenue from halfway up the hill between Fourth and Fifth Streets. (The director claimed he took Dinning and Crowley and a small camera downtown early on a Sunday morning to get a few establishing shots without having to pay for city permits; the rest of the film's street scenes were done on a backlot.)

This Rebel Breed (Warner Bros, 1960)

Bunker Hill costars in this preachy but action-packed teen exploitation movie about undercover cops going after a drug-dealing, racist high school gang. Rita Moreno and her Mexican-American family live at 227 Bunker Hill Avenue, formerly owned at the turn of the century by a downtown lawyer and later judge named George Holton. Her brother is approached by a local gang member (Richard Rust) about dealing drugs at the small park of benches at the corner of Third Street and Bunker Hill Avenue (the same benches used in both *M* and *Angel's Flight*). A more extensive scene is shot a block east, at the corner of Third and Grand Avenue, beginning with a cattycorner shot from the New Grand Hotel toward a liquor store on the southeast corner (formerly the Angels Flight Pharmacy), where Mark Damon is following Moreno. She walks diagonally eastward across the street to a small house at 523 West Third Street, where she learns

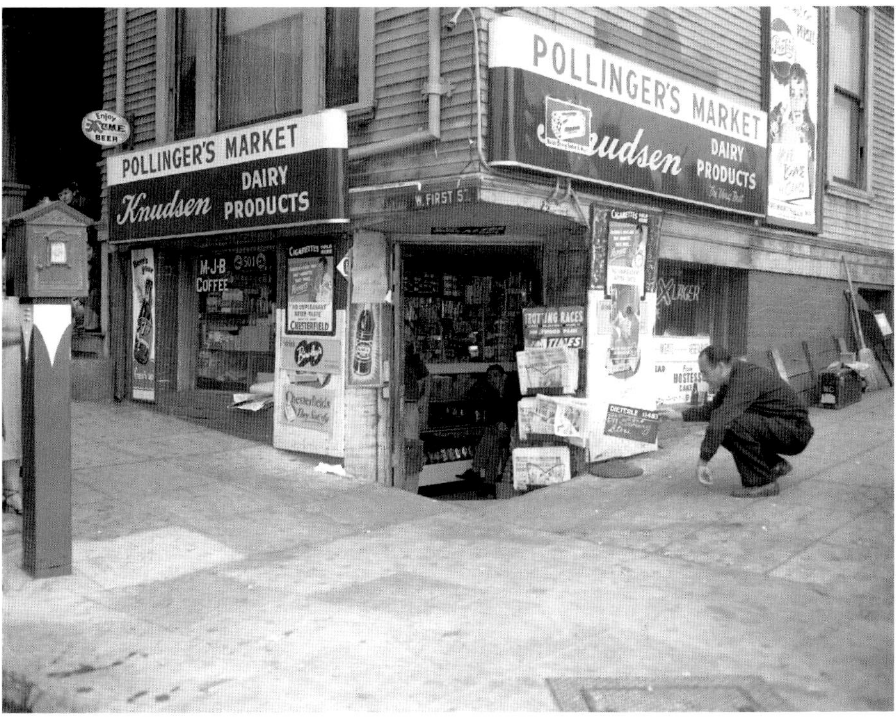

The clapper boy starts the scene, signaling William Holden to walk into frame at Pollinger's Market, 601 West First Street, at the corner of Grand Avenue in *The Turning Point* (1952). *Bison Archives.*

from her doctor that she's pregnant. (This is the Beebe house where the shoemaker, William Varney, lived in Kent Mackenzie's *Bunker Hill 1956* documentary four years earlier.) Then she walks west, past a dry cleaner at 525 Third Street that's built within the Lovejoy—a sprawling apartment building on the northeast corner that fronts at 529 Third; she turns north on Grand, where we can see the Dome Hotel Apartments in the distance at the southwest corner of Second Street. Then, with a few creative cuts, the scene moves another block east as she climbs to the top of the Third Street steps (with the Angels Flight platform just out of frame) and ends up at the Plaza Mission Church several blocks away, near Olvera Street. Other scenes of a black neighborhood are filmed at a house at 201 Bunker Hill Avenue (which was used three years later in the opening scene of *Dime With a Halo*); on a hillside slum pathway on what looks like the western slope of Bunker Hill; and on a street that looks like a part of Bunker Hill even though one visible address, 7615, did not exist on any street on Bunker Hill. (Alpha Home Entertainment; Oldies.com)

THE TURNING POINT (PARAMOUNT, 1952)

Crusading prosecutor Edmond O'Brien and his old friend William Holden, a newspaper reporter, are out to break the local syndicate in this adaptation of a Horace McCoy short story. The film, whose working title was *This Is Dynamite*, was shot mostly on location all over downtown Los Angeles and especially on Bunker Hill. When O'Brien's father, a crooked cop (Tom Tully), is being tailed by Holden, he switches from a car to a taxi on Olive Street behind the building at 500 West Third (Los Amigos, the gang headquarters in *Cry Danger*) and takes it to the Gladden Apartments at 100 South Olive (also used in *The Brasher Doubloon*). Holden keeps an eye on the Gladden from Pollinger's corner grocery at 601 West First Street, meant to be cattycorner from the Gladden but actually a block west at the northwest corner of Grand. In one impressive shot, Holden and Alexis Smith (and the camera) ride up Angels Flight, with the camera panning across to the Sunshine Apartments at 421 West Third Street, where a witness is hiding. Holden and Smith walk down the Third Street steps from the Olive Street station to the Sunshine, but several thugs are standing guard all around the porch. Not far away, in the 400 block of Second Street above the Second Street tunnel, Tom Tully is gunned down on the north side of the street in front of a grocery store beneath the Argyle

Apartments, the same place where Sally Forrest tried to steal a baby three years earlier in *Not Wanted*, right next to the dry cleaning shop that was Cesar Romero's bookie joint in *Once a Thief* in 1950. The mobster that kills Tully is then shot down next door in front of the Rio Grand Apartments at 425 West Second. There's also a scene in which Holden chases a witness through an upper hallway of the Hotel Vendome at 231 South Hill Street that leads to the rear on Clay Street. Despite Bunker Hill's presence in the film, it is never named because the film takes place in what's described at one point as "this fine Midwestern city." The Sunshine's address is given as "446 Pond Street," and the shooting in the store beneath the Argyle Apartments takes place at "34th and Skylar." *Variety* (September 16, 1952) took note of it, saying, "While LA is not the locale of the story, its streets furnish interesting action backdrops."

The Unfaithful (Warner Brothers, 1947)

Pulp writer David Goodis wrote the script for this Somerset Maugham-inspired (but uncredited) story about a Beverly Hills housewife (Ann Sheridan) who kills what is apparently a nighttime intruder. It's essentially an old-fashioned melodrama, but director Vincent Sherman, who was not known for film noir work, enlivened it with plenty of location work all over Los Angeles, from the Ambassador Hotel to the Burbank Airport to downtown's Bradbury Building (where Sheridan's attorney, Lew Ayres, has an office) and Los Angeles City Hall. There are two detailed scenes on Bunker Hill. The victim's wife (Marta Mitrovich) gets on Angels Flight at the Olive Street station and reads about his death on the front page as she rides it down to Hill Street; on Hill Street we also see Royal Liquors on the northwestern corner and the Belmont Hotel just north of it in the 200 block. Near the end of the film, when an art dealer takes Sheridan's husband (Zachary Scott) to the widow's apartment, they emerge from the west end of the Third Street tunnel, turn north and park at the El Mar Apartments at 235 South Hope, where the camera follows them into the lobby and upstairs into a hallway. (This block of Hope Street, with a large retaining wall on its east side, was also used in *M.*) (Warner Bros Archive Collection)

When Kelly Came Home (Independent, 1960)

See *Gangster's Revenge*.

Where the Sidewalk Ends (1950)

Otto Preminger directed this well-regarded film about a New York police detective (Dana Andrews) whose violent nature undermines his job. Though most exteriors were shot in Manhattan, the New York subway was "doubled" by the more manageable underground station beneath the Pacific Electric Terminal Building at 437 South Hill Street. (Fox Video)

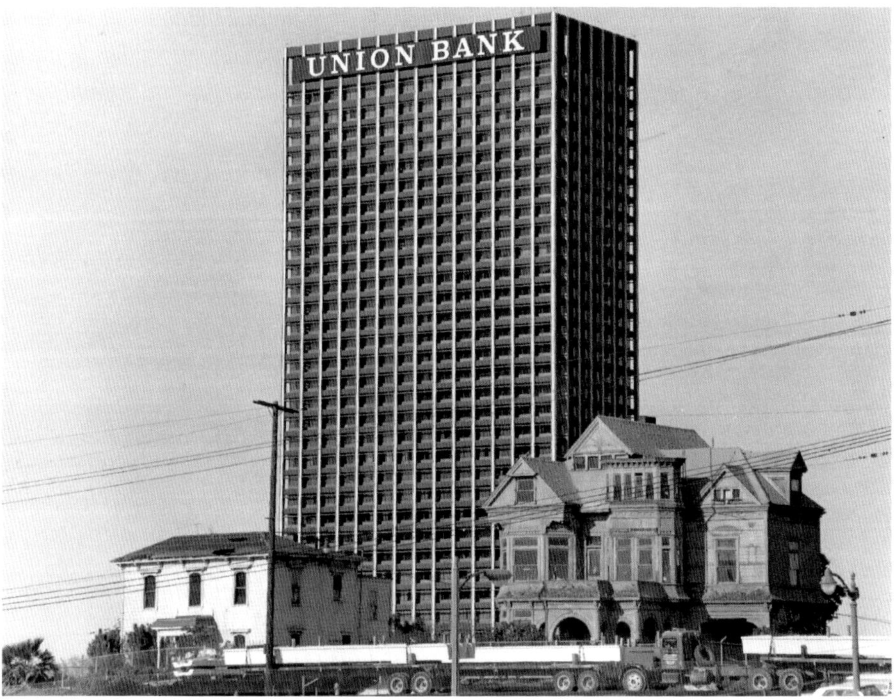

Dwarfed by the new Union Square Bank Building, the 1882 Castle and its neighbor, an 1880 house locally called the Salt Box, wait to be hauled away from what used to be Bunker Hill Avenue. Their removal in March 1969 brought an end to the world of old Bunker Hill. *Security Pacific Collection/LAPL.*

While the City Sleeps (RKO/Warner Bros, 1956)

Newspapermen Dana Andrews, George Saunders and Thomas Mitchell compete to track down serial killer John Barrymore Jr. Andrews chases Barrymore through the subway tunnel that runs beneath Bunker Hill from the Pacific Electric Terminal Building at 437 South Hill Street. (Warner Bros Archive Collection)

Woman on the Run (Universal, 1950)

Ann Sheridan runs around San Francisco hoping to find her estranged husband (Ross Elliot) before tabloid reporter/hit man Dennis O'Keefe tracks him down. Much of the film was shot on the streets of San Francisco and at the Carmel Amusement Park in Carmel, but the lengthy opening scene, in which Sheridan's husband witnesses a murder, was filmed on the Hill Street terrace above the southern end of the Hill Street tunnel. Elliot walks his dog up the same steps where a year earlier, in *The Set-Up*, Audrey Totter took a night stroll down to the balustrade above the tunnel to watch the streetcars and buses pass beneath her. This same spot had once been used regularly during the silent era (e.g., Harold Lloyd's *Look Out Below*, 1926) to build fake building tops for acrobatic scenes, with downtown Hill Street in the background. (The other end of the roughly block-long tunnel, near Temple, was prominently used in *Criss Cross* the year before.) As the cops arrive, this scene in *Woman on the Run* also shows some of the houses in the 100 block of North Hill Street at the top of the stairs.

Work (Essanay Film Company, 1915)

Wallpaper-hanger Charlie Chaplin and his boss have a job at the Bradbury mansion in this silent short. They arrive at the corner of Court and Hill Streets and go up the front steps to the porch. The interiors were shot in a studio.

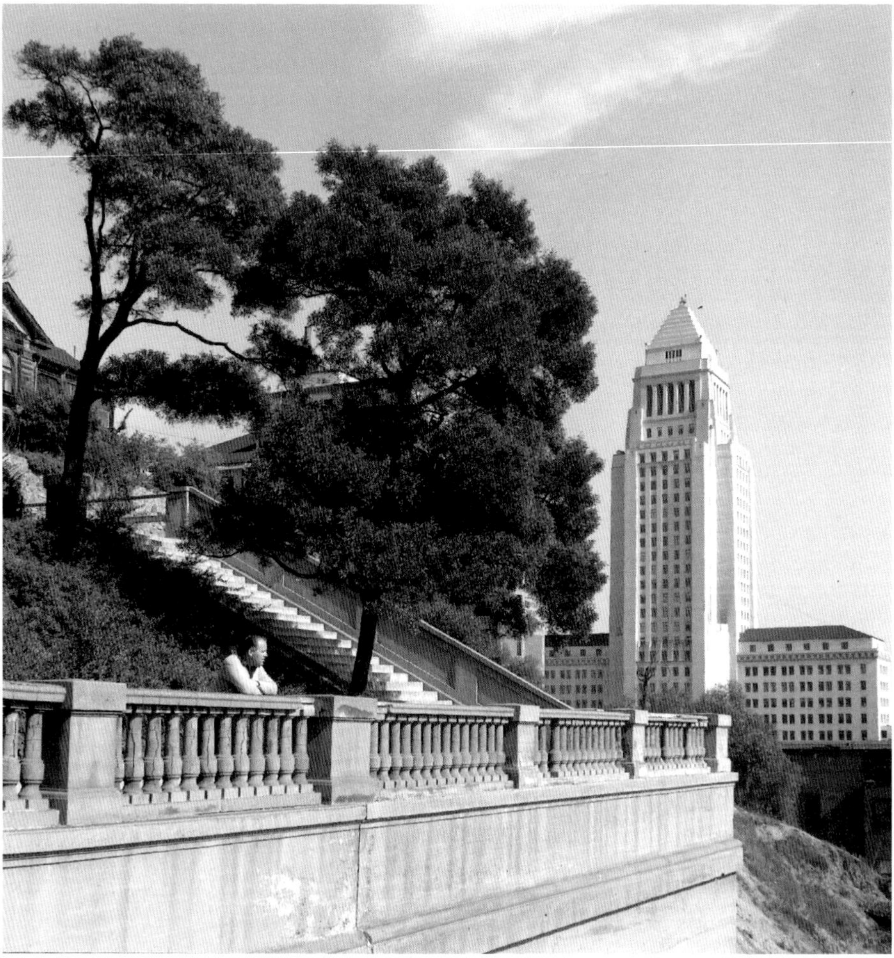

California History Room, California State Library, Sacramento.

BIBLIOGRAPHY

Sites

http://americanfilmnoir.com
www.angelsflight.com
www.electricearl.com/af
www.electricearl.com/bh
www.onbunkerhill.org

Books

Adler, Pat. *The Bunker Hill Story*. Glendale, CA: La Siesta Press, 1968.

Avila, Eric. *Popular Culture in the Age of White Flight*. Berkeley: University of Southern California Press, 2004.

Bixby Smith, Sarah. *Adobe Days*. Fresno, CA: Valley Publishing, 1974.

Cain, Paul. *Fast One*. Berkeley, CA: Black Lizard Press, 1987.

Chandler, Raymond. *The Big Sleep*. New York: Vintage Books, 1988.

———. *The High Window*. New York: Vintage Books, 1988.

———. *The Midnight Raymond Chandler*. Boston: Houghton, Mifflin Company, 1971.

———. *The Simple Art of Murder*. New York: Vintage Books, 1988.

Ciment, Michael. *Conversations with Losey*. New York: Methuen & Co., 1985.

Comer, Virginia L. *Angels' Flight: A History of Bunker Hill's Incline Railway*. Los Angeles: Historical Society of Southern California, 1996.

Davis, Mike. *City of Quartz: Excavating the Future in Los Angeles*. New York: Vantage Books, 1992.

———. *Dead Cities*. New York: New Press, 2002.

Fante, John. *Ask the Dust*. Santa Barbara, CA: Black Sparrow Press, 1980.

———. *Dreams of Bunker Hill*. Santa Barbara, CA: Black Sparrow Press, 1982.

Fante, John, edited by Seamus Cooney. *Selected Letters: 1932 to 1981*. New York: HarperCollins, 2002.

Ford, Peter. *Glenn Ford: A Life*. Madison: University of Wisconsin Press, 2011.

Greco, J. *The File on Robert Siodmak in Hollywood: 1941–1951*. Dissertation.com, 1999.

Gruber, Frank. *The Pulp Jungle*. Los Angeles: Sherbourne Press, 1967.

Halliday, Jon. *Sirk on Sirk*. Boston: Faber & Faber, 1971.

Haver, Ronald. *A Star Is Born: The Making of the 1954 Movie and Its 1983 Restoration*. New York: Alfred A. Knopf, 1988.

Hirsch, Foster. *The Dark Side of the Screen*. New York: Da Capo Press, 2001.

———. *Joseph Losey*. Boston: Twayne Publications, 1980.

Klein, Norman M. *The History of Forgetting: Los Angeles and the Erasure of Memory*. London: Verso, 1997.

Klein, Norman M., and Martin J. Schiesl. *20th Century Los Angeles: Power, Promotion, and Social Conflict*. Claremont, CA: Regina Books, 1990.

Leahy, James. *The Cinema of Joseph Losey*. New York: A.S. Barnes & Co., 1967.

Moyer, Daniel and Eugene Alvarez. *Just the Facts, Ma'am: The Authorized Biography of Jack Webb*. Kaua'i, HI: Writers Direct, 1999.

Naremore, James. *More Than Night*. Berkeley: University of California Press, 1998.

Politi, Leo. *Bunker Hill Los Angeles*. Palm Desert, CA: Desert-Southwest, 1964.

Porfirio, Robert, Alain Silver and James Ursini, editors. *Film Noir Reader 3*. New York: Limelight Editions, 2001.

Pugsley, William; photographs by Roy W. Hankey. *Bunker Hill: Last of the Lofty Mansions*. Corona Del Mar, CA: Trans-Anglo Books, 1977.

Richardson, Carl. *Autopsy: An Element of Realism in Film Noir*. Metuchin, NJ: Scarecrow Press, 1992.

Ryan, Don. *Angel's Flight*. New York: Boni and Liveright, 1927.

Slide, Anthony. *DeToth on DeToth: Putting the Drama in Front of the Camera*. Boston: Faber & Faber, 1996.

Starr, Kevin. *Material Dreams: Southern California Through the 1920s*. New York: Oxford University Press, 1991.

Turner, Timothy G. *Turn Off the Sunshine*. Caldwell, ID: Caxton Printers, 1942.

Weaver, John D. *El Pueblo Grande: A Non-Fiction Book About Los Angeles*. Los Angeles: Ward Ritchie Press, 1973.

Publications

Adams, Sam. "*The Exiles* Is an Excavation." *Los Angeles Times*, November 15, 2009.

"Artist Helps Preserve History on Bunker Hill: Glendale Woman Painter Finds Nostalgic Mementos." *Los Angeles Times*, April 1, 1956.

"Bunker Hill Mansions Moved to New Home." *Los Angeles Times*, March 17, 1969.

"Bunker Hill Property Sold for $2,050,000." *Los Angeles Times*, December 27, 1956.

"Bunker Hill Relics Suffer a New Setback." *Los Angeles Herald-Examiner*, December 10, 1968.

Byrne, Julie. "Bunker Hill Fashion Shoot." *Los Angeles Times*, July 22, 1965.

Dimendberg, Edward. "From Berlin to Bunker Hill: Urban Space, Late Modernity, and Film Noir in Fritz Lang's and Joseph Losey's *M*." Ohio University School of Film, *Wide Angle* 19.4, 1997, 62–93.

Fischer, Greg. "The Big Life of Prudent Beaudry." *Downtown News*, December 5, 2011.

Fleisher, Matthew. "Exiles on Main Street." *L.A. Weekly*, August 15–21, 2008.

George, David. "Film As Literature." *Jerusalem Post Magazine*, August 8, 1980.

Goodman, Ezra. "*Once a Thief*." *L.A. Daily News*, December 18, 1950.

———."Post-War Motion Pictures." *American Cinematographer*, May 1945.

Graham, Aaron W. "Little Shop of Genres: An Interview With Charles B. Griffith." *Senses of Cinema*, Issue 35, Interviewed in August 2004.

Harford, Margaret. "Los Angeles Locale Marks *Turning Point*." *Hollywood Citizen-News*, January 15, 1953.

Harvey, Steve. "Prime Parking for Only 5 Cents." *Los Angeles Times*, September 12, 2009.

Herbert, Ray. "Fabled Bunker Hill Finally Hits Bottom." *Los Angeles Times*, May 12, 1966.

Hift, Fred. "*Criss Cross*." *Variety*, January 15, 1949.

Hoffman, Irving. "*Act of Violence* Megging Lauded, Film Just So-So." *The Hollywood Reporter*, January 31, 1949.

Hogan, William. "*Sudden Fear* Suspends Hard Way." *San Francisco Chronicle*, August 1952.

Kistler, Robert. "Holdout Resident of Hotel on Bunker Hill Departs Quietly." *Los Angeles Times*, June 4, 1969.

Leibowitz, Ed. "Committee of One." *Los Angeles Magazine*, June 2003.

Loukaitou-Sideris, Anastasia, and Gail Sainsbury. "Lost Streets of Bunker Hill." *California History* 74 (1996): 394-407.

Manners, Dorothy. "*Cry Danger* Laid in L.A." *Los Angeles Examiner*, February 23, 1951.

"Mayor Calls for Blighted Area Cleanup." *Los Angeles Times*, February 27, 1956.

Melvin, Edward F. "Down the Double-Cross Trail." *Christian Science Monitor*, March 13, 1951.

Myerson, Harold. "A Tale of Two Cities." *American Prospect*, May 17, 2004.

New York Times. "*Sudden Fear*, Cleverly Turned Melodrama, Is New Bill at Loew's State." August 8, 1952.

Ridley, Jim. "Soul and the City." *L.A. Weekly*, August 15–21, 2008.

Scheuer, Philip K. "Drama of Violence Thrilling." *Los Angeles Times*, January 20, 1949.

———. "Los Angeles Setting For Hard-Boiled Drama." *Los Angeles Times*, February 23, 1951

———. "Melodrama Suspenseful, Effective." *Los Angeles Times*, October 8, 1948. .

———. "*Turning Point* Cracks Down on Crime, Graft." *Los Angeles Times*, January 15, 1953.

Schrader, Paul. "Notes on Film Noir." *Film Comment*, Vol. 8, No. 1, Spring 1972.

Sloan, Lloyd L. "*Criss Cross*: Los Angeles Background Seen in New UI Film." *Los Angeles Citizen News*, January 20, 1949.

Thomas, Kevin. "Ford, Rita Victims of Film 'Trap'." *Los Angeles Times*, February 18, 1966.

Warren, Geoffrey. "The Transparent Man Not Very Solid Movie." *Los Angeles Times*, February 27, 1960.

Webb, Jack, and Peter Martin. "The Jack Webb Story." *Cosmopolitan*, May 1954.

ABOUT THE AUTHOR

Jim Dawson is a graduate of West Virginia University and a longtime resident of Hollywood. He is the author of over a dozen books, including *Los Angeles's Angels Flight* (2008), as well as a short documentary called *Los Angeles's Bunker Hill* (2011) on the Criterion Collection's Blu-ray/DVD reissue of the 1955 film noir classic *Kiss Me Deadly*.

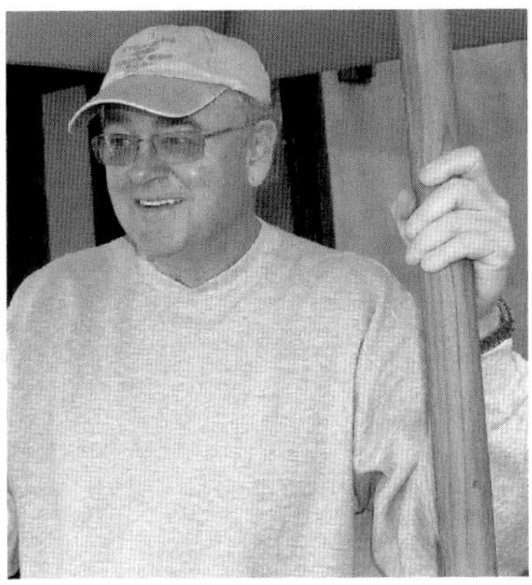

Copyright Leonard Auslender.

Visit us at
www.historypress.net

This title is also available as an e-book